Realist Magic:
Objects, Ontology, Causality

New Metaphysics

Series Editors: Graham Harman and Bruno Latour

The world is due for a resurgence of original speculative metaphysics. The New Metaphysics series aims to provide a safe house for such thinking amidst the demoralizing caution and prudence of professional academic philosophy. We do not aim to bridge the analytic-continental divide, since we are equally impatient with nail-filing analytic critique and the continental reverence for dusty textual monuments. We favor instead the spirit of the intellectual gambler, and wish to discover and promote authors who meet this description. Like an emergent recording company, what we seek are traces of a new metaphysical 'sound' from any nation of the world. The editors are open to translations of neglected metaphysical classics, and will consider secondary works of especial force and daring. But our main interest is to stimulate the birth of disturbing masterpieces of twenty-first century philosophy.

Timothy Morton

Realist Magic: Objects, Ontology, Causality

OPEN HUMANITIES PRESS

An imprint of MPublishing – University of Michigan Library, Ann Arbor, 2013

First edition published by Open Humanities Press 2013
Freely available online at http://hdl.handle.net/2027/spo.13106496.0001.001

Design by Katherine Gillieson
Cover Illustration by Tammy Lu

ISBN-13 978-1-60785-202-5

Open Humanities Press is an international, scholar-led open access publishing collective whose mission is to make leading works of contemporary critical thought freely available worldwide. Books published under the Open Humanities Press imprint at MPublishing are produced through a unique partnership between OHP's editorial board and the University of Michigan Library, which provides a library-based managing and production support infrastructure to facilitate scholars to publish leading research in book form.

MPublishing
www.publishing.umich.edu

OPEN HUMANITIES PRESS
www.openhumanitiespress.org

Contents

For Simon

Acknowledgments

First and foremost, Graham Harman brought this book into being in almost every sense. He compelled me to become an object-oriented ontologist, through the ingenious device of brilliant, seductive prose. And as series editor he has been a most helpful, generous partner in putting this book together.

Ian Bogost, one of the founders of object-oriented ontology (OOO), gave me the title at a highly spiced brainstorming session in Los Angeles in December 2010, and since then has shared his thinking in the most generous ways possible.

There many people whose more than inspiring ideas and kind words have helped me on this project, including but not limited to: Jamie Allen, Jane Bennett, Bill Benzon, Paul Boshears, Rick Elmore, Paul Ennis, Rita Felski, Dirk Felleman, Nathan Gale, Bobby George, Thomas Gokey, Joseph Goodson, Peter Gratton, Liam Heneghan, Eileen Joy, Julia Reinhard Lupton, Douglas Kahn, Ken Reinhard, Tom Sparrow, McKenzie Wark, Cary Wolfe, and Ben Woodard.

This book is dedicated to my son Simon. Anyone who has trouble imagining causality as magical and uncanny need only consider the existence of children.

List of Figures

Everything profound loves the mask.

– Friedrich Nietzsche

What constitutes pretense is that, in the end, you don't know whether it's pretense or not.

– Jacques Lacan

As kingfishers catch fire, dragonflies draw flame;
As tumbled over rim in roundy wells Stones ring;
like each tucked string tells, each hung bell's
Bow swung finds tongue to fling out broad its name;
Each mortal thing does one thing and the same:
Deals out that being indoors each one dwells;
Selves—goes itself; *myself* it speaks and spells,
Crying, *What I do is me: for that I came.*

– Gerard Manley Hopkins

Introduction

Objects in Mirror are Closer than They Appear

Nature loves to hide.

– Heraclitus

I love the disturbing corniness of the P.M. Dawn song "Set Adrift on Memory Bliss" and the accompanying video, in particular the extended mix that features footage from Spandau Ballet's song "True," which provides the backbone of the tune.[1] The corniness of the tune and the video is a little threatening, and it has a personal resonance for me. I heard it emanating over and over again from my brother's bedroom, in the summer of 1992, while he was rapidly descending into schizophrenia.

It was so sad to watch Steve doing this: it was as if he was saying goodbye to his mind. He kept listening to it over and over. And of course, that's what the song does: it attends to an affective state, memory bliss, over and over, as a way to say goodbye to someone—or to hold them in mind, not letting go. We just can't be sure. It's why the song works. It's a hip-hop song, made of pieces of other songs, samples. The song is almost like something you'd sing over one of your favorite records, a cherished object you play over and over again. And of course these pieces of objects are also elegiac, also about holding on to the feeling of something slipping away, being faithful, being true, but knowing that you are losing something. Treasuring an illusion, while kissing it goodbye. I found this so poignant in my brother's listening to this tune, my own cherished memory of my brother which I turn over and play again and again, reciting it to you now, like an ancient Greek rhapsode, the original rappers, the guys who memorized swathes of Homer and Hesiod and, as they say of musicians, *interpreted* them.

The song is a reading, an interpretation, of a Spandau Ballet song ("True"), which itself seems to be trying to copy or evoke something, to do justice to something, in the way that Number 1 hits so often do, as if they were busy quoting one another in some strange heaven for pop tunes. Prince Be certainly knows how to allude to everything, from Joni Mitchell to Wham!'s "Careless Whisper" to the Pointer Sisters' "Neutron Dance" to A Tribe Called Quest's "Bonita Applebum," quaintly renamed "Christina Applecake," to his own song "Reality Used to be a Friend of Mine." There is even a cameo shot of Julian Lennon, from his tribute to his father, "It's Too Late for Goodbyes."[2]

You could almost believe that the lost objects are right here—and they are right here, in the form of colors, sounds, words—one inside the other like Russian dolls: that inset piece of Spandau Ballet, corniest of New Romantic songs (there you go again: new Romantic), displaced amidst the strange psychedelia of P.M. Dawn, yet paid homage to at the same time. And yet those aesthetic forms are about absence and loss and illusion. Something is gone, and my fantasy of that thing is gone. Losing a fantasy is much harder than losing a reality. Yet here it comes again, that chorus, endlessly sampled—at least for the six minutes of eternity that the song carves out. You feel set adrift in the periodic cycling of presence, of the present, of a present that is full of absence, hesitation, mourning. In this respect, Prince Be might be the reincarnation of William Wordsworth.

Things are there, but they are not there: "That's the way it goes." The line suggests how things function, how they execute, how they have already disappeared. They have withdrawn, yet we have traces, samples, memories. These samples interact with one another, they interact with our us, they crisscross one another in a sensual configuration space. Yet the objects from which they emanate are *withdrawn.*[3] This doesn't mean that in every object there are, say, subsections 1, 2 and 3 and then Mystery Subsection 4 (the withdrawn section). This thought assumes objects can be broken into pieces somehow. Withdrawal means that at this very moment, this very object, as an intrinsic aspect of its being, is incapable of being anything else: my poem about it, its atomic structure, its function, its relations with other things ... Withdrawal isn't a violent sealing off. Nor is withdrawal some void or vague darkness. Withdrawal just is the unspeakable unicity of this lamp, this paperweight, this plastic portable telephone, this praying mantis, this frog, this Mars faintly red in the night sky, this cul-de-sac, this garbage can. An open secret.

The title of this book is a play on the literary genre of *magic realism*. Later in the twentieth century, writers such as Gabriel García Márquez developed a writing that incorporated elements of magic and paradox. In magic realist narratives, causality departs from purely mechanical functioning, in part to resist the seeming inevitability of imperialist "reality," in part to give voice to unspeakable things, or things that are almost impossible to speak according to imperialist ideology. *Realist Magic* argues that reality itself is not mechanical or linear when it comes to causality. Indeed, causality is a secretive affair, yet out in the open—an open secret. Causality is *mysterious*, in the original sense of the Greek *mysteria*, which means things that are unspeakable or secret. *Mysteria* is a neuter plural noun derived from *muein*, to close or shut. *Mystery* thus suggests a rich and ambiguous range of terms: secret, enclosed, withdrawn, unspeakable. This study regards the realness of things as bound up with a certain mystery, in these multiple senses: unspeakability, enclosure, withdrawal, secrecy. In this book I shall be using these terms to convey something essential about things. Things are *encrypted*. But the difference between standard encryption and the encryption of objects is that this is an unbreakable encryption. "Nature loves to hide" (Heraclitus).

The title *Realist Magic* is also meant to provoke thoughts about philosophical realism, the idea that there are real things. Realism is often considered a rather dull affair, with all the panache and weirdness on the antirealist side of the debate. We shall see that this is far from the case. The trouble with many theories of causality is that they edit out a quintessential element of mystery. Moreover, this might be a defining feature of theories of causality. It seems elementary that a theory of causality should put "understanding" in the place of mystery. Causality theories are preoccupied with explaining things away, with demystification. A theory of cause and effect shows you how the magic trick is done. But what if something crucial about causality resided at the level of the magic trick itself?

To think this way is to begin to work out an *object-oriented* view of causality. If things are intrinsically withdrawn, irreducible to their perception or relations or uses, they can only affect each other in a strange region out in front of them, a region of traces and footprints: the aesthetic dimension. Let us explore an example.

P.M. Dawn's song "Set Adrift on Memory Bliss" is disturbingly sweet, yet a strange sound cuts through the sweetness. A high-pitched glockenspiel sound, a periodic sound. A cycling sound, like the sound of a musical box. A slightly maddening sound. The notes are strange, pitched oddly, dissonantly, in relation to the soothing sway of the Spandau Ballet sample. Like a broken children's toy, something slightly mad, something slightly threatening. Sparkling as it rotates, a cold sliver of death, an absence of affect. No warm blood in that sound, it's a broken object stuck in repetition, atonal, slightly reminiscent of the beginning bars of *Pierrot Lunaire*.

That musical box rotation is the secret of the whole song—a sense of being stuck, of coexisting with these cycling processes. Grief is the photograph of an object buried deep inside you: every so often it releases some of its photons into the bloodstream. Grief is the footprint of something that isn't you, archaeological evidence of an object. Freud said that the ego is the record of abandoned object cathexes.[4] Like a petrified slab of ancient mud with a dinosaur's footprint in it. Like a glass whose shape was molded by blowers and blow tubes and powdered quartz sand. Every aesthetic trace, every footprint of an object, sparkles with absence. Sensual things are elegies to the disappearance of objects.

That sound, that broken musical box coldness, is the echo of a nonhuman world. A little fragment of the nonhuman, embedded in the soft warmth, indigestible. As if you could wipe away all the other sounds on the record and you would just be left with that. It intrudes. Yet it's so much more delicate, so much more childish, so much more just pure twinkling, than anything else.

Doesn't this tell us something about the aesthetic dimension, why philosophers have often found it to be a realm of evil? The aesthetic dimension is a place of illusions, yet they are real illusions. If you knew for sure that they were just illusions, then there would be no problem. But, as Jacques Lacan writes, "What constitutes pretense is that, in the end, you don't know whether it's pretense or not."[5] You can never know for sure, never know if it's an illusion. "She was right though, I can't lie." Yet Prince

Be is so tuned to the possibility that he could be seduced by the memory: "An eye for an eye, a spy for spy, / Rubber bands expand with a frustrating sigh ... I feel for her, I really do." I know this much is true. Reality is *like* an illusion, with the stress on that ambiguous *like*.

Intense yet tricksterish, the aesthetic dimension floats in front of objects, like a group of disturbing clowns in an Expressionist painting or a piece of performance art whose boundaries are nowhere to be seen. Prince Be has a very fine sense of this when he says "I think it's one of those déjà vu things, / Or a dream that's trying to tell me something ... Reality used to be a friend of mine." It's a maddening dimension for my brother, who finds it hard to look at pictures of smiling Buddhas, because he thinks they are enjoying the confusion too much. They aren't quite sincere, there must be something wrong with them, that Mona Lisa enigma could conceal a void, absolutely nothing at all, or a *meontic* void, a nothingness. Just a smile. If there are only objects, if time and space and causality, as I shall argue, emergent properties of objects—if all these things float "in front of" objects in what is called the aesthetic dimension, in a nontemporal, nonlocal space that is not in some beyond but right here, in your face—then nothing is going to tell us categorically what counts as real and what counts as unreal. Without space, without environment, without world, objects and their sensual effects crowd together like leering figures in a masquerade.

With their claustrophobic intimacy, this crowd of Expressionist things prevents anything like an "ideology of the aesthetic" from forming. In this book the aesthetic just isn't optional candy on top of objects, nor is it some dating service that bonds them together (since they are ontologically separated). As part of the project of *object-oriented ontology* (OOO), the philosophy whose first architect is Graham Harman, this book liberates the aesthetic from its ideological role as matchmaker between subject and object, a role it has played since the days of Kant.

Realist Magic is an exploration of causality from the point of view of object-oriented ontology. I argue that causality is wholly an *aesthetic* phenomenon. Aesthetic events are not limited to interactions between humans or between humans and painted canvases or between humans and sentences in dramas. They happen when a saw bites into a fresh piece of plywood. They happen when a worm oozes out of some wet soil. They happen when a massive object emits gravity waves. When you make or study art you are not exploring some kind of candy on the surface of a machine. You are making or studying causality. *The aesthetic dimension is the causal dimension.* It still astonishes me to write this, and I wonder whether having read this book you will cease to be astonished or not.

The advantages of such an approach are manifold, but perhaps the best is that this approach to causality can include all kinds of phenomena that other theories have trouble with. An OOO theory of causality can, for instance, include shadows and fear, language and lipstick, alongside billiard balls and photons.

The reason why art is important is that it's an exploration of causality, which as we know since post-Newtonian physics involves a lot more than just little metal balls clunking one another … entities interact in a *sensual ether* that is (at least to some extent) nonlocal and nontemporal.[6] That's how objects can influence one another despite the fact that they are enclosed from all forms of access, as my argument will outline. So when old fashioned art criticism speaks of timeless beauty, it is saying something quite profound about the nature of causation, not about spuriously universal human values.

Even if we rule out plausible causal sequences like "His anger made him hit the irritating old man" and focus only on "physical" causation, there are some mysterious things that seem to manifest in the causal realm that an OOO approach can explain quite well. Aesthetic-causal nonlocality and nontemporality should not be surprising features of the Universe. Quantum physics notwithstanding, even electromagnetic fields and gravity waves are nonlocal to some extent. At this moment, gravity waves from the beginning of the Universe are traversing your body. Maxwell and other pioneers of electromagnetism imagined the Universe as an immense ocean of electromagnetic waves. And then of course there's the real nonlocal deal—the quantum mechanical one. Consider the aesthetic shape of an electromagnetic field (how birds navigate, using tiny quantum magnets in their eyes).[7] Since at this level matter just is information, theoretical physics is already in an aesthetic conceptual space. Even the atomist Lucretius imagined causality working through aesthetic "films" emitted by objects.[8] But the arguments in this book go beyond a fanciful exploration of theoretical physics. They can be applied to any sort of entity whatsoever, not just the kind the physicists study.

One advantage of arguing that causality is aesthetic is that it allows us to consider what we call consciousness alongside what we call things. The basic quantum level phenomenon of action at a distance happens all the time. Thinking of a black hole is far safer than being in the vicinity of one, yet somehow thinking links us to it. Bertrand Russell denies physical action at a distance, arguing that causation can only be about contiguous things. If there is any action at a distance, he argues, then there must be some intervening entities that transmit the causality. In a wonderful passage Russell argues thus:

> [W]hen there is a causal connection between two events that are not contiguous, there must be intermediate links in the causal chain such that each is contiguous to the next, or (alternatively) such that there is a process which is continuous.[9]

Yet isn't this an elegant definition of the aesthetic dimension? Action at a distance happens all the time if causation is aesthetic. What is called consciousness is action at a distance. Indeed, we could go so far as to say that consciousness-of anything is action at a distance. Empirical phenomena such as mirror neurons and entanglement bear this out. Thus to be located "in" space or "in" time is already to have been caught in a web of relations. It is not that objects primordially "occupy" some existing region of spacetime, but that they are caught in the fields of, and otherwise "spaced" and "timed" by other entities. Minimally, what physics calls action at a distance is just the existence-for-the-other of the sensual qualities of any entity—an argument this book shall elucidate as we proceed.

Now in Plato's time they used to call action at a distance *demonic*. It was the action of demonic forces that mediated between the physical and nonphysical realms of existence. This is what Socrates says about art in the *Ion*: he compares art to a magnet in a string of magnets, from the Muse, goddess of inspiration, to the artist, to the work, to the performer, to the audience, all magnets linked by some demonic force.[10] We call this demonic force electromagnetism, but it's remarkably similar to Plato's insight: the electromagnetic wave transmits information over a distance; a receiver amplifies the information into music coming through the speakers of the PA system so you can hear P.M. Dawn. In an age of ecological awareness we will come again to think of art as a demonic force, carrying information from the beyond, that is, from nonhuman entities such as global warming, wind, water, sunlight and radiation. From coral bleaching in the ocean to the circling vortex of plastic bags in the mid Atlantic.

The trouble is, all this art is a translation, a metaphor for something. There is a profound ambiguity in the notion of interpretation, which Socrates notes. What is a just interpretation? What is justice, when it comes to a work of art? Socrates decides that a work of art isn't an accurate picture of something. It's a performance of something, some inner demonic force. And when the San Francisco Symphony Orchestra interprets a Mahler symphony, it doesn't mean that they tell you exactly what it means. They just play it. Yet within interpretation as performance and delivery we encounter a further ambiguity: between spontaneity, something emerging seemingly from nothing and reading, skill, expertise. Improvisation, as Derrida pointed out, is a kind of reading in which reading and writing are not so easy to distinguish. "The camera pans the cocktail glass, Behind a blind of plastic plants … " ("Set Adrift on Memory Bliss"). Why this deep ambiguity? Because the aesthetic dimension just is an ambiguous self-contradictory, tricksterish, illusion dimension; any theory that edits this out isn't worth the candle.

You start to read yourself, as a performer. Miles Davis asserted—at least this was attributed to Miles Davis, perhaps it's simply one of those sayings that float around in the demonic aesthetic dimension—that you have to play a long time to sound like yourself. Improvisation is music that listens to itself. It tunes. Art is a tuning, a *Stimmung*. And in an age of decisive awareness of nonhumans—that is, in an age when even instrumentalists such as Richard Dawkins and Republican Congresspeople have to mop their brows when global warming causes a heatwave—ecological art is going to be more and more about this kind of tuning.

That's the trouble with tuning. It's not about correct or incorrect interpretation, though surely some interpretations *are* better than others, since there are real objects. Like in jazz, a better solo would reveal something about the metal and the curvature and the size and the spittle of a trumpet; a good solo is when the instrument takes you over.[11] When the audience applauds an incredible solo, they are trying to touch the inside of a trumpet. The fact that trumpets can be manhandled in this way—or are they trumpet-handling humans?—to release what Harman calls their "molten core," tells us something about objects in general.[12] Because this never works absolutely—no solo ever exhausts the trumpet—there is that feeling that there is always more of the object than we think. One object—say an oud, a lute—can be attended to, attuned to, in different ways that bring out strange hidden properties of that object. In this sense playing an oud is like doing phenomenology. You are attending to the inner structure of the object, allowing yourself to be taken over by it. An oud is roughly the same object as a lute. How come you can get such different sounds from it, such different translations? The answer is the way things withdraw from total access. And this would be why Le Trio Joubran kills with their ouds, while a good player of Dowland is merely exquisite. Because there are real ouds, real lutes, no matter whose fingers are sliding up and down their necks.

It's not about adopting some position outside of the universe, some perfect meta position, some perfect attitude. That is just impossible, in an object-oriented universe, and in the current ecological emergency, just unfeasible. Even if you go to Mars, you are going there in relation to the emergency on planet Earth, as Kim Stanley Robinson's novels make so painfully clear. No, when you tune you are making another object. Tuning is the birth of another object: a tune, a reading, an interpretation. A rhapsodic rap about listening to Spandau Ballet and remembering your ex-lover. Every tune becomes an elegy for the disappearance, that is, the fundamental ontological secrecy, of an object or objects.

Yet when you tune, real things happen. You are affecting causality. You are establishing a link with at least one other actually existing entity. You are painting a black hole—the black hole is here, its horrifying opacity is right here, in the painting, yet not here. You are doing a drip painting: you are dripping about paint, like the way writing about music is like dancing about architecture. In OOO terms, this is what all objects are doing with each other. After all, no object truly contacts another one. They really only share what Harman calls their "notes." So architecture columns (or whatever it does) about human relationships. And dogs sniff about trees (nicely, "about" can also mean "around"). And pencils pencil about pencil sharpeners. The storm storms concerning the chimney it blows through. The calculator calculators concerning the bank balance I'm anxious about. The birds bird about the BP oil slick, telling us about it in bird metaphors. The train trains about the flash of lightning. The camera on the side of the track cameras about it. The photon photons about the electron. And weather weathers about global warming. And writing writes about music. Just like dancing about architecture.

Paintings have always been made of more things than humans. They have been made of paint, which is powdered crystals in some medium such as egg white or oil. Now when you put the painting on the wall, it also relates to the wall. A fly lands on it. Dust settles on it. Slowly the pigment changes despite your artistic intentions. We could think of all these nonhuman interventions as themselves a kind of art or design. Then we realize that nonhumans are also doing art all the time, it's just that we call it causality. But when calcium crystals coat a Paleolithic cave painting, they are also designing, also painting. Quite simply then, the aesthetic dimension is the causal dimension, which in turn means that it is also the vast nonlocal mesh that floats "in front of" objects (ontologically, not physically "in front of").

You are working directly with people's optic nerve and field of vision, as in a Bridget Riley painting. You cause the optical system to vibrate, creating interference patterns. Your painting is a device, a machine, an object that has causal effects. In reality. Aboriginal Australian painter Yukultji Napangati makes devices that scintillate in just this way, that lurch towards you in front of the painting, that threaten your sense of propriety. Napangati was one of the nine people who walked out of the Outback in 1984, some of the last Neolithic humans on Earth. This is what she makes: devices to talk to the spirit world, to allow the demonic force to assault you. In the flesh, not so much in a jpeg, they act like a dozen superimposed Bridget Rileys: the patterns just interlock and suggest layer upon layer of movement and hypnotic scintillation. They are frightening. And they are also paintings of where a small group of women wandered over some sandhills, doing a ritual here, digging for some roots there. An interpretation.

Objects and Non-Objects: $p \wedge \neg p$

The demonic aesthetic and the demonic causal are just a whisper apart from one another in thinking. Descartes worries precisely about action at a distance: perhaps he is being controlled by demons.[13] His refusal to accept this possibility leads to the *cogito*. Descartes mistrusts the sense of being deceived, using the Law of Noncontradiction to eliminate it. Many philosophers reproduce the bright line Descartes draws here, including speculative realist Quentin Meillassoux, who separates reason from belief with a laser-like certainty.[14] This separation has to do with real things that are not just thoughts in the (human) mind. Meillassoux argues that the stability of the universe makes it appear (but only appear) as if it could not have arisen by chance.

Yet physics argues that the appearance of stability is a function of randomness. Random patterns are the ones that seem regular. Clumping is a feature of true randomness. Meillassoux seems to take the idea that randomness equals instability, just like those he is refuting. He decides to eject the idea of randomness, because it implies some order, some law—he is trying to prove that there is no reason why things happen. This is only the case with mechanistic systems, such as dice (Meillassoux's example) and billiard balls (Hume). Quantum entanglement is truly random. What does this mean? It means for instance that in certain highly repeatable conditions the likelihood of a photon being polarized in a certain direction is totally uncertain before a "measurement" takes place. This is why quantum phenomena are incredibly good at generating random numbers.

"Totally uncertain" means that no matter how much information you have, you won't be able to predict the state of the photon. This is patently not the case with dice and billiard balls. *Totally uncertain means uncertain in itself, rather than when we measure.* One explanation for this total uncertainty is that a photon is in two or three different orientations simultaneously. This violates what Meillassoux takes to be the fundamental law (the one law he chooses not to violate), *the Law of Noncontradiction*. What does this violation mean? It means that you sure can apply "probabilistic reasoning" to the universe, and that far from being "meaningless" (Meillassoux), this is how incredibly basic things seem to operate.[15]

What would it mean not to eliminate the demonic dimension from causality? I do not encounter patterns and relations that are resolved in my mind into paintings, mud and glasses. These things encounter me directly, as themselves. But more precisely, every entity throws shadows of itself into the *interobjective* space, the sensual space that consists of relations between objects, carving out its own version of Plato's cave. It is like the poem by Gerard Manley Hopkins that provides one of this book's epigraphs:

> As kingfishers catch fire, dragonflies draw flame;
> As tumbled over rim in roundy wells
> Stones ring; like each tucked string tells, each hung bell's
> Bow swung finds tongue to fling out broad its name;
> Each mortal thing does one thing and the same:
> Deals out that being indoors each one dwells;
> Selves—goes itself; *myself* it speaks and spells,
> Crying, *What I do is me: for that I came.*[16]

This *myself* has an uncanny dimension. Like the person who assures you they are being sincere, can we ever really believe that objects don't play tricks with us? Again: "What constitutes pretense is that, in the end, you don't know whether it's pretense or not."[17] Duns Scotus speaks of the *haecceity* of a thing, its *thisness*, and Hopkins translates this into verse.[18] Yet the thisness is not imposed from without, objectively. It wells up from within. Hopkins himself says so explicitly: *What I do is me.* Quite so: it is a case of *I* versus *me*. In this difference between a reflexive and a nonreflexive personal pronoun, we detect archaeological evidence of the Rift (Greek, *chōrismos*) between a thing and its appearance. That concept, the Rift (I shall now begin to capitalize it), is highly significant in this book.

What Hopkins gives us then is not a brightly colored diorama of animated plastic, but a weird stage set from which things stage their unique version of the Cretan Liar Paradox: "This sentence is false." To speak otherwise is to have decided in advance what things are, which contradicts the way the poem itself forces us to experience things. "Tumbled over rim in roundy wells / Stones" are felt and heard before we hear what they have to say for themselves against the walls of the well and in the deep water within: the first line is an invisibly hyphenated adjective, tumbled-over-rim-in-roundy-wells. The adjective takes almost as long to read as it might take for an average stone to hit the water. The adjective draws out the stone, just as the dragonflies "draw flame." The stone becomes its tumbling, its falling-into-the-well, the moment at which it is thrown over the rim. Then splash—it's a stone alright, but we already sensed it as a non-stone.

All the things by which we specify the object are not the object. By *we* I mean humans, lavatory brushes, quasars and durum wheat, and the object in question itself. We have a very strange situation then, in which there are objects, and there are qualities and relations between these objects and other objects. There is a *chōrismos*, an irreducible gap. Qualities and relations are much the same thing, since they are born in interactions between the object and 1+*n* other things. A cinder block is hard and cold to a fly, it's stubbly to my finger, it's fragile to a well-placed karate chop. It's invisible to a neutrino. Think about a zero-degree *dark object*, some object that may or may not be behind a red curtain. It strictly has no qualities for us, yet this very lack of relationship is itself a kind of relationship, as if the dark object radiated some kind of energy that passed through us.

The qualities of the object are not the object. Objects then are both themselves and not-themselves. In defiance of the Law of Noncontradiction—a law that has never been properly proved—objects present us with the following paradox: objects are both objects and non-objects. All objects are open secrets, like the Liar: *This sentence is false.* Or like Russell's set paradox: the set of things that are not members of themselves.

We are now in a region of thinking traversed by logicians such as Graham Priest, who work on things that can be self-contradictory, in violation of the supposedly universal Law of Noncontradiction (LNC). The Liar, the Russell set paradox, and Kurt Gödel's Incompleteness Theorem all point to the possibility that this law does not always hold. For instance, Gödel establishes that for every logically coherent system, there must be at least one theorem that the system cannot prove, *in order for that system to be true* on its own terms: something like "This sentence cannot be proved."

Such entities seem to stretch the limits of thought, limits that some philosophers want to keep brittle and rigid—or else they insist that some things in reality just aren't logical at all. Let us suppose that we can voyage beyond these limits without departing from logic. What kind of logic would we need? Priest and Jay Garfield imagine that "Contradictions at the limits of thought have a general and bipartite structure":

> The first part is an argument to the effect that a certain view, usually about the nature of the limit in question, transcends that limit (cannot be conceived, described, etc.). This is *Transcendence*. The other is an argument to the effect that the view *is* within the limit—*Closure*. Often, this argument is a practical one, based on the fact that Closure is demonstrated in the very act of theorizing about the limits. At any rate, together, the pair describe a structure that can conveniently be called an *inclosure*: a totality, Ω and an object, o, such that o both is and is not in Ω.
>
> On closer analysis, inclosures can be found to have a more detailed structure. At its simplest, the structure is as follows. The inclosure comes with an operator, δ, which, when applied to any suitable subset of Ω, gives *another* object that is in Ω (that is, one that is not in the subset in question, but is in Ω). Thus, for example, if we are talking about sets of ordinals, δ might apply to give us the least ordinal not in the set. If we are talking about a set of entities that have been thought about, δ might give us an entity of which we have not yet thought. The contradiction at the limit arises when δ is applied to the totality Ω itself. For then the application of δ gives an object that is both within and without Ω: the least ordinal greater than all ordinals, or the unthought object.[19]

The first paragraph describes well the phenomena catalogued by OOO: things withdraw, which means that they limit what one can think about them. Things also contain other things that are not strictly them—just as a zebra is not reducible to its atoms, from an OOO point of view, and yet a zebra is composed of just these particular atoms. Objects are thus *inclosures* in Priest's and Garfield's terms. They are "closed"—a zebra is not a giraffe—and yet not closed—they contain things that are not themselves. When we study beings, we find at least one thing in them—this is Priest's and

Garfield's delta—that are "both in and not in" them. To be a thing, on this view, is to be riddled with contradiction.

Consider the well-known Sorites paradox: what constitutes a heap? One grain of sand doesn't constitute a heap; neither do two; nor do three; and so on. If we go on like this, we have ten thousand grains of sand that do not constitute a heap. Or consider a bald man's head. Adding one hair means that he is still bald; two hairs, ditto; three, ditto. We discover there's no magic number in which bald flips into hairy.

These paradoxes occur in the real world. Consider being in a doorway: are you inside or outside the room? Consider the status of a poem's title: is it the beginning of the poem or outside of it? Consider a frame: is it where the picture stops, or still part of the picture? Consider a first person narrative. Is the narrator who is telling the story identical with the narrator about whom the story is being told? In many cases, authors or stories play with the irreducible gap between these two I's. Every object says "myself." But in saying "myself" the object is also saying "I am at this very moment lying," "This sentence is false."

Charles Darwin's *The Origin of Species* is based on paradoxes that involve *dialetheias*—contradictions, "double truths." You just can't specify when one species ends and another begins, just as you can't specify the first little old lady who said the word "shizzle."[20] In fact, so dire is the paradox of evolution that Darwin should have used some kind of wink emoticon, had one been available, and scare quotes: *The "Origin" of "Species" ;)*. The punchline of Darwin's book is that *there are no species and they have no origin*. Yet every day we see skinks, kiwis and sheep, not to mention slime molds, viruses and mushrooms, uniquely themselves. These lifeforms are made of other lifeforms, which in turn are made of non-living entities, all the way down to the DNA level and beyond. Yet they are unique and specifiable as this actual slime mold, this little patch of bright yellow looking like a spot of dog's vomit at the end of my cul-de-sac.[21] A slime mold is a non-slime mold, or as one philosopher puts it, a rabbit is a non-rabbit. I take this to mean not that no rabbit exists, but that there is a real rabbit whose essence is withdrawn.[22]

Objects are non-objects. I do not mean a non-object in the sense that for François Laruelle there is an unspeakable, radical immanence that no philosophy can speak—nay, that philosophy must actively exclude in order to exist, hence his invention of "non-philosophy" to account for this radical immanence.[23] An object is a non-object not because it is "really" something else, a void or some featureless lump or a moment in my reflective process—but *because an object isn't something else*. The "selfness," the Duns Scotus-like haecceity, of a thing baffles everything around it with its radiant, barbed identity. Blake wrote about seeing infinity in a grain of sand.[24] He was technically correct: this is a very OOO insight. And he precisely means not that some abstraction underlies a grain of sand, but, as he puts it, this "minute particular" is irreducible to anything else at all. Reality, on the OOO view, is a dense thorn bush spiked with diamond tipped thorns that dig into my flesh from every angle—that *are* my flesh. To find oneself in an OOO universe is to allow the thorns to sting you, a little more each day.

But wait, there's more. There are objects and non-objects. In other words, there is an object and there are all the things that are not that object; some of those things are the relations the object is caught in with other objects; some of those things are straightforwardly other objects. Mathematical objects, for instance, on this view, are unreal objects that have to do with the qualities and relations of real objects. "Two" does not exist outside the countability of some objects as two. Two means *countably two*—two is computable two, not some Platonic two floating in some beyond. We can describe two by describing what some objects, for instance a counting machine, do when they encounter objects that are countably two.

If objects are irreducibly secret, causality must reside somewhere in the realm of relations between objects, along with things like number, qualities, time, space and so on. This is congruent with the last century of physics. For Einstein, space and time are also emergent properties of objects: objects don't float in a neutral void but emanate waves and ripples of spacetime. Clocks run faster in orbit above Earth than they do on Earth's surface. This congruency is a good sign that an object-oriented theory of causality is on the right track. But it's not strictly necessary: if anything the necessity goes the other way around. In other words, quantum theory and relativity are valid physical theories to the extent that they are object-oriented.

Causality floats in front of objects, figuratively speaking. It doesn't lie underneath them like some grey machinery. Another way of saying this is that causality must belong to the aesthetic dimension. To study the aesthetic dimension, then, is to study causality. Art students and literary critics have a reason for celebrating. Not because reality is a construct, but amazingly, because it isn't. Precisely because reality is real—that is, encrypted against access by any object, including a probing human mind—the aesthetic dimension is incredibly important.

Objects withdraw, yet they appear: $p \wedge \neg p$ (*p* and *not-p*). And objects can contain beings that are not themselves, thus exemplifying Russell's paradoxical (and for him, illegal) set of things that are not members of themselves. Now to some people, this means that objects can be anything, since anything can result from a contradiction (*ex contradictione quodlibet*, ECQ). There are good reasons for supposing that ECQ doesn't hold just because LNC doesn't hold.[25] The fact that contradictions can be true doesn't necessarily imply that just anything can be true (triviliasm). The fact that baldness is vague doesn't imply that being bald could manifest as sprouting azaleas from the top of your head.

Any attempt to reduce the dialetheic properties of objects—they are both themselves and not-themselves at one and the same time—is doomed. Such attempts to smooth out the terrain of things are rife in metaphysics: objects are made of atoms; or they are substances decorated with accidents; or they are components of a machine; or they are instantiations of a process; and so on. The very attempt to introduce consistency creates more drastic inconsistencies, as if objects were viral, sneakily upgrading themselves in the face of the attempt to make them behave. If we started with $p \wedge \neg p$ we wouldn't need to specify some originary entity outside the universe, some kind of prime mover or causeless cause (God) that makes it all work. There is enough dynamism in $p \wedge \neg p$ already for things to start working all by themselves. If you really want to be an atheist, you might have to consider dropping mechanism and relationism in favor of the object-oriented view.

Meillassoux rules violations of LNC out of court totally. Then he lets them back in a little bit, via a consideration of paraconsistent logics—that is, logical systems that employ seeming paradoxes but in a relatively constrained way. Meillassoux constrains their constraint even further by policing paraconsistency—he holds that they have only to do with databases and other software entities.[26] Meillassoux is afraid that if LNC is breached, philosophy opens the door to belief and restrains thinking. The fundamental difference is that I hold that contradictory beings exist—that this is what existence is in some deep sense. In other words, violations of LNC such as the Liar paradox ("This statement is false") exist as archaeological evidence of something in the ontological realms. The fact that consistent systems are also incomplete (Gödel) is also compelling, despite what Meillassoux says about logical systems and inconsistency. There are plenty of paraconsistent theories that pertain not to software but, for instance, to the way hydrogen atoms behave, and the way waves propagate.

OBJECTS IN MIRROR ARE CLOSER THAN THEY APPEAR

An ontological insight is engraved onto the passenger side wing mirrors of every American car: *Objects in Mirror are Closer than They Appear*. What we take to be the object "behind" its appearance is really a kind of perspective trick caused by a habitual normalization of the object in question. It is my habitual causal relationship with it that makes it seem to sink into the background. This background is nothing other than an aesthetic effect—it's produced by the interaction of 1+*n* objects. The aesthetic dimension implies the existence of at least one withdrawn object. To put it another way, in order for anything to happen, there has to be an object in the vicinity that has nothing to do with the happening in question. For instance: the pixels out of which these words are made as I type them on my Macbook don't care what you are reading right now. That's why you can read these words (or at least, it's one reason why).

And now here is Professor Morton's handy *shoplifting* advice. *Always do it in front of the camera*. Don't try to hide what you're doing. The only time I got caught (I know of what I speak) is when I tried to hide it. Why? If you do it in front of the camera, no one watching will be able to believe what she is seeing. Do it slowly, deliberately, right in front of security. The sense that causality must be happening "behind" objects is a phenomenological illusion. When one object (for instance me) transitions from a certain set of objects to another set, it briefly undergoes the uncanny realization that *not-at-homeness is always the case*, that sensual relations are never the real thing. What we call causality, say when a finger depresses a light switch, is an uncanny moment that happens in front of the encrypted objects, when a strange object perturbs a domain that has achieved a *necessarily, structurally false* ontic familiarity. The thorn tips of reality are hiding in plain sight, right in front of the camera.

Causality is already happening: the light switch rests on the wall, the wall supports the switch, electrons are flowing in the wire, the wall is part of a house. All these are causal statements from this point of view. What we call causality is just an uncanny disruption of a metastable system of entities that only appears to be real because it lasts longer than the moment of the "cause." Mechanistic and other forms of "behind the scenes" theories of causality must therefore be seen as a desperate attempt to normalize this uncanny state of affairs.

The weird clownlike demons that float in front of objects are up to all kinds of tricks. Think about radiation. A unit of radiation is some kind of quantum, such as a gamma ray. It's very hard to see a gamma ray in itself. You have to cause it to be deflected in some way, or to mark some inscribable surface such as a photographic plate. So you can see gamma rays when they illuminate a body, like in an X-ray photo. Gamma rays tune to us, gamma ray-pomorphizing us into a gamma ray-centric parody of ourselves. Radioactive materials are wonderful for thinking about how causality is aesthetic. At the quantum level, to see something just is to hit it with a photon or an electron: hence to alter it in some way. Every seeing, every measurement, is also an adjustment, a parody, a translation, an interpretation. A tune and a tuning.

Now scale this up to think about nuclear radiation from plutonium, the entity that exists distributed over Earth for 24.1 thousand years. This entity is nothing but the sum of all the gamma, alpha and beta ray inscription events occurring throughout the 24.1 thousand year period. It is the living history of plutonium. The dust in Nevada. The dust of Bikini Atoll. Bikinis. All the glass-like substances created when nuclear bombs explode. The sound of the bomb radiating out into the atmosphere. The shock waves that produce seismic effects. The half-life of plutonium and uranium. That monstrous pool of melted uranium at Chernobyl, which you can only look at in a photograph unless you want to die quickly. Photons striking the uranium record it on a photographic plate or in the memory of a digital camera. Software samples this image at a certain rate, creating a jpeg that you are now seeing. The jpeg introduces gaps in the image because of its unique sampling rate and its lossy compression. Everywhere we look, aesthetic–causal events are occurring.

Time to start again, from scratch. Consider again Yukultji Napangati's painting *Untitled*, 2011, which resides in the Art Gallery of New South Wales, highly commended for the 2011 Wynne Prize. At a distance it looks like a woven mat of reeds or slender stalks, yellowed, sun baked, resting on top of some darker, warmer depth. A generous, relaxed, precise, careful yet giving, caring lineation made of small blobby dots. The warmth reminds you of Klee. The lines remind you of Bridget Riley. As you come closer and begin to face the image it begins to play, to scintillate, to disturb the field of vision. It oscillates and ripples, more intense than Riley. This is a painting about, a map of, a writing about, a lineation of women traveling through the sandhills of Yunala in Western Australia, performing rituals and collecting bush foods as they went. The painting is a map of an event unfolding in a two-dimensional rendering of a higher dimensional phase space.

Then something begins. What? You begin to see the "interobjective" space in which your optic nerve is entangled with the objects in the painting. The painting begins to paint right in front of you, paint the space between your eyes and the canvas. Layers of perception co-created by the painting and the field of vision begin to detach themselves from the canvas in front of you, floating closer to you. This "floating closer" effect is associated with the phenomenology of uncanniness.

The painting gazes. Intersecting shards of patterns within patterns, patterns across patterns, patterns floating on top of patterns. A constant mutagenic dance between the levels of patterns. The painting is a device for opening this phenomenal display. It comes lurching towards you, hypnotizing you and owning you with its directives of sandhill, women, rituals, bush food, walking, singing, lines. You feel gripped by the throat with the passion of the imagery. All the hairs on your arms stand up and the painting has you in its electromagnetic field. The painting dreams. Causality begins.

What does this mean? I do not access Napangati's painting across a space. The image is not a mute object waiting to have its meaning supplied by a subject, nor is it a blank screen; nor is it something objectively present "in" space. Rather the painting emits something like electromagnetic waves, in whose force field I find myself. The painting powerfully demonstrates what is already the case: space and time are emergent properties of objects. For Kant, "space is the pure form of sensible intuition": what must be given in advance in order for objects to be intuited.[27] Relying on Newton, Kant thinks space as a box. But in this book, space is emitted by objects.

That this fact is common to relativity and to phenomenology should give us pause. Perhaps just as remarkable is the fact that relativity and phenomenology arose roughly synchronously towards the beginning of the twentieth century. Just as Einstein discovered that spacetime was the warped and rippling gravitational field of an object, so Husserl discovered that consciousness was not simply an empty limpid medium in which ideas float. Consciousness, as revealed by phenomenology, is also a dense, rippling entity in its own right, like the wavering water of Monet's contemporary water lily paintings: the water that is the true subject of those paintings.

The aesthetic form of an object is where the causal properties of the object reside. Theories of physical causation frequently want to police aesthetic phenomena, reducing causality to the clunking or clicking of solid things.[28] It is not the case that a shadow is only an aesthetic entity, a flimsy ghost without effects. Plato saw shadows as dangerous precisely because they do have a causal influence.[29] When my shadow intersects with the light sensitive diode, the nightlight switches on. As stated above, when a quantum is measured, it means that another quantum has intersected with it, altering it, changing its position or momentum.[30] Aesthetics, perception, causality, are all almost synonyms.

When the light-sensitive diode detects my shadow, it perceives in every meaningful sense, if we only accept that objects exert an aesthetic influence on one another (*aisthēnesthai*, Greek "to perceive"). When I am caught in another's gaze, I am already the object of causal influences. Causality does not take place "in" a space that has been established already. Instead, it radiates from objects. The gaze emanates from the force field of a Napangati painting. It gathers me into its disturbing, phantasmal unfolding of zigzagging lines and oscillating patches.

There is no such thing as a phenomenologically empty space. Space is teeming with waves, particles, magnetic seductions, erotic curvature and menacing grins. Even when they are isolated from all external influences, objects seem to breathe with a strange life. A tiny metal tuning fork thirty microns long rests in a vacuum. To the naked eyes of the observers outside, it is breathing: it seems to occupy two places at the same time.[31] There is already a Rift between an object and its aesthetic appearance, a Rift within the object itself. Causality is not something that happens between objects, like some coming out party or freely chosen bargain into which things enter. It pours constantly from a single object itself, from the *chōrismos* between its essence and its appearance. The *chōrismos* gives rise to "blue notes" that both do and do not "express" the object in question, just as a blue note is pitched exquisitely, infuriatingly, impossibly between harmony and dissonance.[32] Objects are blues singing femmes fatales in the seedy cocktail lounge of reality.

An object is therefore both itself and not-itself, at the very same time. ("What is the difference between a duck? One of its legs is both the same.") If this were not the case, nothing could happen. The uncanniness of objects, even to themselves, is what makes them float, breathe, oscillate, threaten, seduce, rotate, cry, orgasm. Because objects are themselves and not-themselves, the logic that describes them must be paraconsistent or even fully dialetheic: that is, the logic must be able to accept that some contradictions are true.[33] Objects are dangerous, not only to themselves, but even to thinking, if it cleaves to rigid consistency. If thinking refuses to accept that objects can be dialetheic, it risks reproducing the dualisms of subject and object, substance and accidents, dualisms that are unable to explain the most basic ontological decision—the one that insists that things are objectively present, as they are. The thing becomes imprisoned in a philosophically constructed cage, a mechanism or in some kind of ideality that falsely resolves the dilemma by shunting everything into a (human) subject. Moreover, thinking itself becomes brittle. The more rigorous the metalanguage, the more susceptible it is to more and more virulent contradictions.[34] Thinking should learn from *Antigone* and bend, like a willow: "Seest thou, beside the wintry torrent's course, how the trees that yield to it save every twig, while the stiff-necked perish root and branch?"[35]

Phenomenology, then, is an essential cognitive task of confronting the threat that things pose in their very being. Without it, thinking is unable to break through the traditional ways of philosophizing that Martin Heidegger calls "sclerotic."[36] After phenomenology, we can only conclude that a great deal of philosophizing is not an abstract description or dispassionate accounting, but only an intellectual defense against the threatening intimacy of things. Moreover, since there is very little difference between what happens to a light sensitive diode and what happens to a human when they encounter a shadow, we can only conclude that there is a strange kind of nonhuman phenomenology, or, as Ian Bogost puts it, an *alien phenomenology*.[37]

The reader will find that the phenomenological approach requires a cycling, iterative style that examines things again and again, now with a little more detail here, then with a little more force there. It's like turning a curiously shaped stone around in one's hands. There are good reasons for this outside the general scope of phenomenology. For a start, thinking objects is one of the most difficult yet necessary things thinking can do—trying to come close to them is the point, rather than retreating to the grounds of the grounds of the possibility of the possibility of asserting anything at all, as Harman puts it in his first outline of OOO.[38] The difficulty lies in the nature of objects themselves and in the two-hundred-year—within a five-hundred-year—within a two-thousand-year—cycle in which thinking has been caught. Moreover, since the OOO view is new in the world, and since the theory of vicarious causation is its most counter-intuitive aspect—though, as I hope to establish, the theory is also one of its most satisfying aspects—the chapter that follows this introduction must reiterate in greater detail some of the themes that have already emerged, in order to lay a foundation for setting out the scope of book as a whole. I shall thus reserve a detailed outline of Chapters 2, 3 and 4 for the end of the first chapter, where it will make much better sense. Before we proceed to the alien phenomenology, Chapter 1 will revolve again around the reasons why the aesthetic dimension is the causal dimension.

Notes

1. P.M. Dawn, "Set Adrift on Memory Bliss," *Of the Heart, of the Soul, and of the Cross* (Gee Street, Island, 1991); available at http://www.youtube.com/watch?v=K11ju_NfnhM.

2. Spandau Ballet, "True," *True* (Chrysalis Records, 1983); Wham! "Careless Whisper," *Make It Big* (Columbia, 1984); A Tribe Called Quest, "Bonita Applebum," *People's Instinctive Travels and the Paths of Rhythm* (Jive Records, 1990); The Pointer Sisters, "Neutron Dance," *Break Out* (Planet, 1984); PM Dawn, "Reality Used to be a Friend of Mine," *Of the Heart, of the Soul, and of the Cross*; Julian Lennon, "Too Late for Goodbyes" (Atlantic, Charisma, 1984).

3. The term "withdrawal" is Graham Harman's translation of Heidegger's term *Entzug*. See Harman, *Tool-Being: Heidegger and the Metaphysics of Objects* (Peru, IL: Open Court, 2002).

4. Sigmund Freud, *The Ego and the Id*, tr. Joan Riviere, revised and ed. James Strachey, intro. Peter Gay (New York: Norton 1989), 24. I am grateful to James Manos for originally suggesting this to me.

5. Jacques Lacan, *Le séminaire, Livre III: Les psychoses* (Paris: Editions de Seuil, 1981), 48.

6. The term is Graham Harman's. See *Guerrilla Metaphysics: Phenomenology and the Carpentry of Things* (Chicago: Open Court, 2005), 33–44.

7. Erik M. Gauger et al., "Sustained Quantum Coherence and Entanglement in the Avian Compass," *Physical Review Letters* 106 (January 28, 2011), DOI 10.1103/PhysRevLett.106.040503.

8. Lucretius, *On the Nature of Things*, tr. William Ellery Leonard (Internet Classics Archive, MIT, http://classics.mit.edu/Carus/nature_things.4.iv.html), 4.26–215. See Levi Bryant, "Of the Simulacra: Atomic Images (Lucretius)," http://larval-subjects.wordpress.com/2012/04/24/of-the-simulacra-atomic-images-lucretius/.

9. Bertrand Russell, *Human Knowledge* (New York: Simon and Shuster, 1948), 491.

10. Plato, *Ion* tr. Benjamin Jowett, available at http://classics.mit.edu/Plato/ion.html (accessed June 25, 2012).

11. I'm grateful to Bill Benzon for an ongoing discussion of these matters.

12. Harman's term comes from *Prince of Networks: Bruno Latour and Metaphysics* (Melbourne: Re.Press, 2009), 215.

13. René Descartes, *Meditations and Other Metaphysical Writings*, tr. and intro. Desmond M. Clarke (London: Penguin, 1998, 2000), 22–24.

14. Quentin Meillassoux, *After Finitude: An Essay on the Necessity of Contingency*, tr. Ray Brassier (New York: Continuum, 2009), 28–49.

15. Meillassoux, *After Finitude*, 100.

16. Gerard Manley Hopkins, *The Major Works*, ed. Catherine Phillips (Oxford: Oxford University Press, 2009).

17. Lacan, *Le séminaire*, 48.

18. John Duns Scotus, *Philosophical Writings*, tr. Allan Wolter (Indianapolis: Hackett, 1987), 166–167.

19. Jay Garfield and Graham Priest, "Nagarjuna and the Limits of Thought," *Philosophy East and West* 53.1 (January, 2003), 1–21 (4).

20. Darwin draws the same analogy with etymology. No study of dialect can specify the very first speaker of a word, for the simple reason that in order to exist, a word has to be repeated: *The Origin of Species*, ed. Gillian Beer (Oxford and New York:

Oxford University Press, 1996). Gillian Beer, Introduction, *The Origin of Species*, xix.

21. I refer to the Dog's Vomit slime mold, *Fuligo septica*.
22. Ray Brassier, "Behold the Non-Rabbit: Kant, Quine, Laruelle," *Pli* 12 (2001), 50–82.
23. François Laruelle, *Philosophies of Difference: A Critical Introduction to Non-Philosophy* (New York: Continuum, 2011).
24. William Blake, *Auguries of Innocence*, 1. *The Complete Poetry and Prose of William Blake*, ed. David V. Erdman (New York: Doubleday, 1988).
25. Graham Priest, *In Contradiction: A Study of the Transconsistent* (Oxford: Oxford University Press, 2006), 5–6, 42, 103, 185.
26. Meillassoux, *After Finitude*, 76–79.
27. Martin Heidegger, *What Is a Thing?* tr. W.B. Barton and Vera Deutsch, analysis by Eugene T. Gendlin (Chicago: Henry Regnery, 1967), 198–199.
28. Dowe, *Physical Causation*, 17, 25, 59, 63–64.
29. Plato, *The Republic*, tr. Desmond Lee (Harmondsworth; Penguin, 1983), 317–324 (514a–520a).
30. David Bohm, *Quantum Theory* (New York: Dover, 1989), 99–115.
31. Aaron O'Connell, M. Hofheinz, M. Ansmann, Radoslaw C. Bialczak, M. Lenander, Erik Lucero, M. Neeley, D. Sank, H. Wang, M. Weides, J. Wenner, John M. Martinis and A. N. Cleland, "Quantum Ground State and Single Phonon Control of a Mechanical Ground Resonator," *Nature* 464 (March 17, 2010), 697–703.
32. It is appropriate to pay homage here to Levi Bryant's "The Mug Blues," a multi-valent pun on essence versus appearance: *The Democracy of Objects* (Ann Arbor: Open Humanities Press, 2011) 87–94.
33. Priest, *In Contradiction* 9–27.
34. Priest, *In Contradiction*, 17–23.
35. Haimon, in *Antigone*, tr. R.C. Jebb, http://classics.mit.edu/Sophocles/antigone.html.
36. Martin Heidegger, *Being and Time*, tr. Joan Stambaugh (Albany, N.Y: State University of New York Press, 1996), 20.
37. Ian Bogost, *Alien Phenomenology or, What It's Like to Be a Thing* (Minneapolis: University of Minnesota Press, 2012), 1–34.
38. Graham Harman, "Object-Oriented Philosophy," *Towards Speculative Realism: Essays and Lectures* (Ropley: Zero Books, 2010), 93–104 (95).

Chapter 1

Like an Illusion

> Surprisingly, the *Viking 1* lander, which remains on Mars, is considered part of the Smithsonian Air and Space Museum.
>
> – Ann Garrison Darrin and Beth Laura O'Leeary, eds., *Handbook of Space Engineering, Archaeology, and Heritage*

In 2011 Saeed Ahmed painted over *Gorilla in a Pink Mask*, a painting by the artist Banksy. As the *Guardian* newspaper makes clear, the wall of a new Muslim cultural center was "covered with graffiti." The online Banksy Forum swiftly denounced the painting-over as "vandalism of the first order."[1] Graffiti makes clear the physical properties of writing, along with its graphic and painterly qualities.

Now we could stop here and consider ourselves to have done some Derridean work.[2] Or we could think in the well-worn grooves of cultural studies, reflecting on the relationship between high and low art. In his defense, Ahmed observed, "I thought [the piece] was worthless. I didn't know it was valuable. That's why I painted over it."

Let us, however, proceed a little further. One of the many intriguing things about graffiti is that it straddles *decorating* and *causing* or *affecting*. Astonishingly, Saeed's erasure of Banksy is capable of being construed as vandalism against graffiti itself. When something is erased it has been affected by some other object. Why? Because there is a profound ambiguity in objects, which is precisely the Rift (Greek, *chōrismos*) between their being and their appearance. This results in appearance having a slightly evil aura, according to some philosophical views. Because you can never be sure. Appropriately enough, a painting of a gorilla in a pink eye mask, the sort worn to a masquerade or by some Lone Ranger, is ambiguous on many levels. Are humans gorillas in pink masks? Is the gorilla male or female? Is pink a girl's color? Is it art? Is it vandalism? We can ask the final two questions *because art is always already vandalism*. And what is vandalism? Why, causality …

One could read *Realist Magic* as an extended meditation on the conundrum of *Gorilla in a Pink Mask* and its whitewash fate. Why study or make art? Because when you do so, you are exploring causality. A bonus feature of *Realist Magic*, then, will be to place the arts and their study at a central point in the affairs of the world. Notice that my argument is the inverse of the usual anti-utilitarian one, which argues that artistic things are only meaningful insofar as they correlate reality with humans. Such arguments abound these days and they are just asking for trouble. "We know very well that the universe is just a machine of particles, but we must make it meaningful for us somehow"; or "For humans it's deeply significant even though we are insignificant"; or "Useless things are really useful in some other way." There are many variants of this justification of the aesthetic. All of them are just art as whistling in the dark. In this book, by contrast, I shall argue that *there is no dark*. It's *all* aesthetics, all the way down, the mechanistic view or eliminative materialist views being precisely one aesthetic effect among many, but taken as real: absurdly, as more real than others, as if to say that a clunking and whirring sound were more real than other sounds. How can one aesthetic effect be more real than another? To assert otherwise is to fall prey to some kind of theology, even if it comes dressed as scientism. (Heidegger and Derrida call it *ontotheology* when a philosophy says that all things are *x*, but some things are more *x* than others.)

The Mystery of the Cinder Block

And so to business. There's no way to break the object-oriented ontological news gently, so we must perforce commence with a rough and ready version. The proposition that begins the next paragraph says something that is given to me in experience. For this reason alone I find it hard to trust, because as an avid reader of poetry, I am liable to mistrust statements of all kinds. Yet as you read this book you will see that the following statement could not have been otherwise, nor could there have been another way to begin. Only insofar as you make it through the book, will you discover the remarkable, strange, totally non-given quality of the proposition.

There are objects: cinnamon, microwaves, interstellar particles and scarecrows. There is nothing underneath objects. Or, better, there is *not even nothing* underneath them. There is no such thing as *space* independent of objects (happily contemporary physics agrees). What is called *Universe* is a large object that contains objects such as black holes and racing pigeons. Likewise there is no such thing as an *environment*: wherever we look for it, we find all kinds of objects—biomes, ecosystems, hedges, gutters and human flesh. In a similar sense, there is no such thing as *Nature*. I've seen penguins, plutonium, pollution and pollen. But I've never seen *Nature* (I capitalize the word to reinforce a sense of its deceptive artificiality).

Likewise, there is no such thing as *matter*. I've seen plenty of entities (this book shall call them *objects*): photographs of diffusion cloud chamber scatterings, drawings of wave packets, iron filings spreading out around a magnet. But I've never seen *matter*. So when Mr. Spock claims to have found "Matter without form," he is sadly mistaken, as is Henry Laycock, who asserts the same thing.[3] You can now buy a backpack that is made of recycled plastic bottles. But an object doesn't consist of some gooey substrate of becoming that shifts like Proteus from plastic bottle to backpack. First there is the plastic bottle, then the production of the bag ends the bottle, its being is now only an appearance, a memory of the backpack, a thought: "This bag is made of plastic bottles."

This is a book about realism without matter. Matter, in current physics, is simply a state of information. Precisely: information is necessarily information-for (for some addressee). Matter requires at least one other entity in order to be itself. Matter is "materials-for":

> The work is dependent on leather, thread, nails, and similar things. Leather in its turn is produced from hides. These hides are taken from animals which are bred and raised by others.[4]

Nature likewise is "discovered in the use of useful things."[5] I take *use* here to apply not only to humans, but also to bees with their flowers and hives, chimpanzees with their digging sticks, slime molds with their wet pavements. This is not an argument about how humans impose meaning on mute things. It's an argument about the fact that what humans call matter and Nature are ontologically secondary to something else. A sort of backward glance confers the material status of matter and the natural status of Nature: the backward glance not of a cognizing being, necessarily, but of a task accomplished. The key turns in the lock: "Oh, that's what the key was for." There must, then, be something "behind" or "beyond" matter—and object-oriented ontology (OOO) gives us a term for this: simply, what is behind matter is an *object*.

Instead of using matter as my basic substrate, I shall paint a picture of the Universe that is realist but not materialist. In my view, real objects exist inside other real objects. "Space" and "environment" are ways in which objects sensually relate to the other objects in their vicinity, including the larger objects in which they find themselves. Sometimes humans have called some of these sensual relationships *Nature*. Then we run into all kinds of difficulties and frankly ideological confusions. A snail is Nature, perhaps—but a cooked snail isn't? Or a cartoon of a snail? Or an irradiated snail?

There is no space or environment as such, only objects. Moreover, in the succession of these objects, there is also *no top object*: no entity that lords it over the rest, whose reality is superior to or more powerful than theirs, one ontotheological object to rule them all. Although this may seem startling, the reason why is quite straightforward. If there is no space separate from objects, then a top object would imply either: (1) this object is unlike every other object and really is "space" for all the rest; or (2) this object floats or sits inside some kind of "space"—which on this view would simply be the inside of another object. When physicists try to think about the Universe as an entity in its own right, they soon run into the edges of this problem. Thus some physicists have suggested a bubble multiverse in which our one is simply one of many—which strictly pushes the problem back a stage further:

where does this foam come from and in what is it sitting? God's hot tub, perhaps. OOO is more comfortable with the implication of this assertion—a potentially infinite regress—than it is with ontotheological top objects.

For much the same reason, it's evident that there is *no bottom object*, either, no smallest entity that subtends all the others, somehow more real than them. An object withdraws from access. This means that its own parts can't access it. Since an object's parts can't fully express the object, the object is not reducible to its parts. OOO is anti-reductionist. But OOO is also anti-holist. An object can't be reduced to its "whole" either. The whole is not greater than the sum of its parts. So we have a strange *irreductionist* situation in which an object is reducible neither to its parts nor to its whole.[6] A coral reef is made of coral, fish, seaweed, plankton and so on. But one of these things on its own doesn't embody part of a reef. Yet the reef just is an assemblage of these particular parts. You can't find a coral reef in a parking lot. In this way, the vibrant realness of a reef is kept safe both from its parts and from its whole. Moreover, the reef is safe from being mistaken for a parking lot. Objects can't be reduced to tiny Lego bricks such as atoms that can be reused in other things. Nor can they be reduced upwards into instantiations of a global process. A coral reef is an expression of the biosphere or of evolution, yes; but so is this sentence, and we ought to be able to distinguish between coral reefs and sentences.

The preceding facts go under the heading of *undermining*. Any attempt to undermine an object—in thought, or with a gun, or with a particle accelerator, or with the ravages of time or heat—will not get at the encrypted essence of the object. By essence is meant something very different from *essentialism*. This is because essentialism depends upon some aspect of an object that OOO holds to be a mere appearance of that object, an appearance-for some object. This reduction to appearance holds even if that object for which the appearance occurs is the object itself! Even a coral reef can't grasp its essential coral reefness. In essentialism, a superficial appearance is taken for the essence of a thing, or of things in general. Feminism, anti-racism and queer theory are justified in assaulting this kind of essence by any means necessary.

In thinking essentialism we may be able to discern another way of avoiding OOO. This is what Harman has christened *overmining*.[7] The overminer decides that some things are more real than others: say for example human perception. Then the overminer decides that other things are only granted realness status by somehow coming into the purview of the more real entity. On this view, only when I measure a photon, only when I see a coral reef, does it become what it is, in a kind of "upward reduction." But when I measure a photon, I never measure the actual photon. Indeed, since at the quantum scale *to measure* means "to hit with a photon or an electron beam" (or whatever), measurement, perception (*aisthēsis*), and doing become the same. What I "see" are deflections, tracks in a cloud chamber or interference patterns. Far from underwriting a world of pure illusion where the mind is king, quantum theory is one of the very first truly rigorous realisms, thinking its objects as irreducibly resistant to full comprehension, by anything.[8]

So far we have made objects safe from being swallowed up by larger objects and broken down into smaller objects—undermining. And so far we have made objects safe from being mere projections or reflections of some supervenient entity—overmining. That's quite a degree of autonomy. Everything in the coral reef, from the fish to a single coral lifeform to a tiny plankton, is autonomous. But so is the coral reef itself. So are the heads of the coral, a community of tiny polyps. So is each individual head. Each object is like one of Leibniz's monads, in that each one contains a potentially *infinite regress* of other objects; and around each object, there is a potentially *infinite progress* of objects, as numerous multiverse theories are now also arguing. But the infinity, the uncountability, is more radical than Leibniz, since there is nothing stopping a group of objects from being an object, just as a coral reef is something like a society of corals. Each object is "a little world made cunningly" (John Donne).[9]

The existence of an object is irreducibly a matter of coexistence. Objects contain other objects, and are contained "in" other objects. Let us, however, explore further the ramifications of the autonomy of objects. We shall discover that this mereological approach (based on the study of parts) only gets at part of the astonishing autonomy of things.

There are some more things to be said about mereology before we move on. Again, since objects can't be undermined or overmined, it means that there is strictly *no bottom object*. There is no object to which all other objects can be reduced, so that we can say everything we wish about them, based on the behavior of the bottom object. The idea that we could is roughly E.O. Wilson's theory of *consilience*.[10] Likewise, there is no object from which all things can be produced, no *top object*. Objects are not emanations from some primordial One or from a prime mover. There might be a god, or gods. OOO wants to return at least to one of Aristotle's four causes (the formal), but it might be keen to drop two others (final causes, *telos*). If there's no top or bottom object there just is no final cause. If one has modified telos to be "goal-like" rather than "actually final" one has lost what is special about final causes. "Goal-like" behavior is only "goal-like" for some other entity, not a deep property of things. Suppose there were a god. In an OOO universe even this god would not know the essential ins and outs of a piece of coral. Unlike even some forms of atheism, the existence of god (or nonexistence) matters little for OOO. If you really want to be an atheist, you might consider giving OOO a spin. God is irrelevant. She or he just as well might or might not exist. There is no problem either way. With some Buddhists, one could call this position *non-theism* to distinguish it from theism, but also from atheism, which still has some skin in the theism game.

Why? Reductionism and eliminative materialism are locked in eternal combat with their theistic shadow. Mechanism distributes the "hot potato" of telos throughout reality, endlessly passing it from one entity to another, shuffling it under the carpet of as many entities as possible like hash browns on a plate of eggs.[11] A mechanism is always a mechanism-for. A spoon is a machine for holding a piece of boiled egg. Holding is a mechanism of the hands for grasping things like spoons. The hands are machines for holding, writing and countless other tasks. They are made of bones, which are machines for … Thus intelligent design theology is the permanent shadow of mechanistic biology. The only difference is that intelligent design is explicit about teleology: there is a designer. Mechanistic biology, by contrast, is duty bound not to be honest about its teleological impulse.

Scientism is a symptom of a certain anxiety that is released in modernity. The anxiety that thinks a telos or a top or bottom object is a resistance to that great discovery of modernity, fueled by democracy, philosophy and by the emergence of consumer capitalism: nothingness. There is no top being in a democracy, no king or emperor—there is an uneasy, ideal equality between you and me. In modern philosophy, there are no metaphysical givens. And in capitalism, I have a supposedly free choice between these two different types of shampoo, and my factory might as well make shampoo bottles or nuclear bomb triggers.

Since Kant, modern philosophy has been preoccupied with where to put the nothingness that seems to ooze out everywhere. Kant puts the nothingness in the gap that opens up between the real and the (human) known. For Hegel, nothingness is an inert blankness that must be overcome—OOO considers this move to be a regression from Kant and not helpful. For the object-oriented ontologist, nothingness is not a blank void or simply the gap between (human) knowing and what is real. It is what the theologian Paul Tillich calls a *meontic* rather than an *oukontic* nothing.[12] This meontic nothing is what Heidegger talks about, constantly.

Nothingness, rather than absolutely nothing: and this nothingness pervades things like myriad cracks in the shell of a boiled egg. Because a thing withdraws, it disturbs us with an excess over what we can know or say about it, or what anything can know or say about it—this excess is a nothingness, not absolutely nothing, but not something to which one can point. If we could point it out, it would be right there, and we would know it—but the withdrawal of a thing cannot be located anywhere on its surface or in its depth. I break a piece of chalk to find out what it is. Now I have two problems where previously I only had one.[13] Nihilism, which argues that the void is more real than anything that appears, is perhaps a way to cover up this more anxiety provoking nothingness with an absolute nothing: a defense against the key discovery of modernity. Nihilism wants to empty its pockets of everything, including the space in the pocket—as if one could pull the nothingness out of the pocket itself, to rid oneself of the inconsistency of the thing. "Believing in" nothing is a defense against nothingness, a metaphysics of presence disguised as a sophisticated undermining of all presence.

Yet the OOO universe is to be discovered "beneath" nihilism, as if the deep water in which modern thought swims turned out to be hiding a gigantic, sparkling coral reef of things. Nietzsche and Heidegger insist on the importance of overcoming nihilism thoroughly, by traversing it—but both were unable to detect the sparkling coral reef. OOO thinks at a depth that is by definition difficult for humans, to say the least. Much of what it can say must be said by analogy or by metaphor, just as Heidegger intuited that poetic language gave some hesitant glimpse of things. Gone since Kant are the metaphysical islands of fact lovingly worked and reworked by the scholastics. Below the shoals of phenomenological fish—thoughts, hopes, loving, hating, proposing—studied by Husserl in the wake of Kant and Hegel, glides the U-Boat of Heidegger, making its way through the dark waters of Angst-ridden nothingness. But Heidegger's sonar only returns an anthropocentric beep from the universe of things. OOO is like a bathysphere that detaches from the Heideggerian U-Boat to plumb the depths at which the sparkling coral reef is found. At the end of the journey, this coral reef is found not to be under an ocean at all. The entire ocean, with all its darkness, its fish and its floating islands of metaphysical facts, is just a projection of one of the things in the coral reef—the human being. OOO is a Copernican turn within the supposed Copernican turn of Kant, who argued that reality was correlated to (human) acts of synthetic judgment a priori. The crack in the real that Kant discovered—I can count but I can't explain directly what number is, for instance—is only a (human) mental crack among trillions, such as the crack between a polyp and the ocean floor, or between a polyp and itself.

Let us continue to explore the coordinates of the non-theistic universe of OOO. If there is no top object and no bottom object, neither is there a *middle object*. That is, there is no such thing as a space, or time, "in" which objects float. There is no environment distinct from objects. There is no Nature. There is no world, if by world we mean a kind of "rope" that connects things together.[14] All such connections must be emergent properties of objects themselves. And this of course is well in line with post-Einsteinian physics, in which spacetime just is the product of objects, perhaps even a certain scale of object larger than say 10^{-17}cm.[15] Objects don't sit in a spatiotemporal box. It's the other way around: space and time emanate from objects.

To reiterate, if there are no top, bottom, or middle objects, then it is possible that there is an infinite regress of objects within objects, and an infinite progress of objects surrounding objects. This possibility seems less objectionable to OOO than the notion that there is a top object or a bottom object. Thus we must very seriously revise our commonly held theories of time and space, bringing them at least up to date with relativity theory. The mereological properties of objects are startling. There are more parts than wholes, as Levi Bryant argues.[16] An object is like Doctor Who's Tardis in the popular BBC television series: the time-and-space-traveling, shapeshifting craft of Doctor Who. The Tardis is bigger on the inside than it is on the outside. This startling intuition is just one way in which OOO escapes correlationism, reductionism and holism in one fell swoop. If you like, it means that a feature of the Kantian sublime—inner space is bigger than outer space—is extended to all entities. This means that an object can contain things that are not it—an example of the kind of set discovered by Georg Cantor, but ruled illegal by Russell and the logicians of brittle metalanguage. The Kantian sublime is an aesthetic way to detect the nothingness that Kant discovers, the "Unknown = X" that pervades (human) reality.[17] As I have just suggested, this is just one flavor of nothingness, one crack in a universe riddled with cracks.

To reiterate once again: there can be no "top object" that gives meaning and reality to the others, such as a certain kind of God. And there can be no "bottom object," some kind of fundamental particle or ether from which everything else is derived. Likewise, there is no ether or medium or "middle object" in which other objects float. Such a medium has been given many terms and explanations over the years: *periechon* ("surround"), world, environment, Newtonian space and time, Nature, ether, ambience, circumambient fluid.[18] Even the pot of gold at the end of the Standard Model rainbow, the Higgs field, might be an example of an ontotheological "middle object" that gives meaning to other subatomic particles, like a symptom that supplements a set of behaviors, thus undermining their coherence and giving away their inherent absurdity.[19]

How does this happen? OOO finds an explanation in objects themselves. Indeed, the ideal explanation would rely on just one single object—a rather cheeky fact, in a world where interconnectedness is the standard issue of the day in so many areas of life. There are very good reasons for this brazen cheek. If we can't explain reality from just one single thing, we are stuck with a scenario in which objects require other entities to function, and this would lead to some kind of undermining or overmining, which OOO rules out. We shall see that we do indeed have all the fuel we need "inside" one object to have time and space, and even causality.

What are these objects, then, that claustrophobically fill every nook and cranny of reality, that *are* reality, like the leering faces in an Expressionist painting, crammed into the picture plane? On what basis can we decide that there is no top, middle, or bottom object, that objects are bigger on the inside than they are on the outside, that they generate time and space, and so on? It's time to proceed to a concrete example. Come to think of it, let's use something made of concrete.

Think of a cinder block—the more gray and mundane the better. (In English English, this is a *breeze block*; in Australian English a *besser block*.) A butterfly alights on the block. She has a butterfly's eye view of it as her wings brush its stubbly exterior. I feel along the sharp sandy surface of the cinder block. My hands encounter hand-style impressions of the block, testing their slightly careworn softness against the rough texture. An architect makes an exploded view of a cross section of the block. But a cross section of a cinder block is not a cinder block. A finger's impression of a cinder block is not a cinder block. A butterfly's touch on a cinder block is not a cinder block.

Now imagine that the cinder block for some reason has a mind and some rudimentary sense organs, perhaps a nose and a mouth and a crude pair of googly eyes like the talking vegetables on *The Muppet Show*. The block extrudes its tongue and gets a lick of its cool, rough, grainy hardness. Does it know the cinder block as such? It has the taste of itself in its mouth. But the taste of a cinder block is not a cinder block. Imagine the cinder block develops telepathic powers. In a single instant it knows its blockness in its entirety. But knowing a cinder block in a single instant of telepathic communion is not—wait for it—a cinder block!

Perhaps the problem is that I need to see the block as a process, not as some static lump. These days processes do generally seem more charming to more people than seemingly rigid blocks. Perhaps I will get further if I include the way the block was formed from Portland cement and sand in a cast, and the ways the block will be used in building, and the socioeconomic conditions that produced the block. But if I see it this way, I am left with the exact same problem. All I have done is swap the term *process* for the term *object*. Now the process, however I see it, has the same problems as the original block. How can I comprehend this process itself, without translating it into some other form—a discussion, a book, a painting, a series of measurements? Changing the term *object* for the term *process* is only a matter of aesthetic nicety. We are still stuck with the problem of fully grasping a *unit*: the cinder block as such, the process as such.[20] If we imagine that objects are inherently self-consistent—being "static" is an aesthetic defect, too, according to modern taste, though that is very much moot—then we may perforce feel the need to supplement our view with some kind of process philosophy that is able to think change and motion (Bergson, Whitehead, Deleuze). We have thus performed an ontotheological trick. We have arbitrarily decided that some things (processes, flows) are more real than other things (objects). In Chapter 3 I shall revisit the notion of process in considerably more depth. For now we shall have to leave it at that.

Perhaps the problem is that we are three-dimensional beings trying to understand objects that exist in a temporal dimension as well as the three spatial ones.[21] Perhaps if I add another dimension to my description I will "see" the real cinder block. Let's give it a whirl. The approach solves quite a few problems. For instance, I can see that the block has distinct temporal parts that compose is, just as it has spatial ones. This seriously dilutes the problem of the block's persistence: the problem of whether I'm seeing "the same" block as I saw a few minutes ago, or last year. Now the block-last-year is a temporal part of an object that also has the temporal part of the block-a-few-minutes-ago. If I could really see in four dimensions, I suppose that I would see the block as a tube-like structure that consisted of all kinds of fronds and tentacles that depicted how it was made and how it was used. I would see the concrete being poured into the cast at one end of the tube, and the block disintegrating into dust at the other end.

We are, however, left with some significant problems concerning persistence. What demarcates the temporal boundary of the block—its beginning and end? What constitutes the boundary between one temporal segment and another one? Let's imagine that this view is wildly successful: what would the Universe look like if so? The entire Universe is now a single lump of something or other, distributed like some crazy trillion-tentacled octopus throughout spacetime. The block would be one region of this tentacled mass, but in the absence of a successful way to distinguish between the block and the non-block, we are left with a vast sprawl of Cartesian extension. We can see the past and the future and the present as a single sequence—at the cost of losing the specificity of the block altogether. On an extreme version of this view, there are no cinder blocks or mountains or trees or people, because those objects are too inconsistent for the view to handle.[22]

But that's not the really big problem. The real trouble is, none of the temporal block-segments would be the block! The block from last week to next week is just a segment of a world-tubular block.[23] The very attempt to introduce consistency has spawned a nightmare. The more we study the block as a "hunk" of four-dimensional matter, the less we can see it as a block. We are no longer dealing with a block, but what in relativity theory is called a *world tube* that is a mere tendril of a Universal extension lump, segmented into various parts.[24] It doesn't seem as if this way is a great method for getting to know the block either. So if there are any four-dimensional beings out there, I'm afraid their chances of knowing the full block are slim to none, just like the rest of us.

Perhaps Maurice Merleau-Ponty was correct.[25] Perhaps if I can somehow see every single possible angle, every single possible configuration of the block, I can know the block as block. Maybe the ultimate exploded view diagram of the cinder block is available. Imagine that some godlike version of Richard Scarry has written a gigantic children's book called *What Do Cinder Blocks Do All Day?* This marvelous book contains diagrams of every aspect of the block. As fun to read as this may or may not be, it's not the cinder block.

So perhaps we need to get a little tough with our poor block. If somehow I were able to assess every particle of the block, every hole in the block; if I were able to evaporate it and then bring it back to its original state, or drench it with water, shoot it into the Sun, boil it in marmalade—if I were able to do *everything imaginable* to it, wouldn't I know it for what it was? Imagine a wondrous machine, created by an insane genius, a machine that allows me to see every possible aspect of the cinder block, not simply as illustrations or diagrams, but as actual configurations of the block itself. I use the machine. The machine does everything to the block.

As I sit there, grinning happily while the machine does its thing, a thought starts to nag at me. In using the machine, I have automatically excluded the one single accidental encounter that the janitor has with it when, cleaning away the cigarette butts and plastic cups after the party to celebrate the machine's successful functioning, he carelessly stubs his left big toe against one corner of the cinder block and shuffles away, not paying much heed to the ontological cataclysm that has just occurred. Having every single possible encounter with the cinder block rules out only having had *one* encounter with it. "All" experiences of the block are reduced to "not-all."[26] Why? Because neither the machine's billions of encounters, nor the janitor's unique toe-stubbing incident, are the block! The reason: *because there is a real block*. There is no view from nowhere from which I can see the entire block, no *sub specie aeternitatis*.[27]

In this sense, even God (should she exist) has a partial view of the cinder block. I once had a friend who said he wanted to do everything. I seem to remember "killing a man" was somewhat high on his rather late adolescent list. Even if you could do everything, I replied, wouldn't that rule out *only doing some things*? If you could do everything, you would never have the experience of not having done something. Should she exist, an omniscient omnipresent God would envy the most meager and partial knowledge of a few routes around a dull suburban neighborhood.[28]

The three approaches I outlined have some significant family resemblances. The main one is the attempt to iron out inconsistencies in our picture of objects. Throughout this book I shall argue that all attempts to iron out inconsistencies are destined to fail in some way or other. I shall offer an explanation for this—*objects themselves just are inconsistent*. For now, let's continue to do some ironing and see what happens.

Maybe I took the wrong approach. Maybe I was too brutal. Perhaps I have been a Baconian sadist, destroying Nature in order to know it. Maybe if I just sit here and wait patiently, I will see the real block. I wait. I become impatient. I develop all kinds of contemplative practices to stay there looking at the block. I become enlightened. The block still refuses to spill the beans. I train a disciple to take over from me when I die. She sees nothing of the real block, which now has a large crack across the top, inside of which you can see right through it. She starts a religious order that carefully transmits my instructions about how to monitor the block. For tens of thousands of years, cultures, peoples, robots study the block, which is now looking pretty gnarly. A hundred thousand years later, a fully enlightened robot sits monitoring the faint traces of dust hanging in the air where the block used to sit. Still no dice. Even Buddha doesn't know the block in the sense of "know" as "grasp as a definite concept whose reality can be checked against a definite, given thing." When it comes to knowing about cinder blocks, Buddha is just as badly off as God.

Let's give up. Imagine the cinder block all on its ownsome. A scandalous thought perhaps, maybe even impossible to think. The block is not just a blank lump waiting to be filled in by some "higher" object (overmining). The block is not a blob of something bigger or an assemblage of tinier things (undermining). The block is not made real by some medium (the "middle object"). The block is itself. It is specific. It is unique. We might as well think it as a specific, unique real thing. The block already has qualities, such as front, back, and so on. Yet these qualities are only ever aesthetic appearances, no matter whether there is any other "observer" around to see. Yet these appearances are real aspects of the block: it isn't a pyramid, and it doesn't have a swan's neck. The object itself is riven from the inside between its essence and its appearance. This can't simply mean that the cinder block is a lump of substance that has a certain shape and color and that those are its accidents. We have already ruled that out. It must mean that *in itself* the block (essence) is also a non-block (appearance).

The conclusion seems magical, but it's a very ordinary kind of magic. It requires no special features, no supervenient soul or mind or animating force of any kind. It requires that our cinder block have no hidden material squirreled away inside it, no extra folds or hidden pockets of any kind. It only requires that the block *exist*. There is a block, whose essence is withdrawn. *Withdrawn* doesn't mean hard to find or even impossible to find yet still capable of being visualized or mapped or plotted. *Withdrawn* doesn't mean spatially, or materially or temporally *hidden* yet capable of being found, if only in theory. *Withdrawn* means beyond any kind of access, any kind of perception or map or plot or test or extrapolation. You could explode a thousand nuclear bombs and you would not reveal the secret essence of the cinder block. You could plot the position and momentum of every single particle in the block (assuming you could get around Heisenberg's Uncertainty Principle) and you wouldn't discover the withdrawn essence of the block. Ten of the world's greatest playwrights and film directors (let's say Sophocles, Shakespeare, Garcia Lorca, Samuel Beckett, Akira Kurosawa and David Lynch just for starters) could write horrifying, profound tragedies and comedies and action movies about the block and still no one would be closer to knowing the essence of the block. The block itself could evolve a godlike intelligence in which it had omniscient knowledge of itself. The slightest rat dropping, falling from a rafter above the block in the warehouse where I keep it to remind me of the obdurate persistence of things, comprehends the block in an absurdly limited way that rules out the possibility that the omniscient block knows everything about itself.

This blasted cinder block is beginning to get on my nerves so perhaps we had better change the subject. But before we leave it there in the warehouse, let's just reflect on what an elementary yet wonderful discovery we've just made. We live in an infinite non-totalizable reality of unique objects, a reality that is infinitely rich and playful, enchanting, anarchic despite local pockets of hierarchy, infuriating, rippling with illusion and strangeness. In this reality, objects are perfectly straightforward, with no transcendental or hidden aspects. Yet precisely because of this very fact, objects are completely weird: they hide out in the open, under the spotlight. Their very appearance is a kind of miracle.

We could go so far as to suggest the possibility of what Bryant calls a *dark object*, an object that has no relations with any other entity whatsoever. These objects are strictly unthinkable, because if we try, we have already forged some kind of relationship with them. Our theory must allow for the existence of unthinkable objects. But even to talk about this is to involve oneself in a play of contradiction. It's like looking at a red theater curtain, swaying gently, illuminated by spotlights. Is there anything behind it?

Since there is no top object from whose VIP lounge we could survey everything perfectly and properly, no object is properly what it is—not even for itself.[29] The OOO universe is a universe of impropriety, of the improper. Yet we know this because in another sense objects *only* are what they are, nothing more or less, since there is no bottom object to which we could reduce them. Objects are sternly irreducible, yet marvelously improper at one and the same time. Since no object is exempt from the uncanniness we have just discovered in the cinder block, no object is the Philosopher's

Stone that will transmute everything into perfect, obvious, well ordered straightforwardness.

This is a Shredded Wheat world ("Nothing added, nothing taken away" was how it was advertised in the 1970s). But a humble bowl of this sort of Shredded Wheat makes the most coruscating psychedelic lightshow look pale and boring. This is a reality in which the realness of things is in direct proportion to their weird pretense, the way in which things wear perfect replicas of themselves, so that everything is a masquerade, yet absolutely, stunningly real—and for the very same reason. If this isn't enough of a miracle, wait until you have considered how causation works in this reality. This is the main topic that this book explores.

The Rift

We should by now be in a position to think more closely how objects are ontologically riven between *essence* and *appearance*. If we refuse to accept this, we are left with some unpleasant choices. We could go for a world of real non-contradictory objects whose qualities were pasted onto them like stamps on Play-Doh: some kind of default Medieval ontology. Mark Heller gets into this pickle: since he can't accept objects with imprecise boundaries, he is compelled to think objects as mind-numbingly dull "hunks of matter" unrecognizable as spoons, comets or Lego bricks.[30] We not only lose people and concrete and traffic signs, we also lose the briny sparkle of seawater and the cold elasticity of clay. Since there is no genuine way to distinguish between a thing and the matter that surrounds it, Heller gradually reduces the entire universe to one formless lump of extension. Some would prefer there were no tables, quarks or ocean currents rather than accept the Rift.

We could go with sets of non-contradictory relations, in which the "hot potato" (as Harman says) of a bona fide object is passed infinitely down a chain of relationships, never reaching the bottom.[31] Or we could go with nominalism or nihilism, in which objects are only what other objects make of them—these overmining views collapse into the relational one fairly straightforwardly. We could be reductionists who say that some objects, namely tiny ones, are more real than non-tiny ones—*tiny* being a question-begging adjective (tiny for whom or for what?). Or we could be holists who think that objects are simply manifestations of some larger flow, begging the question another way—how does this flow manifest as something different from itself (the question Neoplatonism tries to answer)?

Or we could just drop the requirement that everything in reality conform to a principle that has never been adequately justified, except in some taboo-like sense—thou shalt not think things that are self-contradictory, on pain of being ostracized from logic. If OOO is correct, then Aristotle's critique of materialism and his embrace of different types of causation, including formal causation, has something interesting to tell us; but his originary assertion of LNC (the Law of Noncontradiction) does not.[32]

The intuition that there is something screwy about LNC when it comes to real objects is particularly potent when we think of objects that are especially large and long lasting relative to human scales. For instance, consider global warming, an entity that is made up of sunlight, carbon dioxide, fossil fuel burning engines and so on. Seven percent of global warming effects will still be manifest a hundred thousand years from now, slowly being absorbed by igneous rocks. That's more than ten times all of recorded history so far, a preposterously high number. It's almost inconceivable. Yet we see the effects of global warming all around us: we see charts from NASA that plot temperature rises; we feel rain on our heads at strange times of the year; we witness drought. None of these experiences are directly global warming: they are its aesthetic effects.

Think again about Bryant's dark objects, objects that have no relation whatsoever to other objects. Whether or not these objects actually exist in this reality is open to question. But the fact that OOO allows for their existence is beyond doubt. The trouble is, when we think of objects, we are subject to extreme *observation selection effects*. A thought-about object is no longer an object in total isolation. At least one other object is now relating to it, namely my thinking. It's tempting to think that the Hegelian "correlationist" paradigm arose out of such a phenomenon—trying to think an unthinkable object resulted in an observation selection effect whereby that object was bound up with the thinking of it. Speculative realism starts from the assumption that the world doesn't have to be correlated to some (human) observer in order to exist. This kind of givenness isn't all it's cracked up to be, since humans (and sentient beings in general) are not uniquely good at disclosing it. If neutron stars and RNA also disclose givenness, the existence of a universe without humans is not very much of a problem. (We shall see, however, in the context of thinking about how objects begin, that deep phenomenological probing on givenness can reveal some counterintuitive and powerful insights. It is a profound rather than a superficial givenness, though it is still givenness, and thus falls within the realm of appearance or what Harman, following Heidegger, calls the "as-structure.")

It's ironic, then, that the very objects that are the most removed from relations provoke relationist reactions. Dark objects present us with a paradox—something similar to the Liar or to Lacan's haunting statement: "What constitutes pretense is that, in the end, you don't know whether it's pretense or not."[33] To think them is to think the purest possibility that they might exist. It's the ultimate congruence of withdrawal and tricksterish illusion. Is there something behind the curtain? Objects are unspeakable yet perfectly available. They aren't just lumps of whatever. They appear-as all the time: as a cinder block, as cinder block dust, as wet, fresh smelling concrete in a mold. That's what objects *do*.

Let's return to Heller's hunks of matter for a moment. Heller explores the status of a table as an object. You take little chips out of the table—at what point can you no longer call it a table?[34] This is a version of the Sorites paradox mentioned earlier. I have a heap of sand. I remove one grain. It's still a heap. I can keep going until I have just one grain left. It's not clear at what point, if at all, it stops being a heap. Try it in reverse. If I have one grain of sand, it doesn't make a heap. If I add another grain, it doesn't make a heap either. Now I can carry on with the same reasoning process indefinitely—so I never get a heap, no matter how many tens of thousands of grains I pile up.

Heller is trying to explain the existence of objects, yet he spends a lot of time running again and again into this Sorites buzz saw. Why? Heller thinks that it's because of some inaccuracy in his way of understanding tables. So Heller decides to give up the ghost and talk about objects without any specificity at all. Since you can't tell when a table is a table, you are left to fumble around with well behaved but dull lumps of matter. Perhaps the saddest moment is when Heller decides to build a machine that will do the job for him—and runs into the buzz saw yet again, because how can you design a machine to figure out when the table stops being a table, if you don't know?[35] You are thrown back on your perception.

Sorites paradoxes are said to depend upon vague predicates: "is a heap," for instance, or "is bald." Now we know from Darwin that "is a species" is also a vague predicate. Why? Because evolution is incremental and the difference between one life form and its mutated sibling is not well defined. Likewise "is alive" is a vague predicate. To break the vicious circle of DNA and ribosomes, we need some kind of RNA world consisting of RNA and some non-organic replicator such as a silicate crystal. Vague predicates, in other words, might not be evidence of vague objects. It seems that DNA is a very precise chemical, and that cats are very precise mammals.[36] I certainly don't see the cat as a blurry, vague blob, but as this specific cat, sitting here on this mat. Phenomenology comes to the rescue here, with its discovery of intentional objects. I don't assemble the cat from a rough aggregate of cat pixels, rather the whole cat appears in my consciousness. The precision of my cat awareness seems to be evidence that cats are pretty precise.

This suggests that there are Sorites paradoxes not because reality is vague, but because reality is paradoxical. This means that entities may not be entirely subject to the Law of Noncontradiction (LNC). So Heller can build all kinds of machines for measuring when a table stops being a table. He will never succeed. Why? There is a very fundamental reason, according to OOO. Because any knowledge about a table (mine, a machine's, whatever) is not a table. It's just not possible for my knowledge about tables to replace this table. So there will inevitably be moments where I am stumped as to whether I am seeing a table or not. The table withdraws.

If we're going to have tables and RNA and badgers and silt, in all their specificity, we might have to give up the idea that we can be totally definite about them. If you want to be definite, you may have to accept a universe with all the appeal of a cold lump of gray oatmeal.

Sorites paradoxes also arise from overmining. For instance, there is the common tactic of seeing objects as bundles of qualities: an apple is simply something that is round, juicy, sweet and so on (for my mouth). A cat is this furry thing here on this mat, and if I remove the fur one hair at a time, does it remain a cat? Or, as Peter Geach has suggested, are there as many cats on the mat as there are hairs, so that when I remove a hair, there is a different (kind of) cat on the mat?[37] Overmining tries to conquer the Sorites paradox in the following way. Suppose that that when I put a cup on this thingamajig here, it's a table. This is one way to vanquish the Sorites paradox. The deep problem, however, has to do with the existence of this thingamajig despite me. Sure, it's "as-structured" as a table: I think of it as a table, it is a table for the objects around it, not a squashed banana, and so on.[38] The two issues might meet at some point. Suppose I have a wafer thin table after removing *n* chips. I put a cup on it and it falls right through. I think it's a table but it no longer functions as one. Or I'm camping. I use a handy tree stump as a table, knobby as it is and wobbly as it makes my cup. The thingamajig in each case is quite unique, quite different. The tree stump smells of sap and has insects crawling around it. The badly glued piece of furniture in my kitchen, which I've been abusing with this Stanley knife, smells of baby food and is highly polished on one side.

Peter Unger gives an extreme method of overmining in his analysis of "the problem of the many." A cloud is this puffy thing made of droplets in the sky. Except it isn't: the cloud is made of all kinds of other puffy things that could be seen as clouds. The edges of the clouds are particularly ambiguous, as is the part of a rusty nail where the rust blends into the non-rust.[39] If we go on, we can do the philosophical equivalent of cloud busting. If we rule out the smaller clouds one by one, because they are clearly not the whole cloud, then all of a sudden we have no cloud.[40]

We simply can't undermine a table into little wood chips and find the table in there. Yet we can't overmine the table either. How come I can as-structure either the manufactured furniture or the tree stump (in my perception, my language or my usage) as a table? How come the floor can? Or this small crumb of toast and marmalade? The OOO answer is that they are non-tables. What they are withdraws from access even as I rest my cup on them and say "Hey, nice table." We must tread carefully here, to avoid the thought of overmining. This doesn't mean that there is no table, but rather that how I use the table, including thinking about it, talking about it, resting my teacup on it, is not the table. The whole point is that the table is not simply a table-for (me, my teacup, the floor, the concept *table*). This is not a non-table in the sense that François Laruelle means: there is no unspeakable, radical immanence that no philosophy can speak—that philosophy must banish from its mind in order to utter what for Laruelle are its garbled half-truths. In saying *non-table* I am not suggesting that we laugh at tables or at ourselves for even thinking of such a daft idea as a piece of wooden furniture. Precisely the opposite. The total vividness of this actual table, this *tode ti* (Aristotle), this unit, this unique being here, wooden cousin of the friend of many philosophers, is what is unspeakable, ungraspable. In this respect OOO draws on the powerful insight of phenomenology that I stated above. Again, I don't perceive a thousand cat-like dots that I resolve into a cat, but instead the whole cat is intended by my mind, right there and whole, a fact that seems to be borne out by very recent magnetic resonance imaging of activity in the visual cortex of the brain.[41]

We can't simply say that tables are lumps of blah that we call tables or use as tables. And we can't simply say that tables consist of little lumps of blah. Doing both at the same time (undermining and overmining together) is how contemporary materialism functions.[42] The OOO view thus requires that we seriously modify or drop the idea of matter. Matter is always matter-for. If you use the term *matter*, you've already reduced a unique object to "raw materials-for" something-or-other. I light a match. The match is made of matter? No, it's made of wood from a tree. The tree is made of matter? No, it's made of cells. The cells? And so on down to electrons. The electrons are made of matter? No, they're made of ... and so on. Thinking "matter" is thinking with blinkers on. It suits correlationism.

Yet might we say that a match is wood-for? As in wood-for-lighting-a-fire, for instance? Might it not be possible to believe that "purpose-built" objects are indeed at least to some degree objects-for without thinking that objects are only what they are because they are correlated with some human need or conceptual apparatus? Agreed, insofar as I think you could imagine that objects are purpose built without being a correlationist. Perhaps as long as you realize that they are objects-for "to some degree." By then you've gone quite a long way towards conceding that the match is also wood-for a particle of dust that settles on it. It's also wood-for an ant who climbs over it. It's also wood-for a toy house made of matchsticks. Once you've gotten rid of the idea that it's "raw materials-for" then you have no good reason to cling to the human telos of matches. A non-materialist but realist view might include more entities in its vision of what things are "for" (the as-structure).

Alexander Pope's poem *Windsor Forest* admires the scope of a beautiful forest (which still exists to some extent). Look, says the poem: look at all those potential battleships for the English Navy.[43] Philosophy should do better than that.

The problem with "matter-for humans" exposes a deeper problem, that matter is matter-for anything. Matter isn't what it's cracked up to be, some kind of real substrate of things that emerges as those things. It's part of the as-structure, ontologically secondary to objects. "Matter" is correlationist in that it's always correlated to some entity. Matter is the "out-of-which-it's-built" of an object. It is the object's past, or a past object. When you study it directly, it ceases to be matter. This is a problem for eliminative materialism, which holds that if you can explain what you're studying in terms of supposedly basic material components, then you can eliminate the larger thing that you are explaining in favor of those components. If you don't stop at some metaphysical substrate such as prime matter, you end up with equations in the void—you end up, pretty much, with idealism or nihilism. Since correlationism is hostile to the idea of dogmatic metaphysics, it is at risk of ending up with the void, if it goes the materialist route. The void becomes more real than other entities.

The disturbing thing about the Rift between appearance and essence is that it's undecidable, irreducibly. We can't specify "where" or "when" the Rift "is." The Rift means that we are confronted with an illusion-like reality. The ramifications of this illusion-like reality will become clearer as we proceed.

The Object Called Subject

Is it the case then that what are called objects are merely subjective impressions? Not at all. In this and the following section, I shall draw from some examples in my own experience to demonstrate some facts about objects in general. Not surprisingly, we shall find evidence for the Rift. There is a reason why looking at my experience is an acceptable procedure in OOO: it is simply that I am an object among others. Now the common reaction to the sentence "I am an object" is a handwringing horror, or posthuman thrill, that I am saying that I am just a puppet. Neither of these is the case. Both sides of the artificial intelligence debate (for and against) think that being a subject is a special thing—some kind of qualia appear in consciousness or being a person is an emergent property of lower level cybernetic systems whirring away.[44] We need to rethink what we mean by *subject*. But in many ways what is called *subject* and what is called *object* are not that different, especially not from the OOO perspective.

We are conditioned to think that "subject" is one thing and "object" is another. Here, however, I shall be treating them as exactly the same. What is called "object" in everyday speech is just as removed from an OOO object as the conventional "subject" is. On this view, what are normally called *subject* and *object* are simply aesthetic properties that are shared in some way between objects. Whether this means that OOO compels us to adopt a panpsychist view, namely that your toothbrush is sentient; or whether OOO is claiming by contrast that your sentience is toothbrush-like; both are a little beside the point right now, though we shall shortly revisit the choice.

OOO holds that everything is an object, including the seemingly special one we call *subject*: the one we delight in bestowing upon or withholding from other beings, as if we were custodians of the subjectivity equivalent of the Rock 'n' Roll Hall of Fame. By contrast, some might hold that subjects and objects are very different. For instance, post-Kantian thinking tends to favor the view that you just can't argue against subjective states, whereas you can argue with objective facts. Since, however, where the art lives is the causal dimension, the difference between "subjective" and "causal" is nonexistent. In a modern universe, we would not be able to distinguish subjective states as superior or inferior or whatever. We can only do that about empirical data and selves are not empirical data but transcendental facts. In the OOO universe, aesthetic experience is real and tangible yet unspeakable.

In an OOO universe, the human aesthetic is a little island in a larger ocean. The ocean is the causal ocean. Drugs are good examples of things that seem to straddle the causal and the aesthetic in our everyday speech about objects. One can indeed compare and contrast different kinds of aesthetic "experience." Indeed, this accounts for how psychoactive drugs work in the first place. They disprove by their very existence the rigid line between subjective and objective facts. They act causally on your brain, that is, aesthetically, producing all kinds of phantasm. What we call subjectivity is just a causal event that "happens to us," that we snatch out of the aesthetic continuum of causality and call meaningful, human, whatever. So it's perfectly possible to describe subjective states in detail, as well as to compare them and argue about them. In the following section, I shall attempt to show how some fairly ordinary experiences, such as jet lag, can be thought as a message from the causal ocean. Humans are not that different from other entities, since what minds do is not ontologically that different from what other entities do. Consciousness just is what I shall shortly describe as *interobjectivity*, the configuration space of relatedness. Since they place a high premium on the aesthetic, and since their aesthetics prove in oblique ways that there are nonhuman entities (even within human beings), we can mine Kant and Hegel, not for more insights about how minds and worlds can't know one another, but what the interior spaces of objects are, and what the aesthetic spaces are between them.

Uncanny Causality

What we take to be the object "behind" its appearance is really a kind of perspective trick caused by a habitual normalization of the object in question. Objects are not just themselves—they are uncanny: they are both themselves and not-themselves. It is my habitual causal relationship with them that makes them seem to sink into the background. This background is nothing other than an aesthetic effect—it is produced, in other words, by the interaction of $1+n$ objects. This book names the phenomenon *interobjectivity*. The aesthetic dimension implies the existence of at least one withdrawn object. To put it another way, in order for anything to happen, there has to be an object in the vicinity that has nothing to do with the happening in question—an object that is, in other words, not caught in the mesh of relations.

Let's take an example that I know something about—me. I think this is a legitimate technique, since as Heidegger argues, "any ontology" must "take its guideline from Da-sein itself."[45] In other words, as an object among other objects, I have a clue as to their objectness fairly handy, in my experience of things. The genuine uncanniness of objects, their quality of being themselves and not-themselves, is easy to test when you travel to a strange country. You have jet lag and everything seems weird. Bedclothes and street sounds seem to lurch towards you with unseemly intimacy. When I arrive at a strange new place, the sensual vividness of objects seems to jump out at me in front of those objects. Smells are sharper and more penetrating (the different bacteria coating other objects interacts with my smelling system, I guess). Light switches and plug sockets seem to emanate clownlike parodies of themselves that leer out at me, mocking my incompetence. Washing or shaving becomes a weird, slightly seductive, slightly unpleasant experience. Reality seems closer to me than "normal." Then everything clicks into place, often after a couple of nights of sleep.

In the state of jet lag, things are strangely familiar and familiarly strange—uncanny. Then it hits you: this is the default state of affairs, not the world in which regularly functioning things seem to subtend their aesthetic effects. Your regular house in your regular street is really like this. In truth, their smooth functioning is merely an aesthetic effect to which we have grown accustomed. The smooth world is the illusion! The clown-like weirdness of the uncanny situation you find yourself in, on the other side of planet Earth, groggy with jet lag and fumbling for the light switch, is the reality. The idea that I reach for the light switch across a distance that I can ignore is the illusion. What in fact happens is that the light switch has already appeared uncomfortably close to me, leering at me like a circus clown, without distance at all. My intention to switch it on, and the mechanical action of doing so, implies an interpenetration between me and the light switch that is already in place, like a force field.

At this ontological level there is not much difference between what I, a human with a mind (supposedly) do, and what a pencil does to a table when it rests on that table. Holding, sitting and thinking belong to the aesthetic dimension, that is, the causal realm. There is another realm: the realm of being. Objects of all kinds (me, the cup, the table) occupy both realms. So the shifting, clown-like apparition quality that I experience in my phenomenological space is, I claim, common to the way any object appears to any other object. Every object says "myself" as Gerard Manley Hopkins puts it (see this book's epigraph). But in saying "myself" the object is also saying "I am at this very moment lying," "This sentence is false."

I started wondering why I really, really dislike taking the shuttle bus to the airport. Of course there's the exhaustion involved in getting up super early and accommodating other humans as the airporter stops at address after address. (Nothing like getting up at 3am to reveal the inner misanthrope.) But that's not it, not completely anyway. It's that, in the course of picking up those others, I get a totally different feeling about where I live. The airporter drives down different roads in the pitch darkness of northern California small town night. I soon forget where the heck I am even if it's only a few street away from "normal." The journey becomes a stimulating kind of jazz. Town jazz. Playing my hometown like a jazz player could pick up your trumpet and make it sound different. Not totally different, but uncannily different.

The town becomes uncanny, because its withdrawal becomes obvious. This is not my town. It's like that moment when you put on a new pair of glasses but stretched out in time, involving swaying cars and a small group of strangers. Then you realize how much your world was just a sensual object. Then it strikes you that your regular world *was itself a kind of displacement* of some real object(s). The sense of place is already a displacement. Place is the weird one; space is the reified box. As the airporter rounds the corner of the block just a few streets away from your familiar haunts, you realize that your town is irreducibly withdrawn from access. That the strange dreamlike airporter interior with its reflections of outer lights and bizarre swaying of your body, *is what it is like*. More real than the dream you were just living in. Or a transition to a different dream, and the ironic gap between them. So that what is most uncanny is the sense of *familiarity* you have just left behind. The jazz you took to be a plastic disposable pop song.

Philosophy has perpetually thought causality to be at work "behind" the scenes. Perhaps there is a deep existential reason why it does this. It does seem to parallel the long history what Heidegger calls the forgetting of being, the long march toward objectified lumps. But why? There is also an uncanny parallel with what in psychiatry is properly called *the schizophrenic defense*, in which the schizophrenic imagines all kinds of causal chains and threads to be at work behind his back. What this is blocking is how causality takes place "in front of" things. This "in front of" doesn't mean spatially a few inches away from an objective thing, closer to our eyes. It means that causality is the way objects talk to one another, apprehend one another, comprehend one another: causality is the aesthetic dimension.

Some forms of speculative realism imagine an abyss of dynamism churning beneath things.[46] OOO, by contrast, imagines the abyss to be in front of things. When I reach for the coffee cup, I am reaching into an abyss. By imagining a secret causal mafia behind the scenes, perhaps the schizophrenic is defending herself against the abyss in front of things, in the relationship between the tomato and the serrated knife. The abyss is not a featureless swirl, however. Let us explore it a little.

The Abyss of Interobjectivity

It would now be best to delve a little further into the phenomenon I have been calling *interobjectivity*. The causal dimension—that is the aesthetic dimension—is nonlocal and nontemporal, which is another way of saying that objects are closer than they appear in the mirror of our habitual patterns. Objects are somehow entangled together in the causal–aesthetic dimension—I borrow the image from quantum theory, in which when objects do come very close, they become the same thing. I am not sure what limits the nonlocality and nontemporality of the causal dimension, if anything. There are no empty pockets in physical reality.

There is something that the phenomenologist José Ortega y Gasset calls *ingenuousness*, but which we could also call *sincerity*, after Harman.[47] Sincerity means that you are irreducibly glued to your "intentional objects" (Husserl), your experiences, or, in the words of Buckaroo Banzai, the 1980s cult film character, "Wherever you go, there you are."[48] For instance, if you try to maintain a critical distance towards an experience you are having—there you are, distancing yourself. You just can't jump outside your phenomenological skin or, as Jacques Lacan famously puts it, *there is no metalanguage*.[49] We are shrink-wrapped in reality. Reality is sincere: since there is no metalanguage, there is no way to jump outside of it. Even when you perform a cognitive act such as "going meta," trying to get a purchase on some statement, for instance, *there you are*, doing that. This affects our view of language. On this view, a statement is more like a performance in a ballet or a drama—a deed, as Danièle Moyal-Sharrock puts it.[50]

Relationships between objects are sincere in this respect: they are *sincerities*. Sincerities are fundamentally open, because we can never get to the bottom of them. Who knows exactly what a human way of walking is?

Yet there you are, a human, walking. "Middle objects" such as *background*, *world*, *environment*, *place*, *space* and *horizon* are non-objects, phantoms that we (and maybe some other sentient beings) employ to domesticate this wild and uncompromising state of affairs. In truth, objects are both more real and more illusory than we want to know. Elsewhere I argue that ecological awareness consists precisely in concepts such as *world* and *place* evaporating, leaving behind real entities that are far closer than they appear in the mirror of human conceptuality. So that, in general, human beings are now living through an extended and urgent introduction to OOO, whether they like it or not, whenever they confront phenomena such as global warming and the uncanny resemblances between lifeforms.

Any attempt to reduce the double properties of objects—they are both themselves and not-themselves at one and the same time—is doomed to failure. These attempts to smooth out the terrain of things are rife in metaphysics: objects are made of atoms; or they are substances decorated with accidents; or they are components of a machine; or they are instantiations of a process; and so on. Such smoothing-out also occurs in physics. Nonlocality, for instance, and quantum coherence (the way particles seem to be blurred into one another or occupying several places at once) seem to refute LNC at a basic level of material reality. So theories such as the many worlds explanation get rid of the inconsistency.[51] The trouble is, such theories maintain LNC at the cost of a potentially infinite number of parallel universes that open up to accommodate the inconsistent positions of a quantum. It's a bit like sweeping dust under the rug. It doesn't really go anywhere.

OOO objects are simultaneously enclosed and entangled in a sensual (interobjective) ether. A metaphysical system that doesn't take the *dialetheic* (double-truthed) quality of objects into account is prone to inconsistency in at least one part of its argument. We shall investigate this as we proceed. The very attempt to introduce consistency creates more drastic inconsistencies, as if objects were viral, sneakily upgrading themselves in the face of the attempt to make them behave. It would be better to start with the facts—namely that objects exhibit $p \wedge \neg p$. Such a view has the advantage that we don't need to specify some originary object outside the universe, some kind of prime mover or causeless cause (God) that makes it all work. There is enough dynamism in $p \wedge \neg p$ already for things to start working all by themselves. If you really want to be an atheist, you might have to consider dropping mechanism and relationism in favor of the object-oriented view.

For now, let's simply consider mechanism. Machine-like functioning, which is what our common prejudice often takes causality to be (at least since Newton and Descartes), must only be one specific kind of emergent property of some deeper nonlocal, nontemporal ocean in which things directly are other things. Machines are made of separate parts, parts that are external to one another by definition. What causality *just isn't* is this kind of mechanical functioning, like the metal balls in an executive toy. The click of the balls as they hit one another is a sound that implies the existence of at least one other object—the ambient air that vibrates, causing the click to be heard. How come this click or clunk is more real than other forms of causality such as attraction, repulsion, magnetism, seduction, destruction and entanglement?

Clunk causality implies a determinist view: two balls must be contiguous with one another, the causality only goes in one direction, and there must be at least a necessary, if not a sufficient reason for the clunk in the ball that does the clunking. Yet when we go down a few levels, we discover that quantum behavior is irreducibly probabilistic. What does that mean? It means that indeterminacy is hard wired into the behavior: it's not as if we could clean up our way of analyzing it and it would then look determined. So there are physical reasons why determinism doesn't work: we're talking about both sufficient *and* necessary conditions failing at some point. It means that Hume is in trouble.[52] But there's another big reason not to like determinism. When you have a strong statistical correlation such as the likelihood that you will get cancer if you smoke, and you are a determinist, you can wish that fact away. That's the trouble with the post-Humean view that causes can't be directly seen, only strong correlations between associations of data.[53] Kant was the philosopher who explained a deep reason for the truth of Hume: there is a transcendental crack between appearing and knowing. OOO is part of this lineage insofar as it posits a myriad transcendental cracks—reality is riddled with the Rift. This is the reason why philosophers of immanence are disturbed by OOO: it thinks transcendence, but not beyond things—transcendence is in the cracks in an eggshell in a box of eggs in the supermarket.

Tobacco companies and global warming deniers rely on the common resistance to the nothingness inherent in the realization that there are cracks in the real. There is no "proven link" between smoking and cancer—but *that's evidently not the point*. Likewise, global warming denial takes a leaf out of the determinist notebook. Since there is no obvious link between the rain falling on my head and global warming, it must be untrue. *Or my theory of causality is out of whack*. Large complex systems require causality theories that are non-deterministic just like very small quantum scale ones. Clunking is an illusion that seems to happen to medium-sized objects such as billiard balls, but only when we isolate the clunk amidst a welter of other phenomena.

Clunk causality is in denial about the long history of more subtle approaches to causation. The Arabic philosopher al-Kindi defines all causes as *metaphorical*—apart from God, the unmoved mover (al-Kindi is an Aristotelian theist).[54] Al-Kindi did so when my ancestors were clunking one another (talking of clunks) with crudely fashioned weapons, in the last years of the tenth century AD. Causation is metaphorical—that means that causes are overdetermined. The balls are held in place by a wire frame. The frame sits on a desk. The desk is part of an office in a large corporation. All these entities are causes of the executive toy's clunking sounds. Overdetermination, metaphor—they mean the same thing. Or, in translation, *translation*: *metaphor* is just Greek for *translation*, since *meta* means *across* and *-phor* means *carrying*. This is a far more suitable way to think causality than mechanical clunking. It provides a reason why many forms of empirically observed causation are probabilistic. Overdetermination is particularly evident in cases of omission and prevention. How can we say "His failure to call out caused the accident" without considering the father's reading his email, not looking at the child running into the street, the car without adequate brakes driving too fast down the street, and so on?[55] If we hold that there must be non-metaphorical causes, then omissions and preventions are only counterfactual, and only ontically given causes exist: our theory of causation is then a positivistic one. Omissions and preventions are therefore only ways of talking in shorthand about causal chains. On the view established here, however, it is entirely possible for something to be affected simply by being left alone: omission and prevention are hard wired into the theory of causation, rather than simply being counterfactual ghosts. Meditation, for instance, could be defined as a leaving-alone of objects. This leaving-alone is an omission that has real effects. By allowing objects to remain inconsistent, rather than reducing them to appearances (for me), I act nonviolently. And so on.

One object plays another one. This empty orange juice bottle is playing the table in this airport, waggling back and forth as the table sways due to a wonky leg. Objects are shared by numerous entities in a common sensual space. This shared space is a vast nonlocal configuration space. Phenomena such as human subjectivity—"intersubjective" phenomena that is—occupy small regions of the space of interobjectivity. Every interobjective phenomenon requires $1+n$ real objects. This means that for every interobjective system, at least one real object is withdrawn. Consider a beat. A beat occurs when one tone is canceled by another tone. You make a beat by cutting a continuous tone. The gap between the two is a beat.

Every event in reality is a kind of inscription in which one object leaves its footprint in another one. Interobjective reality is just the sum total of all these footprints, crisscrossing everywhere. It's nonlocal by definition and temporally molten. The print of a dinosaur's foot in the mud is seen as a foot shaped hole in a rock by humans sixty five million years later. There is some sensuous connection, then, between the dinosaur, the rock and the human, despite their vastly differing timescales.[56]

When we return in our mind's eye to the time of the dinosaur herself, we discover something very strange. All we find there is another region of interobjective space in which impressions of the dinosaur are transmitted—tooth marks in a some hapless prey, the frozen stare of the dinosaur as she looks at her next victim, the smooth scaly feel of her skin. More dinosaur prints, even when the dinosaur is alive. Even the dinosaur doesn't know herself entirely, only in a rough translation that samples and edits her being. A mosquito or an asteroid have their own unique sample of dinosar-ness, and these samples are not dinosaurs. Why?

Because there is a real dinosaur, withdrawn from access even from herself. Black holes are right here, in magazines and on the web, as jpegs and gee-whizz pop science essays and sci fi movies. Yet they are not here, evidently. But even if you could somehow climb into one with a video camera, you couldn't know the whole story about black holes. Why? Because your video of a black hole is not a black hole. *Because black holes are real.*

The sum total of all the sampling events by which an object inscribes itself on other objects is a history, in both senses of that wonderfully ambivalent Greek term—since history can mean events and recording. Raindrops splatter on the ground in western California. They record the history of La Niña, a massive weather system in the Pacific. In particular, they record how the Japanese tsunami of 2011 scooped up some of La Niña and dumped it on trees and hills and other objects in the object called the USA. La Niña itself is the footprint of a gigantic object called global warming. Another footprint may well have been the Japanese earthquake itself, since the changing oceanic temperature may have changed the pressure on Earth's crust, resulting in an earthquake.

The quake destroyed four nuclear reactors. Quanta from these reactors, known as alpha, beta and gamma particles, inscribe themselves in soft tissue around the world. We are living textbooks on global warming and nuclear materials, crisscrossed with interobjective calligraphy.

Causation Without Clunking

We are beginning to see how we can do without a mechanistic theory of causation: all to the good, since mechanistic theories just fail to cope with relativity or quantum theory.[57] There is an ontological reason why we need to avoid mechanism. If all objects are unique, there is no sense in which we can specify a mechanical level that somehow chugs along beneath objects. This would require consistent machine parts, and according to the view of OOO, we are just not living in that kind of reality.

There is a far deeper problem. If all objects are unique and enclosed from access, they can never truly be said to touch one another! Harman thus outlines an OOO theory of *vicarious causation*. This may sound absurd on the face of it, but is it? Consider quantum theory for a moment. If objects truly touched one another at the quantum level (down towards the Planck length, 10^{-33} cm), they would *become one another*.[58] Above this level, what we think of as touching has to do with how objects *resist* one another. The fact that I can rest my hand on a cinder block means that the quanta in my fingers are failing to bust through the resistance wells on the surface of the block. From a rather straightforward physics point of view, objects just don't touch one another in the ways we take to be given in our experience. When something touches something, even when it seems to penetrate that something, it's not really fusing with it. *Its quanta are failing to fuse with it.*

Touching, no matter how intimate, involves a necessary aesthetic distance. People commonly think of causality as a clunk that breaks through the aesthetic screen, like Doctor's Johnson's boot. This kind of clunking is one aesthetic phenomenon among many. I am touched, for instance, at this very moment, by gravity waves emanating from the beginning of this Universe. A chemical solution can be touched by a catalyst. Soft tissue is touched by high energy photons such as gamma rays, giving rise to mutagenic effects.

Two deep philosophical traditions have explored how causation can be vicarious: how causation does not have to imply direct touching. One tradition is Islamic; the other is Buddhist. We've looked at Al-Kindi briefly; now consider Al-Ghazali, whom Harman cites as a foil for his theory of vicarious causation. Al-Ghazali was an occasionalist—he held that only God could make anything happen. Fire doesn't really burn a piece of cotton—somehow God magically intervenes and uses the fire as an occasion for the cotton to catch alight.[59] Why is this important for our purposes? Because if objects are withdrawn from one another, there must be some vicarious way in which they affect one another. We don't need it to be God—in fact, we don't need God at all. All the vicariousness we want can be found in the aesthetic dimension in which things are enmeshed.

Now this is remarkably similar to an argument in Mahayana Buddhism. Even the example is similar—it involves fire and fuel. Nagarjuna, the great philosopher of Buddhist emptiness (*shunyatā*), argued that a flame never really touches its fuel—nor does it fail to touch! (Here's a dialetheia again.) If it did so, then the fuel would be the flame or vice versa, and no causality could occur.[60] Yet if they were totally separate, no burning could take place. Nagarjuna argues that if something were to arise from itself, then nothing would happen. Yet if something were to arise from something else that was not-itself, then nothing can happen either. A mixture of these views (both–

and and neither–nor) is also possible, since such a mixture would be subject to the defects of each one combined. For instance, on this view, the idea that things arise neither from themselves nor from something else is what Nagarjuna calls nihilism, on which basis *anything at all* can happen. The logic of causal explanations, he argues, is circular.[61] Emptiness is not the absence of something, but the nonconceptuality of reality: the real is beyond concept, because it is real.

What explains burning? Buddhism is non-theistic, so it isn't God. Instead, it's emptiness. In other words, the lack of an intrinsic, non-contradictory, purely given being means that objects can influence one another. We see flames spurting out of candles all the time, but if the candle were to be touched by the flame, it would simply be part of that object, and a flame can't be burnt—it is the act of burning. Yet if the flame and the candle were separate, we would never see flames jiggling about on top of candlewicks. Causality, according to this view, is like a magical display—there is no physical reason why it is happening. Rather, the reason is aesthetic (magic, display). Furthermore, the magical illusion happens all by itself, withdrawn from perception.

There is no "causation" as such—that's a superficial illusion, a presence-at-hand as Harman would say. Like Al-Ghazali, for whom God provides the causal links between unlinkable objects, a kind of magic happens (without God) and we see flames emerging out of candlewicks and billiard balls smacking one another. There is nothing underneath this display. And the display happens whether "we" observe it or not.

What does this mean? It means that causality is *aesthetic*.

The Trouble with Pretense

The term "withdraw" suggests what snails and turtles do—pulling themselves into some small dark chamber into which it's difficult to see. It suggests some kind of spatial dimension behind or beyond or inside the visible: to draw oneself within, to retire. I rather like this valence. I've spent much of my scholarly life so far sticking up for introversion—heaven knows the hale and hearty environmentalist discourse out there could do with more snail-like behavior. But *withdraw* as an OOO term does not really mean "move to a place behind the current position."

Alongside the term *withdrawal*, this book employs imagery associated with magic, illusion and display. Withdrawal is what happens right under your nose, because, to quote Lacan again, "What constitutes pretense is, in the end, you don't know whether it's pretense or not."[62] Causality is *like an illusion*. If we knew it was an illusion, it would not be an illusion, because we would be sure of its ontological status.

Many indigenous cultures think of Nature not as the reality underneath things, but as the pretense in front of things. The machinations are not happening under the pretense. The machinations *are* the pretense. Causality is happening "out in front of" the object. That's why it's so hard to see. Reality is a trickster and objects behave like playful children—even the black hole at the center of the Milky Way annihilating everything in its path. Such a view is glimpsed in apophatic theories of allegory. Moses Maimonides argues that the literal level is the superficial one. The figurative level is like a golden apple contained in a superfine filigree of silver.[63] From a distance it looks as if we are seeing a silver apple. What we are really seeing is a fine mesh that only appears to be solid. This is the mesh that lies in front of objects. The interconnectedness of everything is a finely woven tissue that floats in front of what elsewhere I have called *strange strangers*: all entities, from Styrofoam and radio waves to peanuts, snakes and asteroids, are irreducibly uncanny.[64] In Harman's terms, this mesh is a *sensual ether*. The real objects are the strange strangers.[65]

The trouble is, when you only have the meshwork, the mask, without the possibility that there's something real underneath it, then you have no play, no pretense, no illusion, no display, no magic. You *know* it's an illusion—so it isn't an illusion. You *know* there is no essence—this *becomes* the essence, a shadowy, inverted form of the very essentialism you are trying to escape. This is the trouble with performance art, or at least the manifestoes of conceptual art. By undoing the difference between art and nonart, by self-consciously getting rid of self-consciousness and professional artists, conceptual art ignores the Rift between essence and appearance, reducing the ontological to the merely ontic. An overall atmosphere of jaded cynicism hangs over it.[66]

By contrast, if there truly "is no metalanguage," as Lacanian and post-structuralist theory has been asserting for decades, even if you are aware that it's an illusion, the illusion still works.[67] A phenomenon (Greek, *phainesthai*, to appear) is both an *appearance* and a *false appearance*.[68] This is why a horror movie can be just as scary the second time around. If there really is no metalanguage, even if you know "it's an illusion," it still functions. For causality to happen, objects don't have to deceive other objects totally. How could they? They are prevented total access. Causality is an illusion-like play, precisely because of the fundamental Rift between withdrawn essence and aesthetic appearance, a "place" of profound ambiguity in the being of a thing. That's why causality works.

The object withdraws from itself. Even the object itself is not an adequate expression of itself, since there is a profound Rift between *essence* and *appearance*. This is by no means the off-the-shelf Aristotelianism with which ontology has been stuck for centuries, including that of Descartes and later. This is not the difference between *substance* and *accidents*. On the OOO view, substance is another "translation" of a withdrawn object by some other entity: say a pair of scales that measures the weight of a cupcake but not its flavor or sex appeal. Somehow "we" have decided that substances are dull boring things like bland tasting plain cupcakes, and that accidents are aesthetic and therefore superficial, like candy sprinkles. Whenever we look for essence, we won't find it—because it exists.

OOO is a form of realism. It's just that any attempt to reify essence becomes an ontotheological preference for one ontic being over another. These beings are all appearances, and appearances are always appearances-for (some other entity). Yet appearances are not just the cheerleaders of some faceless football team of essences. The Rift between essence and appearance itself is what fuels causality. An object is not an illusion. But it is not a non-illusion. Much more threatening than either is what is the case, namely an object that is utterly real, *essentially* itself, whose very reality is formally ungraspable. No hidden trapdoors, just a mask with some feathers whose mystery is out in front of itself, in your face. A miracle. Realist magic. This all means that the skills of the literary critic and the architect, the painter and the actor, the furniture maker and the composer, the musician and the software designer can be brought to bear on the workings of causality.

The History of Substance

Now we can take a step back and assess where we have come. Despite the fact that physics since 1900 has given good reasons for thinking that reality has an essential aesthetic component, the aesthetic is in bad shape in the realm of the humanities. If you want a good defense of art, don't ask a humanist—or even an artist, possibly. They are liable to tell you that art is a lie, a beautiful illusion, deceptive sprinkles on the dry, gray cake of the real. They will tell you that like the cavalry, these sprinkles are brought in when the gray cake starts to fall apart. The sprinkles act as a kind of pathetic fairy dust that might fool deluded saps in the trenches but not the officer class up on the hill, surveying the ideological struggle from an infinite distance. Have humanists in general, despite their extraordinarily creative ways of thinking about causes at work, decided in favor of the default clunk causality, a causality that no explanation of quantum scale phenomena supports?

Perhaps the humanists will tell you that reality is really a special kind of art, a flowing, oozing, lava lamp kind of art. What makes lava lamps work isn't art, however: it's heat and liquids and viscosity and other physical properties. What these materialists mean is that this particular view—an officially sanctioned view we see everywhere nowadays—is the one true view. Thus process relationism becomes a way to police what counts as good and bad art. It may be about lava lamps but it's no different from socialist realism: there's an official way of seeing reality, and woe betide you if you don't cleave to it. Or you call it on aesthetic perception being just a matter of taste. It replies, No: this is about science, this is about the real. It seems as if most humanists don't want to defend art per se, let alone the humanities themselves. The strongest recent defense of the humanities has come from a theoretical physicist, who defended the critical thinking taught in humanities classes.[69] Some humanities scholars have become embarrassed about such things, having painted themselves into a corner: if art is only a beautiful lie, so what? Defenses of the humanities start from this position, which is why they end up anodyne at best.[70]

Art is in trouble, and the reason why has a very long and deep history. This history is intimately connected to the sad story of ontology—how thinking drifted away from it. So far the philosophical movement of speculative realism has traced the story of the demise of the humanities back to Kantian correlationism, the restriction of philosophy to the human–world correlate. Yet the problem goes even further back, to the early Renaissance split between logic and rhetoric. Logic was once considered the first and second parts of rhetoric: *discovery* and *arrangement*, what you are going to say and how you are going to argue it through. Then Peter Ramus and others separated logic from rhetoric. At one stroke, rhetoric was restricted to mere style (Latin, *elocutio*); science as a separate discipline was born; and so was aesthetics. When we say nowadays that someone is being *rhetorical*, we mean that she has style but no substance.

Attitudes to rhetoric have profoundly affected the long history of philosophy. Consider in particular the separation of rhetoric from invention and ordering, or as they could be known, science and logic. This separation, a massive world-historical event, defined earlier metaphysicians as scholastic pettifoggers. Nowadays, that thought means that one is as likely when one hears the word "metaphysics" to imagine a section in a bookstore to be avoided by "proper" thinkers as to imagine philosophy. The separation of logic and rhetoric gave rise to science as a separate discipline and the reduction of rhetoric to style—and the subsequent withering of style into tropology, and the subsequent withering of tropology into metaphor. The Freudian, Nietzschean, and deconstructive strategy is to find a kind of style (*elocutio*) within discovery (*inventio*), the realm of science, and arrangement (*ordo* or *dispositio*), the realm of logic: to subvert logic and science by showing how they include–exclude rhetorical gestures, narrowly considered as style. The eliminative materialist strategy is blithely to ignore rhetoric as a third-class citizen of the republic of knowledge.[71] Significantly, then, deconstruction and eliminative materialism share the same attitude towards rhetoric. So that when we read a Dawkins or a de Man, a Dennett or a Derrida, we are still reading someone fully caught in the Ramist pinball machine that divides style from substance.

The restriction of rhetoric to decorative candy on the surface of meaning went along with the restriction of philosophy. Indeed, the two are intimately related. Descartes drew a line between himself and his predecessors, provocatively stripping things of all but their basic extensionality, and trusting science to take the ontological reins. Yet Descartes himself was hobbled by the weight of ontological tradition. Precisely at the moment at which he thought he was escaping scholasticism, he was only too bogged down in it.[72] The dominant (still dominant) Cartesian view of "constant objective presence" was underwritten by mathematics and physics. This presence was cognized with *intellectio* rather than *sensatio* (Greek, *aisthēsis*).[73] To think reality thus is precisely to edit out the aesthetic dimension. The aesthetic then becomes the mere "personalization" of objects, "subsequently outfitting beings with value predicates."[74] Like an expert criminal, the proto-correlationist thought that makes objects into non-contradictory objective constancy leaves no trace: we just assume that this is the case. OOO has a long row to hoe in this regard, since it must tackle not only two centuries of post-Kantian correlationism, but also five centuries of Cartesian fumbling—fumbling, moreover, a ball that is more than two millennia old: the rather bland ball of substance decorated with accidents.

This affects everything. It's about how ontology has become taboo. It's about how the aesthetic arose as a dimension separate from, even hostile to, rhetoric (consider Kant's opposition to rhetoric).[75] It's about how philosophy has become obsessed with perfect arguments rather than suggestive cognitive work, as Harman puts it.[76] It's why the only alternative to perfect freeze-dried arguments is sheer tropological play. It's why there is a vigorous search for new and improved forms of metaphysics such as the lava lampy materialisms on offer currently, although according to the view offered here, such materialisms regress even from the choice between freeze-dried perfection and powdered void.

OOO takes us out of the interlocking machine that separated substance from accidents and rhetoric from logic. This is precisely because it imagines style as an elementary aspect of causality rather than as candy on top of lumps of stuff bumping together indifferently. Appearances are not simply the cheerleaders for the faceless football team of essences. *Thinking about art is thinking about causality.*

The division of rhetoric and logic, and later the split between aesthetics and science, helped to break the lock theism had on knowledge and art. Yet some strange things carried over, like a hangover headache, from the earlier period, disparagingly dubbed *Medieval* by the modernity that sought to transcend it. First, the notion of infinite space, which had begun as a condemnation by the Bishop of Paris, with Pope John XXI's blessing, of doctrines that limited that power of God in 1277: Thou shalt not imagine that God couldn't create anything he likes. God is powerful enough to create an infinite void; therefore, he did.[77] It took until 1900 for physics and inductive logic to get over that little theistic nugget. Currently we conceive of spacetime as an emergent property of objects, thanks to Einstein, not as a gigantic bowl in which objects float. Why is this important? Because the infinite void underwrites atomism, and therefore mechanism. Moreover, since the causal dimension is not mechanistic, OOO gives us a truly non-theist perspective, not some toy universe that could have been wound up by an intelligent designer. OOO cleans up this mess, by paradoxically returning to a time when logic and rhetoric can be thought together. As we shall see, rhetorical theory provides a working model of many aspects of causation. If you really want to get over the modern period, this is what you have to do. Give up fighting for the value of little pieces of human candy. See the aesthetic dimension as the blood of reality.

In the early modern period, aesthetics became all about how humans perceive, and then that was restricted to how humans perceive specific objects, namely, works of art.[78] Gone was the workmanlike pragmatics of fully-fledged rhetorical theory. Gone was the applicability of rhetoric to a vast variety of walks of life. If we return to a more rounded view of rhetoric, indeed a view that thinks rhetoric as causality, we will be accused of scholasticism. For it is precisely the term *scholasticism* whose usage denotes that we are in modernity. Scholasticism, like the word *weed*, means something that you don't want to have around: philosophy in the wrong place, about the wrong stuff. This is roughly the current sad position of ontology in the scheme of things. Aside from Heidegger, who somehow was allowed into the elite club of modern philosophers, ontology smacks of angels dancing on the heads of pins and unmoved movers and celestial spheres. It smacks, in other words, of a time when Aristotle was taken very seriously. Yet if humans are going to exit modernity—which the current ecological emergency seems to be demanding—then the philosophies that arise will begin to look quite Aristotelian.

After all, it was Aristotle who argued for different forms of causality than mere clunking efficiency, which he thinks is just one of four: material, formal, efficient and final. We can probably agree that in a post-Darwinian age, final causes will not come back tout court. We can let go of teleology, which means that a large chunk of theism just evaporates. In turn, material causes can be dealt with by the various arguments I present here. In a nutshell, "raw materials" are precisely as Marx says, things that come in at one end of the factory door: it doesn't matter what they are, just as long as the factory works on them. Matter, then, is always relational—it's matter-for. Material causes are metonymies, tropes that indirectly evoke another thing: a chair *made of wood*, a chip *made of silicon*. So much for material causes.

It's *formal* causes that are going to make a significant comeback. Formal causation and vicarious causation are part of the same phenomenon. Yet "modern" science since the seventeenth century has been so keen to eliminate all but efficient and material causes. But quantum theory necessitates a revisiting of formal causation. An electron shoots through the hole in a doughnut of electromagnetism, and it responds as if it were within the doughnut. It is probably responding to the shape, the form, the *aesthetics* of the field: this is the Bohm-Aharonov effect, one of the first observed kinds of nonlocality.[79] Likewise birds detect the quantum signature of electromagnetic fields, not actual ions.[80] Nonlocality implies that something very deep about our world is formal, not efficient, or material—that is, aesthetic. Formal causation just is vicarious, in a universe without matter per se or telos. Another term for formal cause is "aesthetic dimension."

If birds navigate by detecting the nonlocal quantum signature of electromagnetic waves, their sense of direction is formal. What are formal causes? Why, the things they study in art schools and literature programs: the *shapes* of things. Given atoms in a void, a causality that focuses on efficiency can tell you how they spin around and clunk each other. But we are not given atoms in a void. We are given a quantum soup in which spacetime itself may well be an emergent property of objects of a certain size. We are given planets and black holes that emit time and space like stones casting ripples on the surface of a pond. We have lifeforms that assume a certain shape depending on the way their genome expresses itself. We have sunlight, balloons, almond butter and aspen trees. We have objects that smack, plop, sparkle and shimmer.

It looks as if contemporary science, and OOO, are both in the business of reviving formal causation, downplaying material causes or even eliminating them. The upshot is that "matter" is only what a unique thing looks like when it's being used/exploited/worked on by some other thing. Efficiency is only an emergent property of formal relationships. Yet for a sense of the contemporary taboo on formal causes, only consider the fate of Rupert Sheldrake, whose 1981 book on what he calls *formative causation* incurred the wrath of the eliminativist editor of *Nature*, so much so that the editor was only too happy to compare himself, astonishingly, with the Catholic church persecuting Galileo. If this sounds like eliminative materialism shooting itself in the foot, that is because it is.[81]

Thus when Harman decided that the only way to explain causality, given withdrawn objects, was through some kind of aesthetic process that he termed *allure*, this was a bold and counterintuitive move indeed. When one object has an effect on another, this must only be through some kind of aesthetic dimension. Thus when the dinosaur we met earlier steps into some mud, she leaves a footprint. She *translates* the mud into dinosaur-ese. She *dinosauromorphizes* it, just as I, a human, inevitably *anthropomorphize* it when I put my hand in it or speak about it. Sixty-five million years later, a paleontologist inspects a fossilized dinosaur footprint. She coexists with the dinosaur and the ancient mud in a nontemporal configuration space, which I have termed *interobjectivity*. She can influence the footprint, and the footprint can influence her, in this shared sensual space. It's as if this level of reality is a vast mesh of crisscrossing lines, marks, symbols, hieroglyphics, riddles, songs, poems and stories.

The kind of causality that best describes objects has to do with information flow, copying, sampling, and translation. A space in which the aesthetic form of an object can exert a causal influence. This means that *clunk causality*—the billiard ball clicks that we visualize as soon as we hear the phrase "cause and effect"—is only one kind of event in a much larger aesthetic dimension that includes all kinds of other events. We can swap theistic and nihilistic voids for withdrawal. Infinity and eternity, which Aristotle rules out (and which Arabic philosophers also ruled out, and Europeans didn't listen), imply empty space, in which objects clunk into each other like stainless steel balls in an executive toy.

Causality has been imagined as a kind of mechanical clunking for several centuries now. Relativity and quantum theory put huge dents in clunk causality. Even electrolysis and electromagnetism put dents in it. But clunk causality works well with a disdain for what is called scholasticism, namely, anything like an attempt do produce an ontological account of reality. But we persist in thinking a clunky mechanist materialism, in which a sub-basement full of whirring machines chugs along and everything is just a manifest image, some kind of candy, on top of this machinery. Clunk causality beats Aristotle's four causes down to one: pure efficiency. We assume we know what reality is made of—matter. And we assume that form is aesthetic appearance, just the decoration on the surface. We already concede to a default ontology that doesn't even want to call itself an ontology.

As I argued above, the Arabic philosopher al-Kindi has a beautiful critique of clunk causality: a clunk is only ever a metaphor. The ball clunking the ball is also held in place by strings attached to a metal frame. They are also the cause of the clunk. The frame sits on a desk in the executive's office. The office is part of a global corporation. And so on, all the way back to the Unmoved Mover: causation is *metaphorical*.[82] Causality is much better thought as translation.

Accepting this changes our view profoundly. Clunking is only one of a vast variety of possible kinds of translation. We have decided that clunking is more real than magnetizing, or seducing, or inducing, or catalyzing, or entangling. Why should a clunking sound be the only genuine metaphor for causality? A genuine metaphor for metaphor—how absurd.

Many readers of Harman's work say that they accept, or are at least prepared to admit, the possibility of withdrawn objects. But *allure* as the engine of causality? Cause and effect as metaphor, as translation? This they find hard. Yet this is the very piece of OOO that I find intuitively the most interesting and compelling. Not only that: the aesthetic account of causality is fully in line with the most profound scientific theories of physical reality. It's this essential piece of OOO that *Realist Magic* explores, in three phases that correspond to how objects come into being, persist, and cease to be.

Objects Are Hypocrites

Let's begin by outlining how we could use rhetorical theory to think about causality. We could rewrite the whole of rhetoric as object-oriented by *reversing the implicit order of Aristotle's five parts of rhetoric.* The five parts are invention (or discovery); ordering (or disposition); style; memory; and delivery. Instead of starting with invention and proceeding through disposition to elocution, then on to memory and delivery, we should start with *delivery*. Delivery is precisely the physicality of *rhēma*, speech. Demosthenes used to practice his delivery by filling his mouth with pebbles and walking uphill. Pebbles and hills played a part in Demosthenes' rhetoric. But rhetoric is far more concerned with nonhuman entities than that.

Reversing the order explodes the teleology implicit in common assumptions about rhetoric (common for instance in university level composition classes): first you have an idea, then you figure out how to argue it, then you pour on some nice ear candy, then you recite it or upload it or whatever. Withdrawn objects do not exist in-order-to anything. We often assume that delivery is secondary to rhetoric, kind of like the volume control or the equalizer on a stereo—it's a matter of conditioning the externals of rhetoric. This isn't what Demosthenes and Cicero thought. Asked to name the most important parts of rhetoric, Demosthenes replied "First, delivery; second, delivery; third, delivery"—at which point his interlocutor conceded, but Demosthenes was ready to go on.[83]

If we rethink delivery not as a bottle into which the already-existing argument is poured like a liquid, nor as an envelope that delivers the message like mail, but as a physical *object* and its *sensual medium*, we will be thinking of it like Quintilian, who says of great actors that "they add so much to the charm of even the greatest poets, that the verse moves us far more when heard than when read, while they succeed in securing a hearing even for the most worthless authors, with the result that they repeatedly win a welcome on the stage that is denied them in the library."[84] The object-oriented explanation for this is that the voice, an object with its own richness and hidden depths, translates the words it speaks—a spooky evocation of the encrypted heart of objects not via revelation but via obscurity—as if (as if, mind you) it were summoning forth an obscure dimension of language. Quintilian discusses Quintus Hortensius, whose voice must have "possessed some charm" for people to rank him second only to Cicero, given how awful his written speeches appeared.[85] Now before the reader accuses me of logocentrism, realize that it's not that voice really gives access to the hidden depth of meaning—it's that voice is an object in its own right, vibrating with uncanny overtones. Like ekphrasis (heightened, vivid description), like metaphor, voice leaps forth towards us, unleashing its density and opacity. Voice has what Harman calls *allure*, the sensual energy of the dimension in which causality happens.[86]

We can proceed from thinking of voice as an object in its own right to asserting that a pencil resting against the inside of a plastic cup is a delivery of a pencil, a certain kind of physical posture similar to a loud voice or a cajoling whine. A house is delivery, disporting its occupants and its rooms and its backyard into various configurations. A record player is delivery, as is an MP3 player. A book is delivery. A waterfall is delivery. A computer game is delivery. A spoon is delivery. A volcano is delivery. A ribbon is delivery. A black hole is delivery. Working backwards through the five parts of rhetoric from this expanded sense of delivery, we would end up at *inventio*. We could say that *inventio* was actually object withdrawal—a dark or reverse *inventio*, "covery" rather than "discovery."

Object-oriented rhetoric is not the long march towards the explicit, but a gravitational field that sucks us from delivery to withdrawal, from the sensual into implicit secrecy and silence. Aristotle's *Rhetoric* depends on silence, because rhetoric needs listeners: so the second part of his magnum opus is devoted to the painstaking elucidation of different types of affect, different styles of listening. Harman argues that metaphor makes even the sensual qualities of objects, which seem readily available to us, seem withdrawn.[87] What metaphor does, then, is not unlike another trope, which the old manuals call *obscurum per obscures*: describing something obscure *by making it seem even more obscure*.[88] Percy Shelley was very fond of this trope—his images endarken rather than enlighten.[89] If we generalize this to the whole of rhetoric, object-oriented rhetoric becomes the way objects obscure themselves in fold upon fold of mysterious robes, caverns, fortresses of solitude and octopus ink. Discovery and enclosure are, as Heidegger argues, very closely related.[90]

While *thinking about* an object takes us from delivery to (dis)covery, *being* an object is a matter of all the different parts of rhetoric happening at one and the same time. Instead of looking at the five parts of rhetoric as a step by step recipe for making meaning explicit ("first you pick a subject, then you organize your argument..."), we could see them as *simultaneous* aspects of any object that render that object mysterious and strange yet direct and in your face. Accounting for them this way prevents us from distorting them as present-at-hand (Heidegger, *vorhanden*) entities or metaphysical substances decorated with accidents: there's a plastic cup and now we add some color, now we see it has a certain shape, and so on. This simultaneity of aspects accounts for what musicians call *timbre*, a word that conjures up the substantiality of timber. A note played on a plastic cup sounds very different from the same note played on a smoothly polished wooden cylinder. Timbre is the sensual appearance of an object to another object, in contrast to Xavier Zubíri's *notes*, which are aspects of the hidden dimension of a thing.[91] So rhetoric in an object-oriented sense is the way the timbre of an object manifests.

If we started with delivery, the availability of a sensual object, we'd immediately unfurl a host of mysterious qualities that spoke in strange whispers about the object of which they are aspects. Delivery deforms both what it delivers and the deliveree, stuttering and caricaturing them, remixing and remastering them.[92] Working backwards, the sensual object persists (*memoria*), it displays a unique "style" (*elocutio*), it organizes its notes and parts (*dispositio* and *ordo*), and it contains what Harman calls a "molten core" that withdraws from all contact (*inventio*).[93] The plastic cup does this to the pencil. The garden does this to the house. The plastic cup even does it to itself. The parts of the cup "deliver" the whole in a more or less distorted way, accounting for various aspects of its history and presenting the cup with a certain style, articulated according to certain formal arrangements—and finally, these qualities themselves are uncannily unavailable for present-at-hand inspection.

The molten core of a thing is wrapped within the delivery. Latin gives us a clue about this by translating the Greek for delivery, *hypokrisis*, as either *actio* or *pronuntiatio*.[94] We get the word "hypocrisy" from *hypokrisis*.[95] It stems from the verb to *judge* or *interpret*—objects interpret themselves. Yet in so doing they are like actors, both dissembling and generating an entirely fresh set of objects—as an orchestra "interprets" a score by playing it. For instance, *hypokrisis* can signify the tone or manner of an animal's cry. The cry expresses the animal, yet it's also an object all its own. *Pronuntiatio* is more like the manifest appearance of an object to another object. It speaks to the dissembling part of *hypokrisis*. *Actio* sounds more like execution (Heidegger's *Vollzug*), the dark unfolding of an object's hidden essence. *Actio* speaks to the way objects magically foam with being.

Objects, then, are hyprocrites, forever split from within. I'd rather live in a hypocritical Universe than a cynical one. We've had quite enough of that, a symptom of how the standard philosophical game for two hundred years has been "Anything you can do I can do meta." During this era, philosophy has more or less tacitly agreed that leaping away from objects into the beyond is the mark of true philosophy and intelligence.

Is it not possible to imagine that an object-oriented rhetorical theory might account for vicarious causation, the only kind of causation possible between ontologically vacuum-sealed objects? Harman talks about "elements" or "quality objects"—the aspects of sensual objects that somehow communicate with one another.[96] Could my strange reverse rhetoric supply a model for this? Is it possible then that an element resembles a phrase, or a rhetorical period? Harman hints that the linguistic trope of metaphor might be alluring precisely because it gives us a taste of some kind of deeper causality.[97] Can we imagine the interaction between a pen and a wooden table as made up of rhetorical phrases and periods, whereby the elements of one object persuade another? Consider the Latin root of persuasion (*suadeo*), which has to do with how one object urges, impels, induces or sways another.[98] The aesthetic, in other words, is not a superficial candy coating on the real, but is instead the lubrication, the energy and the glue of causality as such. To think so is truly to exit the Ramist machine.

The Play of Phenomena

Objects are forms of delivery, which means that *objects are hypocrites*—which in turn means that they are actors. The most comprehensive way to think causality is to think drama. Let us explore the difficult and surprising facts that this hypothesis brings up.

In the essay "Experience," Emerson writes of the "evanescence and lubricity of all objects, which lets them slip through our fingers then when we clutch the hardest."[99] Not only is this a description of how humans (fail to) know objects, but also it's a rather elegant image for what happens between any objects whatsoever. In what now sounds like an OOO joke, Emerson says that this dynamic whereby our clutching objects causes them to slip from us is "the most unhandsome part of our condition." There is a play on the notion of handiness (German, *Zuhandenheit*) that one can't fail to miss if one is an object-oriented ontologist. In his tool-analysis, Heidegger draws a distinction between tools that are *zuhanden* (to-hand) and *vorhanden* (present-at-hand). Heidegger argues that when we just use a tool, it disappears into its functioning; it appears when some breakage (or our aesthetic framing of it) isolates it from its background. Harman develops this to apply not only to hammers and the like, and between humans (and the like) and hammers (and the like), but also between and within any and all entities.[100] Harman argues that in order to grasp the most consistent version of the tool analysis, we must accept that any event whatsoever—including the use of the hammer as a tool, the very example Heidegger excludes—is a translation of an object into a *vorhanden* parody of itself.

You are wandering around the Tate Britain art gallery in London with a friend. Both of you know something about art and you've studied art history and criticism. You come to the huge, extraordinary collection of Turner paintings. You stop in front of *Rain, Steam and Speed*, a painting of a train emerging from some mist. The train seems like a ghost, swathed in prismatic clouds of color. You have a conversation about the painting. Your friend says: "Turner celebrates 'the Railway Age' and the affirmation of progress embodied by the locomotive with an allegory developed from the Baroque, and in a style deriving from a study of Rembrandt." But you disagree—you reply: "The painting is Turner's protest against the machine despoliation of the environment, in this case a lovely section of the Thames long dear to the painter."[101]

What is going on here? Are both of you correct at the same time? Wouldn't this imply a contradiction, a dialetheia? Fans of Aristotle are wary of violating LNC. So you look for another reason to justify the contradiction. Maybe you should be relativists. Perhaps you belong to different interpretive communities, as the literary critic Stanley Fish has argued.[102] But this argument has two problems. First, it pushes the issue back a stage. Now you have to explain how these interpretive communities exist. Second, and more seriously, do you two really belong to different communities? You went to the same school, you've been friends for two decades, you studied with the same teachers, and so on. This is a common experience in looking at paintings, or reading poetry, or listening to music. The difference wouldn't be possible if there wasn't some basic agreement. So you rule out the Fish solution. After all, one of the pleasures of looking at paintings is informed disagreement.

It appears then that some art-critical contradictions are true.[103] Why? The OOO answer is that there is a profound ontological ambiguity in objects themselves. This ambiguity is reflected in relations between and within objects. We need to explore the nature of this ambiguity some more.

Let's return to the meeting between you and your friend in the Tate Britain. You recall that Immanuel Kant makes some similar observations in his *Critique of Judgment*. The experience of beauty is paradoxical, because it appears as if beauty is emanating from the object, not from yourself. The experience is universalizable: it's as if it should apply to everyone, anyone with a pulse should love what you're loving. You want to send postcards of the painting to all your friends. Yet you realize that it would ruin their experience, if not yours, if you forced them to like what you like. It seems as if you are close to saying that taste is relative. But no—because of the first criterion, which is that beauty appears to emanate from the object. It would spoil it if you felt it coming from inside you. Then perhaps you could assess what neurochemicals were involved and make a drug that would give you the same experience, or double, or triple. Beauty also avoids relativism because of a third component, a nonconceptual quality. There is a *je ne sais quoi* about beauty: Kant argues that no element in the picture can be isolated, and labeled beautiful. I can't find an "active ingredient" of beauty.

Doesn't this mean that beautiful things are irreducible? We can't reduce them to their parts because this would be isolating an active ingredient. We can't "reduce upwards" to the whole, because this would mean that the parts of the painting were expendable components of a machine. This painting is beautiful, but the beauty is nowhere to be found in it. It is a strange, uncanny situation. We are having a powerful experience that gives us goosebumps, makes us cry. Yet when we look for the source of the experience, we can't find it. Yet the source is just this painting, this piece of music, not that one. What is happening?

Isn't there an echo here of something a little bit object-oriented in Kant himself, the father of correlationism? Can't we claim that beauty proves that reality is not solipsistic, or even at its core relativist, since beauty is evidence of the existence of at least one (other) secret object? Indeed, the experience of beauty is a kind of inner evidence of something in me that is not quite me. It seems to come automatically, and there is nothing I can do to manipulate it. For Kant, it is possible to have an experience that is not based on ego—the experience of beauty is precisely this, which is why perhaps he sees it as a crucial part of the Enlightenment project, and why Schopenhauer made a logical enough progression from Kant to Buddhism. The freedom discovered in beauty is profoundly impersonal and thus it's "object-like," if only we can separate "object" from "hard plastic ball" or whatever. It means beyond your ego.

Here it is, the beautiful painting, and I can't quite tell you what is beautiful about it. Some kind of mind meld is happening, some kind of link between the object and myself. And the experience is universalizable, that is, I can share it because it's based on the possibility that everyone could have it. Even though I can't impose my experience on you, I can coexist with you nonviolently as we both experience our inner space. The aesthetic experience that we humans now call "beauty" is a naked experience of relations between entities: between the Turner painting and me; among the brushstrokes in the painting; between me and you, both having the experience; and so on. Why the *je ne sais quoi*? I propose a rather surprising Hegelian solution to this problem: because *the significance of any set of relations is in the future*. Significance contains a vital ingredient of not-yet, to-come. The meaning of an object is another object.[104]

A causal event is a set of relations between objects. All relations are aesthetic, not just ones between humans and objects such as Turner paintings. Thus we must carefully investigate aesthetics for what it says about the "meaning" of (art) events, since this will give us a clue as to how things work in reality. Perhaps one reason why it is so hard to catch causality in the act unless you hold some kind of vicarious or dialetheic view is that the one thing that cannot be done to relations between objects is catch them "before" or "during" the event of their relating. As every good humanities scholar knows, meaning is *retroactive.* No one ever stood furtively on a street corner in twelfth-century Naples, discussing how they were going to shake up the art world: "Let's start this thing, right. Let's invent perspective and travel round Africa, find the spice islands and rediscover Platonism. Let's call it the Renaissance—that sounds catchy."

If causality is aesthetic, then events only "take place" after they have happened! To say this is to make the Hegelian point that for something to happen, it has to happen twice. In scintillating prose, Percy Shelley describes poets as "the hierophants of an unapprehended imagination, the mirrors of the gigantic shadows that futurity casts upon the present"[105] A hierophant is someone who makes the sacred appear, perhaps a shaman rather than a priest. What this closing section of *A Defence of Poetry* claims is that the significance of an artwork is in the future. The poet is a kind of channel or medium who somehow beams the future into the present.

Now Shelley reaches this position from an opening that couldn't be more physicalist, or materialist. Each person (perhaps even "all sentient beings") is a kind of "Aeolian lyre," a sort of wind instrument that is played by external stimuli, and modulates or translates these stimuli into its own unique timbre. Almost every fairly respectable home had one in the eighteenth century, just as now we have iPods with speakers. What are you hearing when you hear an Aeolian lyre? You are hearing the wind, modulated through the strings and the wooden body of the lyre. You are hearing two objects as they relate to one another. Now the lyre can only sound after the wind is interacting with it; and vice versa—and after you have heard the pressure waves created by the vibration, translated by a transducer in your inner ear that turns the pressure waves into electrochemical signals. The significance of the relation is in the future. In this sense, as strange as it sounds, relations are messages in bottles from the future. Their significance is not-yet, constantly.

Heidegger makes a very similar point about the wind: we never hear it directly, only in the doorway, the fireplace, the tree.[106] Direct seeing is not a guarantee of givenness. We tend to think that realness lies in what is obvious, but *Realist Magic* is arguing that realness lies in what is oblique and mysterious. There is no way to catch the wind in the act before it has been modulated by something. The sound of the wind is in its future. It should be possible to see how the seemingly materialist beginning of Shelley's essay joins up with the seemingly idealist end of the essay. That is, if we drop the notions of matter and idea and instead adopt an object-oriented view, we can see that Shelley and Heidegger are only saying that in themselves, entities are withdrawn: what we think of as their "identity" is already a kind of parody of them. And this parodying process is precisely what causality is. Shelley's Aeolian lyre image is wonderfully appropriate for our purposes, since it's an aesthetic object. It seems that the significance of an aesthetic event is in its future.

Nothing speaks more to the futural quality of relations than the phenomenon of dreams. There is something profoundly ambiguous about a dream, often disturbingly so. Why? Because as Freud argues, dreams can be interpreted infinitely because the deep content of dreams is profoundly latent, unconscious.[107] Now dream interpretation is already happening while you are dreaming, for instance in the attitude you are having about the dream. Moreover, this attitude is one of the core meanings of the dream. The brilliance of Freudian analysis is that it decides not to hunt symbols (such as phallic ones), but to investigate the form of the dream, like a literary critic investigating the narrator: who is she, what attitude does she have, what is her mood, her attunenment? There is already a relation in the dream itself, a relation between the dream images and the dreamer. The deep content of the dream is latent, that is, it's withdrawn. Like a good Kantian, Freud asserts that the deep content just can't be accessed, because when you do, it becomes another kind of manifest content, and thus it's relational: it's a set of relations between a content and a content-holder, yet again.

What then if all relations between all objects were like dreams, not just sentient or just human ones between images and image-maker? Consider again two entangled photons. They "don't know what they are" yet: they must be "measured," that is one of them must be polarized in a certain direction, in order for their significance to be revealed. There really are two photons. Then they are "interpreted," that is, physically adjusted. Physical adjustment, interpretation, causality, aesthetics: all these terms say the same thing. This is not an idealist world in which the photons aren't real until they are perceived. No, it's precisely the opposite, even more opposite than the usual materialist or realist account. That is, perception as such is a physical intervention in the world, which means that causality is profoundly aesthetic.

Kantian beauty is a relationship between entities. What Kant calls the sublime is the vertiginous irreducibility of one object to another object. For Kant, the sublime is provoked by another entity (such as mathematical infinite or the vast scope of the Universe), which acts as a trigger, a sort of irritant, that throws the mind back on itself.[108] When this happens, an abyss of freedom opens up. You experience the raw vastness of your inner space. This experience is as it were the quintessence of the nonconceptuality we glimpsed in the experience of the beautiful. The beautiful and the sublime are not so much opposites as they are related like the liquid center and brittle shell of a piece of chocolate. The beautiful is the basic aesthetic experience, whose essence is the unconditional freedom of the sublime. Would it not be possible to assert, then, that the transcendental freedom that Kant finds in the sublime is simply an echo of the essence of a certain entity or object, namely ourselves? And that if there is not very much difference ontologically speaking between ourselves and a cinder block, the Tardis-like openness of all objects is what manifests as the sublime in our particular human experience?

Since this openness is an irreducible aspect of an object's realness, the only way to get an experiential foothold on one is to relate to it. Yet to relate to it is to be caught in an adjustment, an attunement, between myself and the object. This attunement is what Kant calls a vibration, a possibly violent oscillation between my inner space and the object. This vibration gives us the vertigo Kant describes as the sublime. Our relating with objects opens up the abyss of freedom because each relation is a dance on a volcano, an emission from the opaque void of an object. Relations are uncanny and hollow because they dance at the edge of volcanoes.

Time emerges from relations between things. The meaning of an object is in its future, in how it relates to other objects, including those objects that constitute its parts. Relations are hollowed out from the inside by the uncanniness of the objects between which they play. This hollowness just is time. To figure out what a relation is means to build another relation.

Relations thus contain a nullity that collapses forwards as more relations are built onto them. This tumbling nullity is what is called time. Because they are to-come, relations evoke a feeling of process: hence the illusion that things are processes, that process relationism is the most adequate description of how things are. Yet because time emerges from relations we can never specify in advance what they will be. Process relationism is an ontic or ontotheological attempt to pin down exactly what things are, by way of what OOO sees as an inevitable parody of what things are: causal events. Process relationism tries to reduce the intrinsic ambiguity of relations between things. These relations are inherently contradictory, like the relations you have with a Turner painting in the Tate Britain, versus the ones your friend has.

The point is that for relations to be ambiguous, they don't have to be anything at all. We don't have to imagine that an elephant might sprout flowers all over itself when it squirts water over its back. This is our old friend ECQ (*ex contradictione quodlibet*), otherwise known as *explosion*: the idea that if we accept that (some) contradictions are true, then anything could happen. It's clear for instance that our two readings of Turner's *Rain, Steam and Speed* are better than this one:

> *Rain, Steam and Speed* is about a tomato called Ronnie who juggles hardboiled eggs on Titan.

Though causality is aesthetic, my argument means that the occurrence of just anything at all is not inevitable.[109] The trouble is, we will never be able to specify a causal chain in advance without resorting to ontotheology or smuggling in ontic prejudices about what counts as an object or a causal event. As Harman puts it, "a pebble can destroy an empire if the emperor chokes at dinner."[110] If we are prepared to do away with noncontradictory causal relations we should be open to the possibility that anything could happen.

When we subtract the Kantian correlationist distortion, we see that the Kantian experience of beauty is possible simply because a relation between objects has as its basis a strange nonconceptuality, a *je ne sais quoi*. This nonconceptuality requires another relation, an interpretation, to make sense of it, which in turn requires another relation. Since all relations are physical interventions, all aesthetic interpretations are like what psychology calls *acting out*: they do not know what they are about. Causality is like a play or a mime. Imagine a mime who doesn't know what she is miming. She is frantically gesturing to you, asking you to make sense of what she's doing. This is the nature of causality. As Emerson writes, again in "Experience," "There is a certain magic about [a man's] properest action, which stupefies your powers of observation, so that though it is done before you, you wist not of it. The art of life has a pudency, and will not be exposed."[111] OOO simply generalizes this observation to all entities whatsoever. Accounts of causality, among the many different sorts of philosophical accounting for things, frequently wish to strip the mystery from the world. I am arguing that this mystery is a crucial component of causality as such, so crucial that to eliminate it is to fail to understand how causality functions. Why? Because the significance of any action is to-come. Time, space and other aspects of causality happen because of a deep ambiguity in things.

Causality is like a drama. It is no wonder that *drama* simply means "things that are done" or "doing" (Greek), just as *opera* means "works"; and opera and drama both have "acts." Consider again the default positivism of clunk causality. There is a further problem with clunk causality. Its adherents seem hell bent on excluding precisely the aesthetic dimension, identifying it for instance as a realm of "pseudo causation" (Wesley Salmon). This is deeply symptomatic of an uncanny awareness that the aesthetic dimension contaminates the positivistic materialism we have come to accept as the default ontology. At a small scale, aesthetic phenomena just are physical, and vice versa: to measure is at some stage "to hit with a photon," as is "to see." The sorts of things that clunk causality wants to rule out are shadows, sounds, lights and electromagnetic phenomena: a goodly portion of reality.

Not only this: it seems often as if what clunk causality theories want is to catch causality in the act without having to interfere with it, a fantasy that quantum theory has totally disabled. It seems as if the ideal causal event would be a totally invisible and inaudible one. Yet we know from phenomena such as entanglement and superposition that such events, strangely and ironically, refute clunking in other ways, for instance by producing so-called action at a distance. Before they are measured, two photons can be entangled as they emerge from a certain laser: they are capable of acting instantly based on the other's spin and momentum, and so on.[112]

The ideal conditions for clunking to occur are precisely those conditions in which all kinds of spooky non-clunking occurs. I can't mark the photons with some special *x* (as for instance Salmon wants) to prove that they are the same when they emerge from the laser as when they are entangled. To do so would be to alter them in a very significant way. There is an irreducible uncertainty here: indeed the fact that "marking" is causality is the basis of Heisenberg's Uncertainty Principle: "measure" at the quantum level means "alter (momentum, position) by means of another quantum."[113] We can go up to the level of medium-sized objects and find all sorts of parallels. Certainly, I can mark a cricket ball with an *x* to show that it's the same ball when I toss it across the pitch. Salmon gets tied in knots trying to distinguish this kind of mark from a causal interaction. Would it not be more efficient simply to admit that I have already causally tampered with the ball by marking it? Even at this macro level, the ideal cricket ball would just spontaneously land in Salmon's hand and say "Hey, you know I am the same ball you threw from the other side of the pitch, really, I am—trust me." Or perhaps the ball is able to convey its identity over time by telepathy. Somehow Salmon might just spontaneously know that the ball was the same. Which begs the question: a whole area of clunk causality is to account for how things appear to remain the same over time.

This should alert us to the fact that the aesthetic dimension, the dimension of light and sound and vibration and, moreover, their apprehension by all kinds of entities from ears to loudspeakers to photographic plates to human neurons, not to mention the knife that makes the *x* on the cricket ball, is an irreducible aspect of the causal dimension. Indeed, as I shall continue to stress, *the aesthetic dimension just is the causal dimension.*

Thus there are drastic problems for positivistic clunk theories of causation. Some phenomena such as moving lights, shadows and so on can exert real causal effects, yet these are what positivistic clunk causality tries to rule out.[114] This is evident, since they are the effects of certain causes themselves, and we should expect them to act on things in their turn. A shadow can hit a light sensitive diode and turn on a nightlight. Why this is ruled out as a causal event beats me. Why it isn't even mentioned in the mainstream literature is symptomatic of a stunning blind spot. A spotlight hits a surface—say, the frayed red curtain of some slightly degraded cabaret in a small town miles from the metropolis. The audience's pupils contract to take in the brilliance of the bright red circle of the illuminated piece of curtain. Why is this not a causal event? Never mind whether we cross the light with another light or change the filter or the other kinds of example that the clunkers want to use. The stunning thing is why they don't see the simple spotlight's action as a causal event in the first place.[115]

In order for light to hit the curtain, the electric filament or halogen in the bulb has to reach a certain temperature so that the atoms are excited enough to release photons. Light at this scale is particular as well as wavelike: it just does clunk and splash around. In order to illuminate the curtain, the photons must not all be absorbed by the quanta on the curtain's surface. This sounds ever so causal to me, but again, clunk causality wants to rule it out. It's baffling.

Phil Dowe gives the example of someone running alongside the moving spotlight, holding up a red filter so that the light is "marked" like the cricket ball.[116] Yet this marking is not definably "on" the light. Yet if there is no mark, we can't be sure that it's the "same" light as it moves across the curtain. Dowe admits that with this example, the assumption of a fundamental difference between real versus pseudo causality breaks down. Isn't this the real problem—the compulsion to reduce inconsistency results in yet more inconsistencies. Why? The whole discussion seems absurd, down to the example itself: as positivism struggles to police the boundary between physical and aesthetic events, it produces the clownish aesthetic demons that confound its principles. Freudians would take note of the precisely aesthetic, dramatic counterfactuals that positivism produces to police itself: the Sydney Opera House, a light show, a shadow.[117]

I suggest that the reason more inconsistencies appear the more you try to nail down physical versus pseudo causation is that there is an irreducibly aesthetic aspect of causality. To try to catch causality in the act without this aesthetic dimension produces significant paradoxes and aporias in positivistic theory. It seems to come down to the fact that aesthetic phenomena require some $1+n$ extra entities—a field of energy, dilating and contracting pupils, inscribable surfaces, all kinds of mute yet significant entities that are neither inside nor outside the causal process that clunk causality tries to isolate. The $1+n$ suggests a region of entities that we can't account for directly. Again, this tells us something deep about causality. Even more fundamentally, the trouble arises when philosophy tries to smooth out the intuitively obvious Rift between an object and its properties, so as to avoid logical and set-theoretical paradoxes that seem to violate the Law of Noncontradiction (LNC).[118] Consider this: if an object were totally different from its sensual object, we would have a nihilistic situation where an apple could be grasped as an egg or a toaster could be an octopus. Conversely, if an object were totally the same as its sensual object, then we would have an identitarian ontotheology on our hands, and nothing could arise, and moreover, we would have a situation in which beings are ultimately determined by some form(s) of what I've called *top object*.

On the view proposed in this book, LNC can't hold for objects, because there is a radical cut between an object and its sensual qualities, and this takes the form of a contradiction, $p \wedge \neg p$. If we can only accept that these paradoxes are all right, we will have less of a problem accounting for causality. Of course, this will mean showing that the existence of contradictoriness at this level doesn't imply just any old thing at all—trivialism, or *ex contradictione quodlibet* (ECQ). Fortunately, as argued above, there are good reasons for supposing that ECQ doesn't necessarily hold if we let go of LNC.[119] A cut between an object and its manifestation to other objects doesn't mean that the manifestation can be anything at all.

Take the basic phenomenon of motion. Positivistic causal theories have trouble with the simple fact of inertia: the way in which an object continues to move when it's not interfered with, formalized in Newton's First Law.[120] In Chapter 3 I shall argue that motion is much better thought as the result of an inherent ambiguity in objects. If we refuse to think this way, we risk being saddled with all kinds of unsatisfying "ontic" baggage—prejudices that we have smuggled in to our ontology from an unexplained elsewhere.

Causality takes place in an aesthetic dimension that consists of some kind of moving stage set, like a traveling theater. There is a whole media set up involving stages, curtains, props and lighting that produce the causal event—I use the term *produce* in its fully theatrical sense. Notice that I'm not arguing that there must be a human audience, or human producers. The audience might consist of fish or Martians or dust particles. The producers might be black holes or photons or the San Francisco Symphony Orchestra. It might be one of those plays in which the audience is included in the drama.

What is the sense of threat and strangeness that grips you when you enter a circus or a theater? Is it really the case that this is a fantasy space where the normal rules are suspended? Or is it that you realize that *the illusion is on the other side* of the circus tent, in the outside world you took to be real, and that what you are witnessing when you watch drama (Greek: action) is the play of causality? Isn't it the case that you took the world outside the tent to be real precisely because you treated its aesthetic qualities as secondary to its supposedly physical, causal ones?

There are many plays and movies that, after watching them, cause you to see the world that way, for a time. The rotoscoping graphics of *A Scanner Darkly*, for instance, force the audience to see the world outside the cinema that way, at least for a few disorienting minutes.[121] What precisely is the dynamic of this sensation wearing off? Is it that we return to real reality? Or that we superimpose a socially acceptable distance and normality on the world, having had it ruthlessly stripped away in the theater? Or rather, we have the illusion of depth and distance stripped away, the illusion that there is a mechanism underneath the display. Drama undermines the fake perspective that makes things appear to be really happening against some neutral background. You realize that causality is happening in your face, closer than breathing.

Let's revisit the two main ways of avoiding OOO outlined earlier:

1. Undermining. Things are reducible to smaller entities such as particles. Or things are only instantiations of deeper processes.

2. Overmining. Objects are blank lumps with their appearances glued to their superfices, or added by some "perceiver." On both views, objects are basically blah until they interact with other objects. Instead I would rather locate a Rift between appearance and essence within the object itself. Objects on this view are quaking with vitality. But to achieve this we shall have to accept some kind of paraconsistent, possibly dialetheic logic, the kind of logic proposed by Graham Priest, a logic that allows things

to be what they seem, and not what they seem, simultaneously. Otherwise we are back to default substances-plastered-with-accidents.

Now we can discern a third way of avoiding OOO. This would be to claim the inverse of (2):

3. There are no substances, and it's all appearance-for, all aesthetics all the way down.[122]

I want to preserve the Rift between appearance and essence. Why? Because this preserves, paradoxically, the very aesthetic-ness of the aesthetic dimension. Look at it this way. If reality were "aesthetics all the way down" then we would *know* it was "just" an illusion: so it wouldn't be an illusion. We would know that it was pretense—so it wouldn't be pretense. We would have a kind of inverted ontotheology of pure affects without substances. Let's quote Lacan once more: "What constitutes pretense is that, in the end, you don't know whether it's pretense or not." Until thinking is ready to accept that objects can be intrinsically unstable, both essential and aesthetic at the same time, we are stuck with options (1)–(3), all of which are ways of avoiding OOO.

Once we accept this inherent instability, the Rift between essence and appearance, we don't need to have objects pushed around by processes or particles, or others' perceptions of them. They can do just fine on their own. This seems to be the case with a single quantum, which appears visibly to occupy more than one place at once, to "breathe" in the words of physicist Aaron O'Connell.[123] In that case, as a rough and ready rule, let's assume that causality happens in three acts, just like in a play—if we include the aesthetic dimension it might be appropriate to see aesthetic phenomena as distorted archaeological evidence of causality.[124] Act one is how things begin. So on with the show.

Aristotle remarks that dramas have a beginning, middle, and end.[125] When he says this, he means something more than the first page, the last page, and the total number of pages divided by two. Aristotle means that there are phenomenologically distinct qualities of beginning, persisting and ending. Likewise, I have divided this book into three subsequent chapters that correspond to the beginning, middle, and end of an entity. Why? I mean, is there any deeper fact that this arrangement accounts for, or is it just helpful in terms of formal organization? It does indeed seem that there is some kind of ontological cut between arising, persisting and ceasing. So much does this appear to be the case that I shall argue that it's difficult, perhaps impossible, to specify that the "same" entity is involved in arising, dwelling and ceasing. This is just one of the inconsistencies and double-truths that we shall have to get used to in an object-oriented ontological account of reality. Beginning, middle and end are after all different formal parts of a novel or a play or a movie. Hollywood directors talk instinctively about acts one, two and three of a movie. I argue that there is some reason for this talk: they are talking, in however distorted a way, about how causality really works.

Somewhat provocatively, and somewhat against my own intuitions, I have decided to call the phases of an object "birth," "life" and "death." This is not meant to suggest that objects are "alive" if by that you are to think of me as a vitalist. However, it seems to me that the common or garden understanding of what objects are is far too mechanistic and reified. I agree with Jane Bennett that it might be useful, if only for the sake of imagining things more openly, to inject a little bit of animism into the discussion.[126] For reasons I give throughout, it would be better if we had some term that suited neither vitalism nor mechanism. This approach seems quite congruent with what we know about lifeforms: that they are made of non-life.[127] And it seems congruent with what OOO holds about objects: they are not just lumps of dullness. The best I can think of is appending some kind of negation to life and death, so that objects become *undead*. But explaining this will take some time: so birth, life and death remain in the chapter titles.

The following chapter, "Magic Birth," explores the origin of an object. This is done in two related ways: through a thought experiment that imagines a nursery for objects in the shape of the pond at the end of the street on which I live; and through an analysis of Cantor's transfinite sets that restores the dialetheic paradoxes that some interpretations struggle to omit—most notably, in our time, the ontology of Alain Badiou that is based on the Zermelo-Fraenkel interpretation of Cantor. The chapter then moves to an alien-phenomenological account of the beginning of an object, drawing from aesthetic theories of beginning (*aperture*) and the sublime.

("Alien phenomenology" is Ian Bogost's term.) Chapter 2 argues that how an object begins consists, in short, in the *opening of a fresh Rift* between essence and appearance. For Badiou, the existence of an entity means that it is identical with itself. In *Realist Magic*, however, the existence of an entity is the existence of a Rift within identity.

Chapter 3, "Magic Life," accounts for the persistence of objects. Since time is an emergent property of objects, this persistence is not just haphazard loitering in a preexisting street called Temporality Avenue. Every object "times," in the sense of an intransitive verb such as "walk" or "laugh." The present moment, which many philosophical systems (such as Augustine's) take to be more real than past or future, is here examined as a deceptive, shifting zone of *suspensions*. Musical and narrative theory is used to elucidate presence, which is never as objective and as given as some suppose. In turn, the fact of motion, and in particular inertia (continuing to exist in the sense of continuing motion), becomes explicable within the framework of OOO. The persistence of things, I argue, is the *suspension of the Rift* between essence and appearance that constitutes an object.

Chapter 4, "Magic Death," is an account of how an object ends. The end of an object is simply the *closing of the Rift* between essence and appearance, and thus the reduction of an object to appearance only. This presents us with a startlingly counter-intuitive fact, that the appearance of an object is that object's *past*, while the essence of an object is the *future* of the object. If the main term for the alien phenomenology of Chapter 3 was *suspension*, the principle term in Chapter 4 is *fragility*. I give an OOO definition of fragility based on an interpretation of Gödel's Incompleteness Theorem, which traces its ancestry to Cantor's discovery of transfinite sets, explored in Chapter 2. Badiou supposes an object's end to be the termination of its identity with itself. Because he cleaves to LNC, a plague of Sorites paradoxes threatens to arise: when something is nearly dead, how identical is it with itself? Where is the line? The view that ending is the closing of a Rift, a return to consistency—at least in a certain region of reality—is not afflicted with these paradoxes, because it does not imagine objects in what amounts to a positivistic manner.

Realist Magic ends with a brief conclusion about what it has accomplished. I conclude that what the book amounts to is a return to a weird non-theistic Aristotle, less preoccupied with final causes and the Law of Noncontradiction. This Aristotle is summoned at the moment at which humans become aware of their ecological impact on Earth.

Notes

1. Stephen Bates, "Banksy's Gorilla in a Pink Mask" Is Painted Over," *The Guardian* (July 15, 2011), http://www.guardian.co.uk/artanddesign/2011/jul/15/banksy-gorilla-mask-painted-over (accessed September 16, 2011). See Bobby George, [formerly http://dreamduke.tumblr.com/post/7657062564/bansky].
2. In particular, consider *The Truth in Painting*, tr. Geoffrey Bennington and Ian McLeod (Chicago and London: University of Chicago Press, 1987).
3. John T. Dugan, *Star Trek*, "Return to Tomorrow," first broadcast February 9, 1968; Henry Laycock, "Some Questions of Ontology," *The Philosophical Review* 81 (1972), 3–42. See Arda Denkel, *Object and Property* (Cambridge: Cambridge University Press, 2007), 188–194.
4. Martin Heidegger, *Being and Time*, tr. Joan Stambaugh (Albany, N.Y: State University of New York Press, 1996), 66.
5. Heidegger, *Being and Time*, 66.
6. The term *irreduction* is derived from Bruno Latour: *The Pasteurization of France*, tr. Alan Sheridan and John Law (Cambridge, Mas.: Harvard University Press, 1993), 191, 212–238.
7. Graham Harman, *The Quadruple Object* (Ripley: Zero Books, 2011), 7–18.
8. This is not the place to get into an argument about quantum theory, but I have argued that quanta also do not endorse a world that I can't speak about because it is only real when measured. This world is that of the reigning Standard Model proposed by Niels Bohr and challenged by De Broglie and Bohm (and now the cosmologist Valentini, among others). See Timothy Morton, "Here Comes Everything: The Promise of Object-Oriented Ontology," *Qui Parle* 19.2 (Spring–Summer, 2011), 163–190.
9. John Donne, *Holy Sonnets* 15, in *The Major Works: Including* Songs and Sonnets *and Sermons*, ed. John Carey (Oxford: Oxford University Press, 2009).
10. Edward O. Wilson, *Consilience: The Unity of Knowledge* (New York: Knopf, 1998).
11. Harman uses the term *hot potato* to describe the way relationist theories include–exclude the object: *Guerrilla Metaphysics: Phenomenology and the Carpentry of Things* (Chicago: Open Court, 2005), 82.
12. Paul Tillich, *Systematic Theology 1* (Chicago: University of Chicago Press, 1951), 188.
13. Martin Heidegger, *What Is a Thing?* (Chicago: Henry Regnery, 1967), 19–20.
14. Martin Heidegger, *What Is a Thing?* 243.

15. Albert Einstein, *Relativity: The Special and the General Theory* (London: Penguin, 2006); Petr Horava, "Quantum Gravity at a Lifshitz Point," arXiv:0901.3775v2 [hep-th].

16. Levi Bryant, *The Democracy of Objects* (Ann Arbor: Open Humanities Press, 2011), 73–77, 152, and in particular 208–227.

17. Immanuel Kant, *Critique of Pure Reason*, tr. Norman Kemp Smith (Boston and New York: Bedford/St. Martin's, 1965), 51.

18. Leo Spitzer, "Milieu and Ambiance," in *Essays in Historical Semantics* (New York: Russell and Russell, 1948; repr. 1968), 179–316.

19. I note in passing that physicists Stephen Hawking and Basil Hiley have both wagered that there is no Higgs.

20. Ian Bogost thinks objects as units: *Unit Operations: An Approach to Videogame Criticism* (Cambridge: MIT Press, 2008).

21. Mark Heller, *The Ontology of Physical Objects: Four-Dimensional Hunks of Matter* (Cambridge: Cambridge University Press, 2008), 1–29.

22. Heller, *Ontology*, 75.

23. This is the case on Heller's own admission: *Ontology*, 47–49, 68–109.

24. David Bohm, *The Special Theory of Relativity* (London: Routledge, 2006), 159–174, 175–176.

25. Maurice Merleau-Ponty, *Phenomenology of Perception*, tr. Colin Smith (New York: Routledge, 1996), 67–69.

26. This is the Lacanian not-all set: see Bryant, *The Democracy of Objects*, 250, 253, 255–257.

27. This is Spinoza's phrase: *Ethics*, ed. and tr. Edwin Curley, intro. Stuart Hampshire (London: Penguin, 1996), 174.

28. This is far more peculiar than simple skeptical empiricism, which says that the object is perceived in different ways by different perceivers. It's also strikingly different from idealism, in which to be perceived is to exist. There really is an object there and my experience of it is not just "a different take on the same thing." My relationship with the object constitutes an entirely unique realm. This refreshes the Buddhist idea that different sentient beings inhabit different sorts of reality. Far from *esse est percipi* idealism, what this means is that there are real objects and that they are withdrawn. If a hell-being drinks a glass of water, she tastes molten lead. If a hungry ghost drinks a glass of water, she tastes a glassful of pus. To microbes, the water is their home. To humans, the water slakes their thirst. How can water do all this? Because it exists.

29. This is to extend and modify the notion that "there is no metalanguage," in other words, there is no privileged place outside of reality from which we can view it correctly. OOO cashes out this principal tenet of post-structuralism better than post-structuralism did. By returning to phenomenology, OOO allows for an all encompassing "sincerity" that makes cynical distance impossible. Yet at the same time, this particular sincerity is charged with irony, like a thunderstorm filled with electricity. And by raising the stakes from epistemology to fundamental ontology, OOO prevents any kind of smugness or distance from creeping its way into the attitude that "there is no metalanguage" codes for.

30. Heller, *Ontology*, 84.
31. Harman, *Guerrilla Metaphysics*, 82.
32. Aristotle, *Metaphysics*, tr. and intro. Hugh Lawson-Tancred (London: Penguin, 2004), 88, 89–97, 98–103.
33. Jacques Lacan, *Le séminaire, Livre III: Les psychoses* (Paris: Editions de Seuil, 1981), 48.
34. Heller, *Ontology*, 70–72, 80–81.
35. Heller, *Ontology*, 94–96.
36. David Lewis, "Many, but almost One," in John Bacon, Keith Campbell and Lloyd Reinhardt, eds., *Ontology, Causality and Mind: Essays in Honor of D. M. Armstrong* (Cambridge: Cambridge University Press, 2008), 23–42 (26–28).
37. Arda Denkel, *Object and Property* (Cambridge: Cambridge University Press, 2007), 82–83, 211–212. Peter Geach, "Ontological Relativity and Relative Identity," in Milton K. Munitz, ed., *Logic and Ontology* (New York: New York University Press, 1973), 287–302.
38. I use Graham Harman's Heideggerian notion of the as-structure: *Tool-Being: Heidegger and the Metaphysics of Objects* (Peru, IL: Open Court, 2002), 8–9, 40–49.
39. Lewis, "Many, but almost One," 23.
40. Peter Unger, "The Problem of the Many," *Midwest Studies in Philosophy* 5 (1980), 411–467.
41. Shinji Nishimoto et al., "Reconstructing Visual Experiences from Brain Activity Evoked by Natural Movies," *Current Biology* 21 (2011), 1–6, doi:10.1016/j.cub.2011.08.031.
42. Harman, *The Quadruple Object*, 13–16.
43. Alexander Pope, "Windsor Forest," The Poems of Alexander Pope: a One-Volume Edition of the Twickenham Text, with Selected Annotations, ed. J. Butt (London and New York: Routledge, 1989).
44. See Margaret A. Boden, ed., *The Philosophy of Artificial Intelligence* (Oxford and New York: Oxford University Press, 1990).
45. Heidegger, *Being and Time*, 22.
46. Iain Hamilton Grant, "Suprematist Ontogony and the Thought Magnet," Object-Oriented Thinking, Royal Academy of Arts, July 1, 2011.
47. José Ortega y Gasset, *Phenomenology and Art*, tr. Philip W. Silver (New York: Norton, 1975), 63–70; Harman, *Guerrilla Metaphysics*, 39, 40, 135–143, 247.
48. W.D. Richter, Dir., *The Adventures of Buckaroo Banzai across the Eighth Dimension* (20th Century Fox, 1984).
49. Jacques Lacan, *Écrits: A Selection*, tr. Alan Sheridan (London: Tavistock, 1977), 311.
50. Danièle Moyal-Sharrock, "Words as Deeds: Wittgenstein's 'Spontaneous Utterances' and the Dissolution of the Explanatory Gap," *Philosophical Psychology* 13.3 (2000), 355–372.

51. See for example David Deutsch, *The Fabric of Reality: The Science of Parallel Universes—and Its Implications* (London: Penguin, 1998).

52. Phil Dowe, *Physical Causation* (New York: Cambridge University Press, 2000), 14–29.

53. Judea Pearl, *Causality: Models, Reasoning, and Inference* (Cambridge: Cambridge University Press, 2010), 78–85.

54. Al-Kindi, "The One True and Complete Agent and the Incomplete 'Metaphorical' Agent," in *Classical Arabic Philosophy: An Anthology of Sources*, tr. and intro. Jon McGinnis and David C. Reisman (Indianapolis: Hackett, 2007), 22–23.

55. Phil Dowe, *Physical Causation*, 123–145.

56. This connection between differing timescales becomes apparent in Werner Herzog's *Cave of Forgotten Dreams* (IFC, Sundance, 2010), a documentary about the Chauvet cave paintings of 30 000BC.

57. David Bohm, *Quantum Theory* (New York: Dover, 1989), iii–v, 167; *The Special Theory of Relativity* (London: Routledge, 2006), 217–218.

58. Casimir forces glue nanoscale cogwheels together: Anon., "Focus: The Force of Empty Space," *Phys. Rev. Focus* 2, 28 (December 3, 1998), DOI: 10.1103/PhysRevFocus.2.28, available at http://physics.aps.org/story/v2/st28, accessed June 27, 2012.

59. Al-Ghazali, *The Incoherence of the Philosophers* tr. Sabid Ahmad Kamali (Lahore: Pakistan Philosophical Congress, 1963). See also Harman, *Guerrilla Metaphysics*, 92–93.

60. Nagarjuna, *The Fundamental Wisdom of the Middle Way*, tr. and commentary Jay L. Garfield (Oxford: Oxford University Press, 1995), 28–30.

61. Eleanor Rosch, "Is Causality Circular? Event Structure in Folk Psychology, Cognitive Science and Buddhist Logic," *Journal of Consciousness Studies* 1.1 (Summer 1994), 50–65.

62. Lacan, *Le séminaire*, 48.

63. Moses Maimonides, *Guide for the Perplexed*, http://www.sacred-texts.com/jud/gfp/gfp008.htm, accessed August 18, 2012.

64. Timothy Morton, *The Ecological Thought* (Cambridge: Harvard University Press, 2010), 14–15, 17–19, 38–50.

65. Harman, *Guerrilla Metaphysics*, 33–44, 77, 81–84, 84–87.

66. Allan Kaprow, "Education of the Un-Artist 1," "Education of the Un-Artist 2," in *Essays on the Blurring of Art and Life*, ed. Jeff Kelley (Berkeley: University of California Press, 2003) 97–109, 110–126; Theodor Adorno, *Aesthetic Theory*, tr. and ed. Robert Hullot-Kentor (Minneapolis: University of Minnesota Press, 1997), 103–105.

67. Jacques Lacan, *Écrits: A Selection*, tr. Alan Sheridan (London: Tavistock, 1977), 311.

68. Heidegger, *Being and Time*, 25; 23–34 are pertinent in this regard.

69. Gregory Petsko, "Save University Arts from the Bean Counters," *Nature* 468.1003 (published online, December 22, 2010), doi:10.1038/4681003a.

70. See for example Martha Nussbaum, *Not for Profit: Why Democracy Needs the Humanities* (Princeton: Princeton University Press, 2012).

71. This affects speculative realism itself. For instance, Quentin Meillassoux's negative view of rhetoric is a direct product of scientific dominance. A default materialist relationism reigns supreme. See Graham Harman, *Prince of Networks: Bruno Latour and Metaphysics* (Melbourne: Re.Press, 2009), 175.

72. Heidegger, *Being and Time*, 89.

73. Heidegger, *Being and Time*, 89.

74. Heidegger, *Being and Time*, 92.

75. See Don Abbott, "Kant, Theremin, and the Morality of Rhetoric," *Philosophy and Rhetoric* 40.3 (2007) 274–92.

76. Harman, *Prince of Networks*, 163–85.

77. Edward Casey, *The Fate of Place: A Philosophical History* (Berkeley: University of California Press, 1997), 106–116.

78. Terry Eagleton, *The Ideology of the Aesthetic* (Oxford: Basil Blackwell, 1990), 1–30.

79. Yuri Aharanov and David Bohm, "Significance of Electromagnetic Potentials in the Quantum Theory," *Phys. Rev.* 115.3 (August 1, 1959), 485–491.

80. Maria Isabel Franco et al., "Molecular Vibration-Sensing Component in *Drosophila Melanogaster* Olfaction," *Proceedings of the National Academy of Sciences* 108.9 (2011), 3797–3802, DOI 10.1073/pnas.1012293108.

81. Rupert Sheldrake, *Morphic Resonance: The Nature of Formative Causation* (Rochester, VT: Park Street Press, 2009).

82. Al-Kindi, "The One True and Complete Agent and the Incomplete 'Metaphorical' Agent," in *Classical Arabic Philosophy: An Anthology of Sources*, tr. and intro. Jon McGinnis and David C. Reisman (Indianapolis: Hackett, 2007), 22–23.

83. Quintilian, *Institutio Oratoria* 11.3. This fourth part of the Loeb Classical Library edition of Quintilian is not readily available in hard copy, but an online version can be found at http://penelope.uchicago.edu/Thayer/E/Roman/Texts/Quintilian/Institutio_Oratoria/11C*.html - 3, accessed August 15, 2012.

84. Quintilian, *Institutio Oratoria* 11.3.

85. Quintilian, *Institutio Oratoria* 11.3.

86. Harman, *Guerrilla Metaphysics*, 142–44, 172–82.

87. Harman, *Guerrilla Metaphysics*, 162.

88. Richard Lanham, *A Handlist of Rhetorical Terms: A Guide for Students of English Literature* (Berkeley, Los Angeles and London: University of California Press, 1969).

89. Timothy Morton, "Introduction," *The Cambridge Companion to Shelley* (Cambridge: Cambridge University Press, 2006), 1–13.

90. Joan Stambaugh, *The Finitude of Being* (Albany: SUNY University Press, 1992), 7–11, 59–70.

91. Xavier Zubiri, *On Essence*, tr. A.R. Caponigri (Washington DC: Catholic University Press, 1980), 46–47. See also Harman, *Tool-Being*, 243–268.

92. Alphonso Lingis, *The Imperative* (Bloomington: Indiana University Press, 1998), 135.

93. Harman, *Guerrilla Metaphysics*, 102–6, 119–21; 161.

94. Charlton T. Lewis and Charles Short, *Latin Dictionary* (Oxford: Clarendon Press, 1879), *actio*, *pronuntiatio*.

95. Henry George Liddell and Robert Scott, *A Greek-English Lexicon: Revised and Augmented throughout by Sir Henry Stuart Jones with the Assistance of Roderick McKenzie* (Oxford. Clarendon Press, 1940), *ὑπόκρισις*.

96. Harman, *Guerrilla Metaphysics*, 164–70, 171.

97. Harman, *Guerrilla Metaphysics*, 172.

98. Lewis and Short, *Latin Dictionary*, *suadeo*.

99. Ralph Waldo Emerson, "Experience," in *The Essential Writings of Ralph Waldo Emerson*, ed. Brooks Atkinson, intro. Mary Oliver (New York: Modern Library, 2000) 307–326 (309).

100. In Harman *Tool-Being*, 19, 24, 28, 35–36.

101. These are genuine quotations from John Gage and John McCoubrey. See Brandon Cooke, "Art-Critical Contradictions," paper given at the American Society of Aesthetics, San Francisco, October 2003.

102. Stanley Fish, *Is There A Text in This Class?* (Cambridge: Harvard University Press, 1980), 147–174.

103. For a trenchant discussion see Brandon Cooke, "Art-Critical Contradictions."

104. I adapt for my own purposes a famous line of Harold Bloom's: "the meaning of a poem can only be a poem, but *another poem—a poem not itself*." *The Anxiety of Influence: A Theory of Poetry* (Oxford: Oxford University Press, 1997), 70.

105. Percy Shelley, *A Defence of Poetry*, in *Shelley's Poetry and Prose*, ed. Donald H. Reiman and Neil Fraistat (New York and London: W.W. Norton, 2002), 509–535 (535).

106. Martin Heidegger, "The Origin of the Work of Art," in *Poetry, Language, Thought*, trans. Albert Hofstadter (New York: Harper & Row, 1971), 15–86 (26).

107. Sigmund Freud, *Interpreting Dreams*, tr. J.A. Underwood, intro. John Forrester (London: Penguin, 2006), 148–149.

108. Immanuel Kant, *Critique of Judgment: Including the First Introduction*, tr. Werner Pluhar (Indianapolis: Hackett, 1987), 113–117.

109. I argue this in contradistinction to Quentin Meillassoux, who gets rid of the principle of sufficient reason in order to maintain LNC: *After Finitude: An Essay on the Necessity of Contingency*, tr. Ray Brassier (New York: Continuum, 2009), 34, 40–42, 48–52, 60, 132.

110. Harman, *Prince of Networks*, 21.

111. Ralph Waldo Emerson, "Experience," *Essential Writings*, ed. Brooks Atkinson and Mary Oliver (Modern Library, 2000), 307–326, 318.

112. Anton Zeilinger, *Dance of the Photons: From Einstein to Quantum Teleportation* (New York: Farrar, Straus and Giroux, 2010), 45–55.

113. Bohm, *Quantum Theory*, 99–115.

114. Dowe, *Physical Causation*, 104–107.

115. Dowe, *Physical Causation*, 64–90.

116. Dowe, *Physical Causation*, 75.

117. Dowe, *Physical Causation*, 75–79.

118. Dowe, *Physical Causation*, 77.

119. Graham Priest, *In Contradiction: A Study of the Transconsistent* (Oxford: Oxford University Press, 2006), 5–6, 42.

120. Dowe, *Physical Causation*, 54, 63.

121. Richard Linklater, Dir., *A Scanner Darkly* (Warner Independent Pictures, 2006).

122. This is Steven Shaviro's position: "Kant and Hegel, Yet Again," http://www.shaviro.com/Blog/?p=991, accessed August 18, 2012.

123. Aaron O'Connell, "Making Sense of a Visible Quantum Object," TED Talk, March 2011, http://www.ted.com/talks/aaron_o_connell_making_sense_of_a_visible_quantum_object.html, accessed June 27, 2012.

124. See Harman, *Guerrilla Metaphysics*, 101–124 for a discussion of how poetic metaphor is archaeological evidence in just this sense.

125. Aristotle, *Poetics*, in Aristotle, Horace and Longinus, *Classical Literary Criticism*, tr. T.S. Dorsch (Harmondsworth: Penguin, 1984). 41.

126. Jane Bennett, *Vibrant Matter: A Political Ecology of Things* (Durham: Duke University Press, 2004), 119–120; Timothy Morton, *The Ecological Thought* (Cambridge: Harvard University Press, 2010), 8, 110, 115.

127. Timothy Morton, "Some Notes towards a Philosophy of Non-Life," *Thinking Nature* 1 (2011).

Chapter 2

Magic Birth

Who's there?

– Shakespeare, *Hamlet*

Brekekekex, ko-ax ko-ax! The frogs were croaking in the pond near the house. There must have been tens of thousands of them. Humans hear the croak and translate it: into the word *croak*, for instance. Aristophanes translated it into the rhythmically fancy *brekekekex, ko-ax ko-ax.*[1] *Croak* or *ko-ax*, it's not too bad a translation, or to use the strict term for the figure of speech, onomatopoeia. Frogs don't go *boing* or *clunk*. They croak. Somehow these nonhuman sounds made it into human language, altered but reasonably unscathed. A new translation has appeared. A fresh Rift has opened up between appearance and essence. *An object is born.*

A wall of croaking filled the night air. Hanging on either side of a human head, a pair of ears heard the sound drifting over the pond towards darkened suburbia. A discursive thought process subdivided the wall of sound, visualizing thousands of frogs. A more or less vivid, accurate image of a frog flashed through the imagination. The soft darkness invited the senses to probe expectantly further into the warm night. On the breeze came the wall of sound, uncompromising, trilling like the sound of frozen peas rattling around inside a clean milk bottle multiplied tens of thousands of times.

While the author was writing the preceding sentence, a whimsical taste for metaphor enjoyed linking the sound of the frogs with the sound of frozen vegetables. (It's not easy being green?)

Air was forced into an elastic sac at the bottom of a frog's mouth. The lungs pushed and the sac inflated, and when released out came the croak. The air was modulated by frog tissues, sampled briefly and repackaged, returning to the ambient atmosphere as a low rasp with high harmonics. The sound was made of myriad waves crisscrossing in the air. Fetid smells of the damp swamp at the edges of the pond drifted indifferent to the frog chorus, reaching the nose of a little girl who said they reminded her of the seaside. The air carried sound and smell and a soft touch to the skin.

A single sound wave of a certain amplitude and frequency rode the air molecules inside the frog's mouth. The wave was inaudible to a mosquito flying right past the frog's lips, but sensed instead as a fluctuation in the air. The wave carried information about the size and elasticity of the frog's mouth, the size of his lungs, his youth and vigor. The wave spread out like a ripple, becoming fainter and fainter as it delivered its message further and further into the surrounding air. Ten thousand feet above the pond, passengers in a plane failed to hear the sound wave, although a faint glint of the plane's landing lights was visible as a brief wink of color reflected from the surface of the water. Reaching the ears of a nearby female frog, however, the sound wave was soon translated into hormones that told her that a young stud frog was close by. The wall of croaking caused the grasses in the pavement next to the pond to vibrate slightly.

Fingers switched on an MP3 recorder outside the suburban house. The wave front entered the microphone along with countless of its sonic cousins. A software driven sampler took 44,000 tiny impressions of the sound per second and stored it in the device's memory.

As the wave front advanced, the shape of the wave remained fairly constant as molecule after molecule translated it into its own vibration. The expanding wave front brushed against the outermost rim of a spider's web, causing the spider to detect in her feet the possible presence of the next meal. Like a plucked violin string, one thread of the web moved slightly back and forth.[2] There were minuscule momentary differences in pressure on either side of the thread. A tiny drop of dew fell from the vibrating thread, impacting on the surface of a stone below, exposing millions of microbes to the surrounding air. Several moments later, the author of a book called *Realist Magic* remembered the sound of the frogs in the pond and wondered what else might have been going on in and around that sound.

Actual, real things are happening at multiple levels and involving multiple agents, as the wave front of the single sound wave from the frog's mouth traverses the pond to my ears. The wave becomes imprinted on the air, on the spider's web, in the human ear. Each packet of air molecules translates the wave from itself to the next packet: trans-late means "carry across," which is also what *meta-phor* means. I hope you are beginning to see how causality and aesthetic "information" are deeply bound up with one another.

Every object is a marvelous archaeological record of everything that ever happened to it. This is not to say that the object is only everything that ever happened to it—an inscribable surface such as a hard drive or a piece of paper is precisely *not* the information it records, for the OOO reason that it withdraws. Precisely for this reason, we can have records, MP3s, hard drives, and tree rings. We can also have the Universe—the largest object we know. Evidence of it shows up everywhere—one percent of TV snow is the Cosmic Microwave Background radiation left over from the Big Bang. The more widespread is the evidence of a thing in the form of other beings, the greater its power and the deeper its past. Thus the more basic a character trait is, the further it has come from the past of a person. Five proteins found in all lifeforms are evidence of LUCA, the Last Universal Common Ancestor, thought to be a gigantic ocean creature with very porous cells. These proteins are now manufactured differently than they were in LUCA, but it is as if our bodies—and the bodies of geckos and bacteria—keep on reproducing them anyway, like lines from the Bible accidentally woven into the everyday speech of a twenty-first century atheist. Likewise Heidegger thought that philosophy had forgotten being so deep in the past that evidence of its forgetting was as it were everywhere and nowhere.

If we could only read each trace aright, we would find that the slightest piece of spider web was a kind of tape recording of the objects that had brushed against it, from sound wave to spider's leg to hapless housefly's wing to drop of dew. A tape recording done in spider-web-ese. Thus Jakob von Uexküll refers to the *marks* (*Merkmalträger*) of the fly in the spider's world.[3] Although the two worlds don't intersect—the spider can't know the fly as the fly, and vice versa—there are marks and traces galore. Thus Giorgio Agamben, interpreting Uexküll's insight, writes about a forest:

> There does not exist a forest as an objectively fixed environment: there exists a forest-for-the-park-ranger, a forest-for-the-hunter, a forest-for-the-botanist, a forest-for-the-wayfarer, a forest-for-the-nature-lover, a forest-for-the-carpenter, and finally a fable forest in which Little Red Riding Hood loses her way.[4]

OOO adds: yes, but let's not forget the forest-for-the-spider, the forest-for-the-spider-web, the forest-for-the-tree, and last but not least, *the forest-for-the-forest*. Even if it could exist on its little ownsome, a forest would exemplify how *existence just is coexistence*. To say that existence is coexistence is not to say that things merely reduce to their relations. Rather, it is to argue that because of withdrawal, an object never exhausts itself in its appearances—this means that there is always something left over, as it were, an excess that might be experienced as a distortion, gap, or void. In their very selves, objects are "a little world made cunningly," as John Donne writes.[5] This is because of the Rift: the being of things is hollowed out from within. It is this Rift that fuels their birth.

Causality as Sampling

Let's return to that wave front of the frog croak. It seems as if each entity samples the wave front in different ways. There is the wave front as sampled by the mosquito as a sheer change in pressure, for instance. The vibrating thread of the spider's web announces the presence of a possible meal in the web to the waiting spider. Yet a single entity, the wave front, is what is being sampled in each moment. It's like a pop song. You can get the CD, the vinyl, the cassette, the MP3, the twelve-inch dance remix, the AIF, the WAV—or you hear it one day blaring out of some cheap transistor radio buzzing with interference. In each case you have a sample, a footprint, of the song. The song has a form. The vinyl has a form. Special tools engrave the vinyl with the form of the song. A laser cuts tiny holes in the plastic surface of a CD, translating the song into a sequence of holes and no-holes.

Let's analyze that MP3 recording of the croaking frogs. It's a translation of the frog sound as much as the word "croak" or Aristophanes' elaborate *brekekekex, ko-ax ko-ax*. First we select two seconds of the croak. A computer terminal translates the sound into a visual image of a wave. A special software application introduces zeroes into the wave so that each little piece of the wave become visible between increasingly stretched out sequences of space. A tiny piece of the wave that is two seconds of frog croak is a sequence of clicks. Speed up the clicks and we have a croak. At a very small scale, the wave is a series of beats, like the beats of a drum. These beats occur when one sound interrupts another. Think of a line. Now introduce a gap into the line—interrupt it: you have two lines. The space between them is a beat. In music composition software, one sample can be broken up according to the rhythm of another one, giving rise to an effect commonly known as "gating." A voice, for example, can break up into the scattered patter of hi-hat beats or snare drum shots, so that a smooth-seeming "Ah" can become "A-a-a-a-a-ah."

Think of a straight line. Then break it into two pieces by chopping the middle third out. Now you have a beat, the space between the lines; and two beats, the lines. Then chop the middle thirds out of those lines. You have some more beats. And more beats-as-lines. Eventually you end up with *Cantor dust*. It is named after Georg Cantor, the mathematician who discovered transfinite sets—infinite sets of numbers that appeared to be far larger (infinitely larger) than other sets of infinite numbers. Cantor dust is weird, because it has infinity pulses in it, and infinity no-pulses. Infinity beats and infinity beats-as-lines: $p \wedge \neg p$. This paradoxical fact is the sort of discovery that reinterpretations of Cantor have sometimes striven to edit out, most notably, the Zermelo-Fraenkel theory preferred by Alain Badiou.[6] We have seen this formula before, in our first foray into the world of fundamentally inconsistent objects. It is not surprising that we encounter it again here. Why?

The amalgam of beats and no-beats is also what happens at a smaller physical scale. Single waves break into and are broken by others. Sound cuts into silence. Silence cuts into sound. We have arrived at a very strange place.

In order for a frog croak to arise at all, something must be there, yet missing! Some continuous flow, say of frog breath inside a frog's mouth, must be interrupted somehow, to produce a beat. There must always be at least one extra sound or non-sound that the beat cuts into.[7] For the mathematically inclined, this is reminiscent of Cantor's astonishing diagonal proof of transfinite sets, that is, of "infinities" larger than the infinity of regular whole numbers, or of rational numbers (whole numbers plus fractions). Say we look at every number between zero and one. Cantor imagines a grid in which you read off each number between zero and one in the series across and down. Yet every time you do this, a number appears in the diagonal line that cuts across the grid at forty-five degrees, a number not included in the set of rational numbers. Astoundingly, something is always left out of the series![8]

We could argue that Cantor had discovered something about entities of all kinds or, as I call them here, *objects*. Cantor discovered that objects such as sets contain infinite and infinitesimal depths and shadows, dark edges that recede whenever you try to take a sample of them. The set of real numbers contains the set of rational numbers but is infinitely larger, since it contains numbers such as Pi and the square root of 2. There appears to be no smooth continuum between such sets. So the set of real numbers contains a set that is not entirely a member of itself—the set of rational numbers sits awkwardly inside the set of real numbers, and it is this paradox that infuriated logicians such as Russell. Their "solution" is to rule this kind of set not to be a set—which is precisely to miss the point.

Returning to our croaking frog, no matter how many times you sample his voice—recording it with an MP3 player, hearing it with your spider's feet, enjoying it as an indistinct member of a thousand-strong frog chorus—you will not exhaust it. And that's not all. The croak itself contains inexhaustible translations and samples of other entities such as the frog's windpipe and the frog's sex hormones. The croak itself is not identical with itself. And no croak sample is identical with it. There is no whole of which these parts are the sum, or which is greater than their sum. There just can't be. Something always escapes, something is always left out for a beat to occur. "Beat" implies "withdrawn object."

What happens when you take the smallest thinkable unit of beat? This is what physicists call a *phonon*. A phonon is a quantum of vibration, just as a photon is a quantum of light. When you pass a phonon through a material sensitive enough to register its presence, such as a tiny supercooled metal tuning fork visible to the naked eye, you see the fork vibrating and not vibrating *at the same time*.[9] Recall that Aaron O'Connell, who designed the experiment, describes this state in a lovely way as "breathing." This breathing is visible to humans. O'Connell employs the analogy of someone alone in an elevator: they are liable to do all kinds of things that they would feel inhibited about in public.[10]

To achieve this magic you have to pass the phonon through a qubit. A qubit, unlike a classical switch, can be ON, OFF, or both OFF and ON. As if to defy our wish to reduce objects to fundamental particles, the tiniest amount of vibration possible, when we preserve its fragile being by passing it through the qubit into a crystal lattice (metal) at just above zero Kelvin (absolute zero), causes nothing and something, overlapped. It's as if the beat and the no-beat happen at once. An extra layer of mystery springs out before our very eyes; this experiment can be seen by humans without prosthetic aids, thus making it extra strange, given standard prejudices about the scale on which quantum phenomena should occur.

The unit of vibration doesn't happen "in" space or "in" time if by that we mean some kind of rigid container that is external to things. It seems as if time itself and space itself are in the production of these differences, these beats, everywhere.[11] But because of the regularity of our timekeeping devices, we humans ironically expect things to behave mechanically, even though physics tells us that this just can't be the case, at least not in some fundamental sense. The gate of a sampler snaps open and closed in one forty thousandth of a second. It records, inscribes, a certain chunk of croak. A quartz crystal in a digital clock in the MP3 recorder vibrates. It tells you that the frog croak was recorded at such and such a time. It tells the time in quartz-ese, just as the metal cogs and springs in an old cuckoo clock tell the time in coggish and springish. "Telling the time" is a telling phrase that reveals more than it lets on. To tell is to speak and thus to translate—electronic quartz vibrations into human, for instance. To tell is also to count or to beat time. The periodic clicks of the frog tell out measured beats.

Reality in this sense is a gigantic pond in which trillions of frog-like entities are croaking at different speeds, across one another, through one another, modulating and translating one another.

Going up a scale or two (and then some), the little night pond with its chorus and its softly swaying reeds and grasses can be seen from a spy satellite in geostationary orbit. A timeless photon bounces off the frog's eye. The photon shoots back into space where it passes through the sampling devices in the satellite's camera. At this scale information fans out at the speed of light into the Universe in a gigantic cone, a cone that Hermann Minkowski called the light cone. If some passing alien vessel equipped with superb telescopes were able to receive photons from the frog's eye, the aliens would be able to figure out when the photons bounced off of the eyeball, and where their ship was in relation to the eyeball. But if the alien vessel passes outside the light cone emanating from the croaking frog, it becomes meaningless to them whether the frog is croaking in their past or their future or their present. There is simply no way to find out. At this macro scale, then, the Universe also seems to behave as if objects in it are mysteriously withdrawn—events start to lose their comparability with other events, so that we can't tell when and where they happen unless we're within a certain range defined by the light cone. If Einstein is right, then this realization also affects the frog himself. Place a tiny clock on the frog's tongue. It will tell a different time from the tiny clock you place on the wing of the passing mosquito as it flies.

Quantum theory and relativity theory put all kinds of limits on seeing our pond as an intricate machine. Machines need rigid parts operating smoothly in an empty container of time and space. The materialists in the infinite-Universe and empty-space-as-container crowd adapted what was ironically a neo-Pythagorean piece of mysticism from Augustine and other theologians, who were the first to argue for infinite space—an argument that was enforced by the Pope himself.[12] Now the Big Bang theory is well established, but most post-Newtonian physicists assumed that the Universe had to be eternal. Yet several hundred years before that, an Arabic Aristotelian not subject to Papal edicts figured it out. Speculative metaphysician al-Kindi used a bit of Aristotle and some clear reasoning to argue that the Universe couldn't be infinite or eternal. Using Aristotle against Aristotle, he reasoned that since a physical thing can't be infinitely large, and since time is an aspect of the physical Universe, the Universe can't be eternal.[13] (Aristotle himself thought that since the motion of the heavens was perfect, the Universe had to be eternal.) If the Universe were eternal, it would have taken infinity days to get to this one. This means that today couldn't arrive. So the Universe isn't eternal.

The last century of physics makes it extremely unlikely that our pond is a machine in any but a fanciful sense. Maybe the croaking of fifty thousand frogs does remind you a little of a department store full of wind-up toys all malfunctioning simultaneously. There is a periodicity, a regular repetition, to the beats, that makes it seem as if what is happening is mechanical. And biology likes to use machinery to imagine how lifeforms do things like croaking. But from the point of view of fundamental physics this machinery is really only a reasonably good metaphor.

Yet for quite some time, at least since the seventeenth century, humans have been used to thinking that causality has something mechanical about it, like cogwheels meshing together or little balls in an executive toy clicking against one another. Yet even when we examine cogwheels and balls, what we find is far more curious than that. For instance, if you make really tiny nanoscale cogwheels, when you place them together you may find that they don't spin, because to all intents and purposes they have become an item. Casimir forces have glued them together even though they haven't properly touched. When a tiny, tiny ball smacks against a crystal lattice, it might bounce off or it might go in—or it might do both.

As we saw in the Introduction, when we think of causality, what we think of is some kind of clunking. But think of the hormones in the frog's endocrine system. In a chemical system, there may be no obvious moving parts, yet a catalyst might cause a reaction to occur. It might not be best to think of the frog's sexual stimulation in terms of one ball hitting another (pardon the awkward double entendre). It might be better to think of a transfer of information—it might be better to think that causality is an *aesthetic* process.

We've seen how events begin via some kind of aesthetic phenomenon. This isn't a quaint notion. In fact, it may be far less quaint than the images of clunk causality. How come nanoscale cogwheels can get glued together through Casimir forces? How come a tiny tuning fork can vibrate and not vibrate simultaneously? How come "past" and "future" are meaningless outside the light cone? Don't all these phenomena compellingly suggest the possibility that when we look for causality like someone opening the hood of a car, to inspect the machinery underneath, we might be looking in the wrong place? The magic of causation, in other words, might be magic in the sense that it happens right before our eyes, in the aesthetic dimension. As stated before, the best place to conceal something is right in front of the security camera. No one can believe it's going on. What remains to be explained, in other words, is not the blind mechanics underneath the hood, but the fact that things seem to happen at all, right here.

Might the search for a causal machine underneath objects be a defensive reaction to the fact that causality is a mystery that happens right under our nose, but that's inexplicable without recourse to the aesthetic, and without seriously revising a whole bunch of assumptions we've made about the world since the seventeenth century? The gradual restriction of philosophy to a smaller and smaller shrinking island of human meaning in a gigantic void only served to confirm these assumptions. In parallel with this sad course of events, the arts and the aesthetic dimension of life are seen increasingly as some kind of fairly pleasant but basically useless candy sprinkles decorating the surface of the machinery. I shall be arguing for the exact opposite. The machinery is the human fantasy, and the aesthetic dimension is the very blood of causality. An effect is always an aesthetic effect. That is, an effect is a kind of perceptual event for some entity, no matter whether that entity has skin or nerves or brain. How can I even begin to suggest anything so outlandish?

One way to start thinking about why it might be compelling and even reasonable to think this way is to examine whether there is anything all that different about my perception and the perception of a frog, or for that matter, the perception of a spider, or indeed of a spider's web. Rather than going the route of claiming that cinder blocks have minds, let's go the other way—let's imagine how being mindful of something is like being a cinder block. We can take comfort here from the hardest of hardcore evolutionary theory. If we think perception is some kind of special bonus prize for being highly evolved, then we aren't being good Darwinians. That's a teleological notion, and if Darwin did anything, it was to drive a gigantic iron spike rather impolitely through the heart of teleology. The frog croaking in the pond is just as evolved as me. He might well have more genes for all I know. Fruit flies have more genes than humans. Genetic mutation is random with respect to present need. Brains are quite ungainly kluges stuck together over millions of years of evolutionary history. Maybe the point is that when a brain styles the world according to its brain-ish ways, this is not unlike how a cinder block styles the world in cinder block-ese. Why?

When I listen to the frog croaking, my hearing is carving out audible chunks of frog croak essence in a cavalierly anthropomorphic way. When the MP3 recorder takes a perforated sample of the same sound forty thousand times a second, it MP3-morphizes the croak just as mercilessly as I anthropomorphize it. The croak is heard as my ears hear it, or as the recorder records it. Hearing is hearing-as. It's an example of what Harman, via Heidegger, calls the *as-structure*. My human ears hear the frog as human ears. The digital recorder hears the frog as a digital recorder. The spider web hears the frog in a web-morphizing manner. The ears otomorphize; the recorder recorder-morphizes. When you hear the wind, you hear the wind in the trees—the trees dendromorphize the wind. You hear the wind in the door: the door doormorphizes the wind.[14] You hear the wind in the wind chimes: the chimes sample the wind in their own unique way.

Interobjectivity Revisited

Another way to say this is that the wind *causes* the chimes to sound. The wind *causes* the doorway to moan softly. The wind *causes* the trees to shush and flutter. The frog *causes* the spider web to waver. The frog *causes* my eardrum to vibrate. It's perfectly straightforward. *Causality is aesthetic.*

This fact means that causal events never ever clunk, because clunking implies a linear time sequence, a container in which one metal ball can swing towards another one and click against it. Yet *before* and *after* are strictly secondary to the *sharing* of information. There has to be a whole setup involving an executive toy and a desk and a room and probably at least one bored executive before that click happens. Clunk causality is the fetishistic reification, not sensual causality!

Objects seem to become entangled with each other on the aesthetic level. Now quantum entanglement is beginning to be quite a familiar phenomenon. You can entangle two particles, such as photons or even small molecules, such that they behave as if they were telepathic. Over arbitrary distances (some think there is no limit) you can tell one particle some information, and the other particle seems to receive the same information simultaneously.[15] Spatiotemporal differences are meaningless when it comes to quantum entanglement. What if this were also the case with salt cellars and fingers, or with ponds and night air, or MP3 players and sound waves? Causality is how things become entangled in one another. Causality is thus distributed. No one object is responsible for causality. The buck stops nowhere, because causality means that the buck is in several places at once. It's two days since I first heard those frogs, and here I am, still writing about them. The entanglement spreads across time. Or rather, I *tell* the time according to the croak rhythms in which I am entangled. "Yesterday" is a relationship I'm having with quartz, sunrise, gravity and a persistent sore throat.

Another way to say this is that causality is interobjective. We began to explore this in the previous chapter. To reiterate, we are fairly familiar with the term *intersubjectivity*. It means that some things are shared between subjects. For instance, I am someone several people think of as Tim. Tim is an intersubjective phenomenon. Small children talk about themselves in the third person because they haven't yet internalized this fact. They refer to themselves as someone else, and in so doing they are speaking the truth. But here I'm claiming that intersubjectivity—indeed, what we call subjectivity in any sense whatsoever—is a human-shaped piece of a much vaster phenomenon: interobjectivity. This has far-reaching implications. It's efficient to describe phenomena such as *subjectivity* and *mind* as interobjective affairs. A brain in a bucket, a brain on drugs, a brain in a functioning forty-year-old man: these are all different interobjective states. Intersubjectivity is just a small zone of human meaningfulness in a vast ocean of objects, all communicating and receiving information from one another, frogs in the pond of the real. Thinking the mind as a substance "beneath" the interobjective sensual realm, a tradition begun by

Theophrastus, results in all kinds of puzzles, as the Arabic philosopher Ibn Rushd pointed out.[16]

Interobjectivity means that something fresh can happen at any moment, because in any given situation—in any given configuration of objects—there are always $1+n$ objects more than needed for information sharing. The frog croak travels across the pond. The water aids the smooth transmission of the sound waves into the ambient air around the pond. But the grasses at the edge of the pond absorb some of the sound, imprinting it with their own slender rustle by canceling some of it out. When I hear the croak as I turn the key in the garage door, I'm hearing a story about air, grasses, water and frogs. It's a frog croak plus n objects. The sound doesn't travel through empty space. It travels through an object in which there reside other objects. For example, the sound travels through a light cone in which various planets, galaxies, and vacuum fluctuations exist. The sound travels through West Coast U.S. suburbia. The sound travels through a society of frogs. There is no *world*, strictly speaking—no *environment*, no *nature*, no *background*. These are just handy terms for the n objects that make it into interobjective relationships with whatever's going on. There is simply a plenum of objects, pressing in on all sides, leering at us like crazed characters in some crowded Expressionist painting.

Interobjectivity is the uterus in which novelty grows. Interobjectivity positively guarantees that something new can happen, because each sample, each spider web vibration, each footprint of objects in other objects, is itself a whole new object with a whole new set of relations to the entities around it. The evidence of novelty cascades around the fresh object. The human-shaped frog croak I hear inspires me to write a chapter in my book on causality. The MP3-shaped frog croak squats in the memory of the chip in the recorder, muscling other data out of the way. The web-shaped frog croak deceives the spider for half a second, luring her toward the source of the disturbance. And a human eyeball remains indifferent to the croak, focused as it is instead on the eyelash that has come adrift on its wet milky surface. Objects are ready for newness, because they have all kinds of pockets and redundancies and extra dimensions. In short, they contain all kinds of other objects, $1+n$.

If an object's beginnings were the beginning of a story, it would be called *aperture*. Since causality is aesthetic, aperture is precisely what we shall call it when a new object is born. What is aperture—what can we learn from aesthetic objects with which we're familiar? Can we extrapolate from this to other kinds of objects and to object–object interactions? For this, we can handily return to Aristotle. His notion of formal cause comes in very useful for thinking about artworks as substances, that is, as objects with a specific shape, a specific contour and line. The deep reason why this will be useful for us is that artworks do origami with causality, folding it into all kinds of unusual shapes for us to study.

Aperture: Beginning as Distortion

Think of a story as a certain kind of form. Aristotle was right about stories. They have a *beginning*, a *middle* and an *end*, he argues.[17] When I first read this I felt exasperated. Tell me something I don't know, Aristotle! Look, here's the beginning of a story (page 1). Here's the middle (total number of pages divided by two). And here's the end (final page). Of course this is not what Aristotle means. What he means is that stories have a *feeling* of beginning (aperture), a *feeling* of middle (development), and a *feeling* of ending (closure). Depending on the story, these feelings can be more or less intense and last for different durations.

Beginnings, middles and ends are sensual. In other words, they belong to the aesthetic dimension, the ether in which objects interact. Any attempt to specify a pre-sensual or non-sensual beginning, middle or end will result in aporias, paradoxes and dead ends. Since objects love to hide, to adopt Heraclitus' well known saying about nature, chasing the way they begin, continue or end will be like trying to find the soap in the bath.

So what is aperture, the feeling of beginning? Maybe thinking this through can give us some clue as to how objects begin. Stories begin with flickers of uncertainty. As the reader you have no idea who the main character is. You have no idea what counts as a big or small event. You have no idea whether the persistent focus of the opening chapter on a living room in suburban London in the late Victorian period will become significant. Every detail seems weird, floating in a bath of potential significance. You are uncertain whether the story proper has begun at all. Is this just a prologue?

Imagine listening to the story on the radio. Imagine switching on the radio at some random moment and catching a snatch of the story. Would you be able to tell, just from the way the narrator was telling the story, whether you were at the beginning, the middle, or the end? If the story happens to be a realist story, written from about 1790 on, you may be in luck. There are quite precise rules for performing aperture, development and closure in a realist narrative. Now obviously I'm not going to argue that real reality corresponds to a realist narrative. But aesthetic realism gives us some useful tools for thinking about how art can convey a sense of newness, familiarity, and finality. And since causality is a kind of art, there is reason enough to do some investigating. Note, however, that a realist novel is not necessarily realist in the way that an ontology is realist. It is just that realist novels have quite clearly defined parameters for what counts as a beginning, a middle and an end.

We've spent some time in a nursery for objects, the pond across the way from my house. Now let's see what happens when we witness the birth of an object. How do objects begin?

Crash! Suddenly the air is filled with broken glass. The glass fragments are fresh objects, newborn from a shattered wine glass. These objects assail my senses and, if I'm not careful, my eyes could get cut. There are glass fragments. What is happening? How many? How did this happen? I experience the profound givenness of beginning as an *anamorphosis*, a distortion of my cognitive, psychic and philosophical space.[18] The birth of an object is the deforming of the objects around it. An object appears like a crack in the real. This distortion happens in the sensual realm, but because of its necessary elements of novelty and surprise, it glimmers with the real, in distorted fashion. Beginnings are open, disturbing, blissful, horrific.

The puzzled questions that necessarily occur to me at the start of a story are all marks of *aperture*, the feeling of beginning. Since aesthetics plays a fundamental role in object-oriented ontology, let's think about the aesthetics of beginning. The feeling of beginning is precisely this quality of uncertainty, a quality well established at the beginning of *Hamlet*, whose first line is a question: "Who's there?"[19] Isn't that the quintessential issue at the beginning of a drama, whether it's a movie or a play? Who is the lead character? Who are we watching now? Are they minor or major characters? How can we tell?

We can't. Only when the movie or play has continued for some time can we figure this out.

Aperture is distortion (anamorphosis), the absence of a reference point. Nothing has happened yet, since "happening" is paradoxical: it requires at least two things to occur, as Hegel argued. In addition, aperture is flexible. It can be stretched and it can be compressed. You can have beginnings that throw you right into the story with little need for figuring out who is who: action movies are good examples. You can have beginnings that take up the entire movie. Beginning is not measurable, but it is definite—it has precise coordinates but these coordinates are aesthetic, not spatial or temporal.

When you begin to read a story—anything that has a narrator—some extra questions arise in your mind. What counts as an event in this story? Am I privy to a major event or an insignificant one? There are some traditional ways of doing this, such as *mise-en-scène* (scene setting). Aperture is the feeling of uncertainty as to the relative speeds and tempos of the story. How can we know yet? Speed and tempo are relative, and thus we need sequences of events to compare. Likewise, the birth of just one object simply is a distortion of the plenitude of things, however slight. Novelty is guaranteed in an OOO universe, since the arrival of a new thing puts other things out of kilter with one another, just as the addition of a new poem changes the poems that went before it. A new thing is a distortion of other things.

There are some tricks realist novelists use to begin stories, to evoke aperture. These tricks are worth exploring, because they tell us something about how causality functions. Consider the beginning of Oscar Wilde's *The Picture of Dorian Gray*:

> The studio was filled with the rich odour of roses, and when the light summer wind stirred amidst the trees of the garden, there came through the open door the heavy scent of the lilac, or the more delicate perfume of the pink-flowering thorn.
>
> From the corner of the divan of Persian saddle-bags on which he was lying, smoking, as was his custom, innumerable cigarettes, Lord Henry Wotton could just catch the gleam of the honey-sweet and honey-coloured blossoms of a laburnum, whose tremulous branches seemed hardly able to bear the

> burden of a beauty so flamelike as theirs; and now and then the fantastic shadows of birds in flight flitted across the long tussore-silk curtains that were stretched in front of the huge window, producing a kind of momentary Japanese effect, and making him think of those pallid, jade-faced painters of Tokyo who, through the medium of an art that is necessarily immobile, seek to convey the sense of swiftness and motion.[20]

"The studio..."[21] With his genius for minimalism, Wilde begins the story with a definite article. *There is already a studio.* Which studio? Huh? Right. That's the feeling of beginning, aperture. To say *The studio* is to reference a studio that somehow preexists the narrative in which it appears. Imagine how it would feel if Wilde had begun his story with "A studio..." We would feel somehow "outside" of the story. We would feel in control. Instead, we find ourselves thrown into an ongoing situation. *There is already at least one object.* This is precisely the "feeling" of aperture. If we were to give it a name, I would call it "plus one," borrowing a term from Alain Badiou: by adding to the plenum of objects, the "plus one" object disturbs the universe.

There is a more traditional way of starting a story: "Once upon a time there was *a studio*..." The opening phrase leads us gently into the narrative realm. The realist use of the definite article, on the other hand, rudely awakens us *in medias res* as Horace puts it.[22] And isn't that how objects begin? Isn't the compelling power of the story itself an echo of real objects, objects that subtend their availability-as, their use-as, their perception-as? Objects that preexist their as-structure? *The beginning of an object is distortion.* Other objects, like readers of a realist narrative, just find themselves in their midst, all of a sudden, in the realm of the plus-one. For this reason, any sense of neat wholeness is imposed on the plenum of objects arbitrarily.

Our analysis of narrative is by no means a superficial glimpse of some trivial fact pertaining to human constructs. Rather, the always-already quality of aperture has ontological implications. Watching a video of the shattering glass, played back ultra-slowly, we will never be able to specify exactly when the glass becomes its pieces. We confront a Sorites paradox not unlike the problem of the fragmenting table in the Introduction. We are only able to posit the existence of glass fragments retroactively. The fragmenting glass does not fragment in some neutral container of time. The glass pieces create their own time, their own temporal vortex that radiates out from them to any object in the vicinity that cares to be affected. An entirely new object is born, an alien entity as far as the rest of reality goes: a sliver of glass traveling at high speed through the air. *There are* fragments of glass; the studio… The plenum of objects is illuminated by the plus-one object: the plenum as plenum is never a stable bounded whole. The plenum is 1+*n*, an indeterminately vast array of objects whose overall impression is of an anarchic crowd of leering strangers, like characters in a painting by James Ensor.

Emmanuel Levinas is the great philosopher of the infinite against the totalizing: of the way just one entity, the real other, the stranger, undermines the coherence of my so-called world. Yet Levinas is also the great philosopher of the "there is," the *il y a*.[23] With hauntingly evocative prose, Levinas describes the *there is* as resembling the night revealed to an insomniac, a creepy sense of being surrounded, not by nothing but by sheer existence. Now this *there is* is somewhat inadequate as far as OOO goes. The *there is* is only ever a vague elemental "splashing" or "rumbling," an inchoate environmentality that seems to envelop you. This vagueness makes Levinas's idea quite different from the fresh specificity that hits you in the arm with its glassy shards, making you bleed; or the studio that seems to be exuding its seductive pull on all the phenomena that encompass it and dwell in it—garden, birds, curtains, dilettantes, paintings, sofas and London.

Nonetheless, the *there is* works somewhat for us in describing the effect of aperture. Surely this is why Coleridge begins his masterpiece *The Rime of the Ancient Mariner* with "It is an Ancient Mariner…" (line 1).[24] Suddenly, there he is, foul breathed, crusty, oppressively abject, lurking like a homeless person at the entrance to the church. The *there is* is not a vague soup but a shatteringly *specific* object. Levinas writes, "The one affected by the other is an anarchic trauma."[25] It's so specific, it has no name (yet); it's totally unique, it's a kind of Messiah that breaks through the "homogeneous empty time" of sheer repetition that constitutes everyday reality.[26] The breakthrough of the plus-one shatters the coherence of the universe. Likewise, the idea that history is taking place within a tube of time is what Heidegger calls a "vulgar illusion."[27] Revolutions strip this illusion bare.

Sublime Beginnings

If we want a term to describe the aesthetics of beginning, we could do worse than use the term *sublime*. The kind of sublime we need doesn't come from some beyond, because this beyond turns out to be a kind of optical illusion of correlationism, the reduction of meaningfulness to the human–world correlate since Kant. OOO can't think a beyond, since there's nothing underneath the Universe of objects. Or not even nothing, if you prefer thinking it that way. The sublime resides in particularity, not in some distant beyond. And the sublime is generalizable to all objects, insofar as they are all *strange strangers*, that is, alien to themselves and to one another in an irreducible way.[28]

Of the two dominant theories of the sublime, we have a choice between authority and freedom, between exteriority and interiority. But both choices are correlationist. That is, both theories of the sublime have to do with human subjective access to objects. On the one hand we have Edmund Burke, for whom the sublime is shock and awe: an experience of terrifying authority to which you must submit.[29] On the other hand, we have Immanuel Kant, for whom the sublime is an experience of inner freedom based on some kind of temporary cognitive failure. Try counting up to infinity. You can't. But that *is* precisely what infinity is. The power of your mind is revealed in its failure to sum infinity.[30]

Both sublimes assume that: (1) the world is specially or uniquely accessible to humans; (2) the sublime uniquely correlates the world to humans; and (3) what is important about the sublime is a reaction in the subject. The Burkean sublime is simply craven cowering in the presence of authority: the law, the might of a tyrant God, the power of kings, the threat of execution. No real knowledge of the authority is assumed—terrified ignorance will do. Burke argues outright that the sublime is always a safe pain, mediated by the glass panels of the aesthetic. That's why horror movies, a truly speculative genre, try to bust through this aesthetic screen at every opportunity.

What we need is a more *speculative* sublime that actually tries to become intimate with the other, and here Kant is at any rate preferable to Burke. There is indeed an echo of reality in the Kantian sublime. Certainly the aesthetic dimension was a way in which the normal subject–object dichotomy is suspended in Kant. And the sublime is as it were the essential subroutine of the aesthetic experience, allowing us to experience the power of our mind by running up against some external obstacle. Kant references telescopes and microscopes that expand human perception beyond its limits.[31] His marvelous passage on the way one's mind can encompass human height and by simple multiplication comprehend the vastness of "Milky Way systems" is sublimely expansive of the human capacity to think.[32] It's also true that the Kantian sublime inspired the powerful speculations of Schelling, Schopenhauer and Nietzsche, and more work needs to be done teasing out how those philosophers begin to think a reality beyond the human (the work of Iain Hamilton Grant and Ben Woodard stands out in particular at present).[33] It's true that in §28 of the Third Critique, Kant does talk about how we experience the "dynamical sublime" in the terror of vastness, for instance of the ocean or the sky. But this isn't anything like intimacy with the sky or the ocean.

In subsequent sections, Kant in fact explicitly rules out anything like a scientific or even probing analysis of what might exist in the sky. As soon as we think of the ocean as a body of water containing fish and whales, rather than as a canvas for our psyche; as soon as we think of the sky as the real Universe of stars and black holes, we aren't experiencing the sublime (§29):

> Therefore, when we call the sight of the starry sky *sublime*, we must not base our judgment upon any concepts of worlds that are inhabited by rational beings, and then [conceive of] the bright dots that we see occupying the space above us as being these worlds' suns, moved in orbits prescribed for them with great purposiveness; but we must base our judgment regarding it merely on how we see it, as a vast vault encompassing everything, and merely under this presentation may we posit the sublimity that a pure aesthetic judgment attributes to this object. In the same way, when we judge the sight of the ocean we must not do so on the basis of how we *think*, it, enriched with all sorts of knowledge which we possess (but which is not contained in the direct intuition), e.g., as a vast realm of aquatic creatures, or as the great reservoir supplying the water for the vapors that impregnate the air with clouds

> for the benefit of the land, or again as an element that, while separating continents from one another, yet makes possible the greatest communication among them; for all such judgments will be teleological. Instead we must be able to view the ocean as poets do, merely in terms of what manifests itself to the eye — e.g., if we observe it while it is calm, as a clear mirror of water bounded only by the sky; or, if it is turbulent, as being like an abyss threatening to engulf everything — and yet find it sublime.[34]

While we may share Kant's anxiety about teleology, his main point is less than satisfactory from a speculative realist point of view. We positively shouldn't speculate when we experience the sublime. The sublime is precisely the *lack of speculation*. Should we then just throw in the towel and drop the sublime altogether, choosing only to go with horror—the limit experience of sentient lifeforms—rather than the sublime, as several speculative realists have done? Can we only speculate from and into a position of feeling our own skin about to shred, or vomit about to exit from our lungs?

Yet horror presupposes the proximity of at least one other entity: a lethal virus, an exploding hydrogen bomb, an approaching tsunami. Intimacy is thus a precondition of horror. From this standpoint, even horror is too much of a reaction shot, too much about how entities correlate with an observer. What we require is something deeper, that subtends the Kantian sublime. What we require, then, is an aesthetic experience of coexisting with $1+n$ other entities, living or nonliving. What speculative realism needs would be a sublime that grants a kind of *intimacy* with real entities. This is precisely the kind of intimacy prohibited by Kant, in which the sublime requires a Goldilocks aesthetic distance, not too close and not too far away (§25):

> in order to get the full emotional effect from the magnitude of the pyramids one must neither get too close to them nor stay too far away. For if one stays too far away, then the apprehended parts (the stones on top of one another) are presented only obscurely, and hence their presentation has no effect on the subject's aesthetic judgment; and if one gets too close, then the eye needs some time to complete the

> apprehension from the base to the peak, but during that time some of the earlier parts are invariably extinguished in the imagination before it has apprehended the later ones, and hence the comprehension is never complete.[35]

The Kantian aesthetic dimension shrink-wraps objects in a protective film. Safe from the threat of radical intimacy, the inner space of Kantian freedom develops unhindered. Good taste is knowing precisely when to vomit—when to expel any foreign substance perceived to be disgusting and therefore toxic.[36] This won't do in an ecological era in which "away"—the precondition for vomiting—no longer exists. Our vomit just floats around somewhere near us, since there is now no "away" to which we can flush it in good faith.

Against the correlationist sublime I shall now argue for a speculative sublime, an object-oriented sublime to be more precise. There is a model for just such a sublime on the market—the oldest extant text on the sublime, *Peri Hypsous* by Longinus. The Longinian sublime is about the physical intrusion of an alien presence. The Longinian sublime can thus easily extend to include non-human entities—and indeed non-sentient ones. Rather than making ontic distinctions between what is and what isn't sublime, Longinus describes how to achieve sublimity. Because he is more interested in how to achieve the effect of sublimity rhetorically than what the sublime is as a human experience, Longinus leaves us free to extrapolate all kinds of sublime events between all kinds of entities.

Longinus' sublime is already concerned with an object-like alien presence—he might call it God but we could easily call it a Styrofoam peanut or the Great Red Spot of Jupiter. The way objects appear to one another is sublime: it's a matter of contact with alien presence, and a subsequent work of radical translation. Longinus thinks this as contact with another: "Sublimity is the echo of a noble mind."[37] Echo, mind—it's as if the mind were not an ethereal ghost but a solid substance that ricochets off walls. We could extend this to include the sensuality of objects. Why not? So many supposedly mental phenomena manifest in an automatic way, as if they were objects: dreams, hallucinations, strong emotions. Coleridge says about his opium dream that inspired *Kubla Khan* that the images arose as distinct things in his mind. This isn't surprising if cognition is an assemblage of kluge-like unit operations (Ian Bogost's term) that just sort of do their thing. It's not that this pen is alive. It's that everything that is meaningful about my mind resting on the pen can also be said of the pen resting on the desk. Consciousness may be sought after in the wrong place by neuroscientists and AI (and anti-AI) theorists: it may be incredibly default. Mind may simply be an interobjective phenomenon among many: a distributed mind that consists of neurons, desks, cooking utensils, children and trees.[38]

Let's consider Longinus' terms. Luckily for OOO there are four of them: *transport*, *phantasia*, *clarity* and *brilliance*. Even more luckily, the four correspond to Harman's interpretation of the Heideggerian fourfold (Earth, Heaven, Gods, Mortals) as a set of descriptions of the basic properties of objects. The trick is to read Longinus' terms in reverse, as we did with rhetoric in general. The first two terms, clarity and brilliance, refer to the actuality of object–object encounters. The second two, transport and phantasia, refer to the appearance of these encounters. It sounds counter-intuitive that brilliance would equate to withdrawal, but on a reading of what Plato, Longinus and Heidegger have to say about this term (*ekphanestaton*) more clarity will be reached.

1. Brilliance. Earth. Objects as secret "something at all," apart from access.
2. Clarity: Gods. Objects as specific, apart from access.
3. Transport: Mortals. Objects as something-at-all for another object.
4. Phantasia: Heaven. Objects as specific appearance to another object.[39]

Each one sets up relationships with an alien presence.

(1) Brilliance. In Greek, *to ekphanestaton*, luster, brilliance, shining-out. *Ekphanestaton* is a superlative, so it really means "the most brilliant," "eminent brilliance." This eminence must mean *prior to all relations*. Longinus declares that "in much the same way as dim lights vanish in the radiance of the sun, so does the all-pervading effluence of grandeur utterly obscure the artifice of rhetoric."[40] Brilliance is what *hides* objects. Brilliance

is the secretiveness of the object, its total inaccessibility prior to relations. In the mode of the sublime, it's as if we are able to taste that, even though it's strictly impossible. The light of this inner magma is blinding—that's why it's withdrawal, strangely. It's right there, it's an actual object. Longinus thus calls this brilliance an uncanny fact of the sublime.

For Plato *to ekphanestaton* was an index of the essential beyond. For the object-oriented ontologist, brilliance is the appearance of the object in all its stark unity. Something is coming through. Or better: we realize that something was already there. This is the realm of the uncanny, the strangely familiar and familiarly strange.

(2) Clarity (*enargeia*). "Manifestation," "self-evidence." This has to do with ekphrasis.[41] Ekphrasis in itself is interesting for OOO, because ekphrasis is precisely an object-like entity that looms out of descriptive prose. It's a hyper-descriptive part that jumps out at the reader, petrifying her or him (turning him to stone), causing a strange suspension of time like Bullet Time in *The Matrix*. It's a little bit like what Deleuze means when he talks about "time crystals" in his study of cinema.[42] This is the jumping-out aspect of ekphrasis, a bristling vividness that interrupts the flow of the narrative, jerking the reader out of her or his complacency. Quintilian stresses the time-warping aspect of *enargeia* (the term is *metastasis* or *metathesis*), transporting us in time as if the object had its own gravitational field into which it sucks us. The object in its bristling specificity.

Longinus asserts that while sublime rhetoric must contain *enargeia*, sublime poetry must evoke *ekplexis*—astonishment.[43] This may also be seen as a kind of specific impact. In strictly OOO terms, ekphrasis is a translation that inevitably misses the secretive object, but which generates its own kind of object in the process. Ekphrasis speaks to how objects move and have agency, despite our awareness or lack of awareness of them; Harman's analogy of the drugged man in *Tool-Being* provides a compelling example.[44] Now if somehow you get it wrong, you end up with bombast: the limit where objects become vague, undefined, just clutter (the word *bombast* literally means "stuffing," the kind found in shoulder pads).

(3) Transport. The narrator makes you feel something stirring inside you, some kind of divine or demonic energy, as if you were inhabited by an alien. "Being moved," "being stirred."[45] We can imagine the sublime as a kind

of transporter, like in *Star Trek*, a device for beaming the alien object into another object's frame of reference. Transport consists of sensual contact with objects as an alien universe. Just as the transporter can only work by translating particles from one place to another, so Longinian transport only works by one object translating another via its specific frames of reference. In so doing, we become aware of what was lost in translation. Transport thus depends upon something much richer than a void: the open secret reality of the universe of objects, the aspect that is forever sealed from access but nevertheless thinkable.

The machinery of transport, the transporter as such, is what Longinus calls amplification: not bigness but a feeling of (as Doctor Seuss puts it) "biggering": "[a figure] employed when the matters under discussion or the points of an argument allow of many pauses and many fresh starts from section to section, and the grand phrase come rolling out one after another with increasing effect"; in this way Plato, for instance, "often swells into a mighty expanse of grandeur."[46] By attuning our mind to the exploding notes of an object, amplification sets up a sort of subject-quake, a soul-quake.

(4) *Phantasia*. Often translated as "visualization."[47] Visualization not imagery: producing an inner object. It's imagery in *you* not in the text. Quintilian remarks that *phantasia* makes absent things appear to be present.[48] *Phantasia* conjures an object. If I say "New York" and you're a New Yorker, you don't have to tediously picture each separate building and street. You sort of evoke New Yorkness in your mind. That's *phantasia*. What I've called the poetics of spice operates this way: the use of the word "spice" (rather than say cinnamon or pepper) in a poem acts as a blank allowing for the work of olfactory imagination akin to visualization.[49] It's more like a hallucination than an intended thought.[50] In stories, for instance, *phantasia* generates an object-like entity that separates us from the narrative flow—puts us in touch with the alien as alien. Visualization should be slightly scary: you are summoning a real deity after all, you are asking to be overwhelmed, touched, moved, stirred.

The suddenness of an alien appearance in my phenomenal space is an apparition. In OOO terms, *phantasia* is the capacity of an object to imagine another object. This depends upon a certain sensual contact. How paper looks to stone. How scissors look to paper. Do objects dream? Do they contain virtual versions of other objects inside them? These would be examples of *phantasia*. How one object impinges upon another one. There is too much of it. It magnetizes us with a terrible compulsion.

We should briefly recap what we now know about the Longinian sublime. Longinus says that sublimity is "the echo of a noble mind." There isn't much difference between human souls, if they exist, and the souls of badgers, ferns, and seashells. The Longinian sublime is based on coexistence. At least one other thing exists, apart from me: that "noble mind," whose footprint I find in my inner space. By contrast, the more familiar concepts of the sublime are based on the experience of just one person. It's my fear and terror, my shock and awe (Burke). It's my freedom, my infinite inner space (Kant). Of course, some object triggers the sublime. But then you drop the trigger and just focus on the state: this is especially true in Kant. And Burke is just about oppression. It's about the power of kings and bombing raids. Why couldn't the sublime object be something vulnerable or kind?

Let's think again about how causality is aesthetic. The sublime, on this view, is how fresh objects are born. Suddenly, other objects discover these shards of glass in their world, fragments of broken object embedded in their flesh, scattered over the floor. It's not so much that Burke and Kant are wrong, but that what they're thinking is ontologically secondary to the notion of coexistence. Longinus puts the sublime a way back in the causal sequence, in the "noble" being that leaves its footprint on you. In this sense, it's in the object, in the not-me. Thus the sublime tunes us to what is not me. This is good news in an ecological era. Before it's fear or freedom, the sublime is coexistence.

Now for an example of the Longinian sublime, take Harman's first great use of the "meanwhile" trope (which Quentin Meillassoux calls the *rich elsewhere*), in his paper "Object-Oriented Philosophy":

> But beneath this ceaseless argument, reality is churning. Even as the philosophy of language and its supposedly reactionary opponents both declare victory, the arena of the world is packed with diverse objects, their forces unleashed and mostly unloved. Red billiard ball smacks green billiard ball. Snowflakes glitter in the light that cruelly annihilates them;

> damaged submarines rust along the ocean floor. As flour emerges from mills and blocks of limestone are compressed by earthquakes, gigantic mushrooms spread in the Michigan forest. While human philosophers bludgeon each other over the very possibility of "access" to the world, sharks bludgeon tuna fish and icebergs smash into coastlines.
>
> All of these entities roam across the cosmos, inflicting blessings and punishments on everything they touch, perishing without a trace or spreading their powers further—as if a million animals had broken free from a zoo in some Tibetan cosmology...[51]

This is nobody's world. This is sort of the opposite of stock-in-trade environmentalist rhetoric (which elsewhere I've called ecomimesis): "Here I am in this beautiful desert, and I can prove to you I'm here because I can write that I see a red snake disappearing into that creosote bush. Did I tell you I was in a desert? That's me, here, in a desert. I'm in a desert."[52] This is no man's land. But it's not a bleak void. Bleak void, it turns out, is just the flip side of correlationism's world. No. This is a crowded Tibetan zoo, an Expressionist parade of uncanny, clownlike objects. We're not supposed to kowtow to these objects as Burke would wish. Yet we're not supposed to find our inner freedom either (Kant). It's like one of those maps with the little red arrow that says You Are Here, only this one says You Are Not Here.

Novelty versus Emergence

Now realize that the novelty of aperture is true for *every* object, not simply for sentient beings and certainly not simply for humans. A kettle begins to boil. Water in the kettle starts to seethe and give off steam. At a subatomic level, electrons are quantum jumping to more distant orbits around the nuclei of atoms. For an atom that is not yet in an excited state, *nothing is happening*. It's only from the point of view of at least one other "observer," say a measuring device like me or like the whistle at the top of the kettle, that the kettle is boiling smoothly. At another level altogether, there are a series of sudden jumps, none of which on its own is the thing we call boiling.

This is the big problem with the now popular notion of *emergence*. The problem is that emergence fails to explain how things begin, because emergence is always emergence-for. Emergence requires at least one object outside the system that is perceived as emergent. Something must already be in existence for emergence to happen. That is to say, emergent properties are *sensual* in OOO terms. Emergent things are manifestations of appearance-as or appearance-for, what Harman calls the as-structure. Emergence requires a holistic system in which the whole is always greater than its parts—otherwise, runs the argument, nothing could emerge from anything. But in an OOO reality, the parts always outnumber the whole. What happens when objects begin is that *more parts* suddenly appear, breaking away from objects that seemed like stable entities. These parts are without wholes, like limbs in some horror movie, flailing around in the void. It's only later that we can posit some whole from which they "emerge."

All the classical definitions of emergence seem to indicate that they are talking about wholes that are more than the sum of their parts, that are relatively stable, that exert downward causality (they can affect their parts), and so on. Current ontological ideology, fixated on process, assumes that emergence is some kind of basic machinery that keeps the world together and generates new parts of the world. The tendency is to see it as some kind of underlying causal mechanism by which smaller components start to function as a larger, super component. If true, this would seriously upset the object-oriented applecart. Why? Because objects are the ontologically primary entities. In an OOO reality, emergence must be a property of objects, not the other way around. In other words, emergence is always sensual.

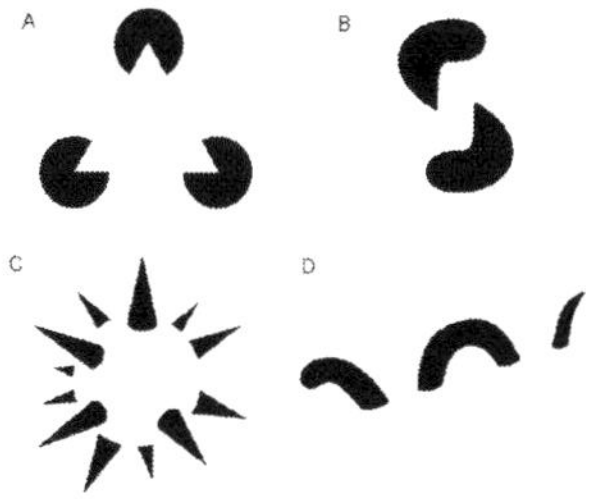

Figure 1: Emergence. From Steven Lehar, *Gestalt Isomorphism and the Primacy of Subjective Conscious Experience: A Gestalt Bubble Model*

Emergence implies $1+n$ objects interacting in what Harman calls the sensual ether.[53] This ether is the causal machinery, not some underlying wires and pulleys. Let's now consider how emergence is really a sensual property of objects. Let's consider an easier kind of emergence—that is, a kind about which it's easier to say that it's sensual, produced in interactions with other entities. There are numerous illustrations of emergence in visual perception.

Pop! A sphere, a triangle, a Loch Ness Monster emerge from the patterns of black on white. According to the theory you don't assemble the forms out of their parts. They emerge out of the fragments of shading and blank space in the picture. Now this kind of emergence clearly requires an observer. It requires, more minimally, an interaction between the image and some other entity. If "observer" sounds too much like a (human) subject, then try this neuroscientific explanation of how it works:

> Although Gestalt theory did not offer any specific computational mechanism to explain emergence in visual perception, Koffka (1935) suggested a physical analogy of the soap bubble to demonstrate the operational principle behind emergence. The spherical shape of a soap bubble is not encoded in the form of a spherical template or abstract mathematical code, but rather that form emerges from the parallel action of innumerable local forces of surface tension acting in unison. The characteristic feature of emergence is that the final global form is not computed in a single pass, but continuously, like a relaxation to equilibrium in a dynamic system model. In other words the forces acting on the system induce a change in the system configuration, and that change in turn modifies the forces acting on the system. The system configuration and the forces that drive it therefore are changing continuously in time until equilibrium is attained, at which point the system remains in a state of dynamic equilibrium, i.e. its static state belies a dynamic balance of forces ready to spring back into motion as soon as the balance is upset.[54]

"[F]orm emerges from the parallel action of innumerable local forces ... acting in unison." What does that mean? It means that emergence is a sensual object. Emergence is relational. Snowflakes, for instance, form in interactions between water crystals and properties of the ambient air through which they fall (temperature, humidity). It would be truly strange if snowflakes magically assembled themselves out of themselves alone, without interactions with anything else. This would mean that there was some kind of mysterious engine of causality working underneath or within them. This kind of deep emergence should strike us as slightly odd—how can something build itself?

No wonder we have trouble thinking of minds. How come patterns of neurons just pop into mentation? However, if emergence is a sensual object produced by neurons plus other entities in their vicinity, there is no problem. There's no need, Harman argues, to see any difference between what my chair does to the floor (which prevents me "from plummeting 30 meters to the cellar" as he puts it memorably), and what my mind does to the floor.[55] That is to say, my chair relies on but also ignores the floor to a large extent, just as my mind does. This is not to claim that chairs are mind-like, but the reverse. Ontologically a mind is like a chair sitting on the floor. The chair rough-hews a chunk of floorness for its distinct nefarious purposes, and so does a mind. We might predict then that "mind" is not some special bonus prize for being highly developed. Which is not to say that what human minds do is exactly the same as what chairs do in every specific. "Mind" is an emergent property of a brain, perhaps, but not all that amazingly different from emergent properties of chairs on floors. And mind requires not simply a brain, but all kinds of objects that become enmeshed with the brain, from eggs to frying pans to credit card bills.

Reality really would be strange if there were some magical property hidden beneath objects. All we need for object-oriented magic, however, are objects. Their interaction generates a sensual ether in which the magic takes place. The best place to do magic is right under your nose. No one can believe it when it's in your face. You suspect some hidden mystery. But as Poe's story "The Purloined Letter" makes clear, the real mystery is in your face.

The anxiety about form and formal causation in modern science and philosophy is probably what gives rise to the mystery and slight fascination or dread surrounding notions of emergence. Somehow we want causation to be clunky, to involve materialities bonking into one another like the proverbial metal balls in the proverbial executive toy. But if causality happens because of shape (as well as, or even instead of, because of matter) then we are forced to consider all kinds of things that materialist science, since its inception, has had trouble with (such as epigenesis). Formal causes are precisely the black sheep of science, marked with a big scarlet letter (S for Scholastic).

Emergence steps in as a kind of magic grease to oil the engine presumed to lurk in the sub-basement of reality beneath objects. Yet emergence is always emergence-for or emergence-as (somewhat the same thing). Consider again the case of the boiling kettle. What is happening? Electrons are quantum jumping from lower to higher orbits. This behavior, a phase transition, emerges as boiling for an observer like me, waiting for my afternoon tea. The smooth, holistic slide of water from cool to boiling happens to me, an observer, just like the way the sphere pops out of the patches of black in Figure 1. Emergence appears unified and smooth, but this holistic event is always for-another-entity. It would be wrong to say that the water has emergent properties of boiling that somehow "come out" at the right point. It's less mysterious to say that when the heating element on my stove interacts with the water, it boils. Its emergence-as-boiling is a sensual object, produced in an interaction between kettle and stove.

Likewise, on this view, mind is not to be found "in" neurons, but in sensual interactions between neurons and other objects. There is some truth, then, in the esoteric Buddhist idea that mind is not to be found "in" your body—nor is it to be found "outside" it, nor "somewhere in between," as the saying goes. There is far less mystery in this view, but perhaps there is a lot of magic. The ordinary world in which kettles boil and minds think about tea is an entangled mesh where it becomes impossible to say where one (sensual) object starts and another (sensual) object stops.

Now the preexistence of $1+n$ objects tells us something about how to think origins. I'm not particularly interested in answering whether the universe is created by a god or not. As far as I'm concerned there could be an infinite temporal regress of physical events. But we can lay down some ground rules for how a god should operate in an object-oriented reality. A god would need at least one other entity in order to re-mark his or her existence. Until the universe was created, there could be no god, in particular. It is simply impossible to designate one being as a *causa sui* (as the scholastics put it) that stands in a privileged relation to all the others.

I use the term *re-mark* after Jacques Derrida's analysis of how paintings differ (or not) from written texts. How can you tell that a squiggle is a letter and not just a dash of paint?[56] This is a genuine problem. You enter a classroom. The blackboard is scrawled with writing. But as you come closer, you see that the writing is actually not writing at all, but the half-erased chalk marks that may or may not have been writing at some point.

Any mark, argues Derrida, depends upon at least one other thing (there's that pesky 1+*n* again). This could be as simple as an inscribable surface, or a system of what counts as a meaningful mark. For there to be a difference that makes a difference there must be at least one other object that the mark can't explain, re-marking the mark. Marks can't make themselves mean all by themselves. If they could, then meaning could indeed be reduced to a pure structuralist system of relations. Since they can't, then the "first mark" is always going to be uncertain, in particular because it's strictly secondary to the inscribable surface (or whatever) on which it takes places. There must be some aperture at the beginning of any system, in order for it to be a system—some irreducible *uncertainty*. Some kind of magic, some kind of illusion that may or may not be the beginning of something.

The idea of an inscribable surface is not an abstract one. A game could be thought of as an interobjective space consisting of a number of different agents, such as boards, pieces, players and rules.[57] This space depends upon 1+*n* withdrawn objects for its existence. A game is a symptom of real coexisting objects. Citing Kenneth Burke and Gregory Bateson, Brian Sutton-Smith made a similar suggestion about the function of play biting in animals. He suggested that play might be the earliest form of a negative, prior to the existence of the negative in language. Play, as a way of not doing whatever it represents, prevents error. It is a positive behavioral negative. It says no by saying yes. It is a bite but it is a nip.[58] In both cases, the urge to play is a means of communicating in a situation in which intelligent creatures have not yet acquired language. A play action is a signal similar to a predator call, except that its referent is to the social world. If you've ever owned a kitten you will see that play biting goes quite far down and quite far in to mammalian ontogeny. Think about what this means. It means for a kick off that what we call language is a small part of a much bigger configuration space. For a word to be a play-bite, a play-bite must already refer to a genuine bite. There has to exist an interobjective space in which "meaning" can take place. The fact that we speak, then, means not that we are different from animals, but that we encapsulate a vast array of nonhuman entities and behaviors. For language to exist at all, there have to be all kinds of objects already in play. All kinds of inscribable surfaces.

Again we encounter some thoughts about the nature of mind. Consider Andy Clark's and David Chalmers's essay "The Extended Mind."[59] The argument is remarkably akin to some implications of Derrida's essay "Plato's Pharmacy." Not that Derrida spells them out—he studiously avoids talking about what is, a sin of omission. But Derrida does argue that there's no sense in which some notional internal memory can be said to be better than external devices such as wax tablets and flash drives.[60] Or more real, or more intrinsic to "what it means to be human," and so on.

Clark and Chalmers seem to echo this when they argue that the idea that cognition happens "inside" the brain is only a prejudice. The best parts of deconstruction, for me, are those parts that *refute* relationism. It's *structuralism* that is purely relationist. Deconstruction constantly points out that meaningfulness depends upon 1+*n* entities that are excluded from the system, yet included by being excluded, thus undermining the system's coherence. These entities can include wax tablets, ink and paper. Whether or not they are "signifiers" is precisely at issue. Meaning arises from the meaningless. It's not relations all the way down.

There is no such thing as meaning in a void, which is why I prefer Derrida's re-mark to Spencer-Brown's roughly contemporaneous Mark.[61] Spencer-Brown's Mark seems to create itself and its conditions for interpretation out of a void, like some proud Hindu or Judaeo-Christian god. Yet there must already be an inscribable surface on which the Mark appears. Marks require a stage on which to strut their stuff. This is the preferred sense in which I take Derrida's term *arche-writing*. Not "everything is signs all the way down"—but everything *isn't*.

Perhaps this is letting Derrida off the hook too easily, since it's quite possible to use his work to underwrite anti-realism, as many have. Yet there is a kind of givenness in Derrida, despite his statements to the contrary. He calls it arche-writing, trace, *différance*, gramma. By contrast, the Mark pretends to be a magic wand or a magic word like Abracadabra. Reality is *like an illusion*—you never know. The way objects appear is *like magic*. If reality were actually, definitely, verifiably magic, we would be in a world designed by a theist or by a nihilist (take your pick). It's time for that quotation again: "What constitutes pretense is that, in the end, you don't know whether it's pretense or not."[62]

Spencer-Brown style theories lead to what is now called emergence. Emergentism wants to catch novelty in the act of its appearance. If that doesn't sound like an impossible task right now, I may not have written this book carefully enough. For something to happen, it must happen twice. An object is always already inside some other object, like writing appearing on a piece of paper. Furthermore, emergence per se is emergence-for. There is at least one "observer"—naturally this observer need not be human or even traditionally sentient. When excited noble gases emerge as photons in a fluorescent lamp, they emerge-for the bathroom off of whose walls the photons reflect. When a cloud of dusty spores emerges as moldy peach rots in a forgotten bowl, the dust emerges-for the currents of air in the deserted kitchen. When a kettle boils unseen, the steam emerges-for the less excited particles in the water on the stove and for the framed photograph on the windowsill, whose glass it coats with a fine layer of mist.

We can trace some of the problems of certain forms of materialism to a fixation on emergence as an ontotheological fact: in this case, emergence is taken not to be emergence-for, but to operate all by itself, a kind of causal miracle. Consider the Marxist theory of the emergence of industrial capitalism. From this standpoint, it turns out that the real problem with Marxism is that Marx is an idealist, or perhaps a correlationist. How can one justify such a fanciful notion? As a matter of fact, there are plenty of ways to do this. For instance we could look at Marx's antiquated anthropocentrism, which his beloved Darwin had blown sky high by the time he put pen to paper. But my argument here is more technical, and pertains to the issue at hand: how do things appear?

Consider chapter 15 of *Capital* 1. There Marx outlines his theory of machines. The basic argument is that when you have enough machines that make other machines, you get a qualitative leap into full-on industrial capitalism. Marx never specifies how many machines this takes. You know it when you see it. If it looks like industrial capitalism, and quacks like industrial capitalism, then... So what this boils down to is a theory of emergence. Capitalism proper emerges from its commercial phase when there are enough machines going ker-plunk or whatever. This is highly reminiscent of the Turing Test.[63] Intelligence is an emergent property of enough algorithms doing their thing, runs the theory. The point is, emergent for whom? If I'm sitting on the other side of the two rooms, and I receive some printouts from each room that look fairly similar, and make me think that an intelligent person is behind the door, then an intelligent person is behind the door. For a theory that tries to explain the whole of social space, this is a significant problem.

That's the trouble with emergentism. Any system requires 1+*n* entities external to it for it to exist and to be measured, and so on. This is Derrida's wonderful conclusion about structuralism. Deconstruction is often confused with structuralism—but it's the latter that says that nothing really means anything, it's all relational. What deconstruction argues is that for any system of meaning, there is at least one opaque entity that the system can't assimilate, which it must simultaneously include and exclude in order to exist.

Emergence is far too slick an umbrella under which to include every causal possibility. Consider the photographs of Myoung Ho Lee. Lee simply adds a huge cloth behind a tree. Then he photographs it, creating an instant aura. It's as if the tree appears inscribed upon a two-dimensional surface like a drawing or a painting. It's a kind of inversion of the surrealist technique that Magritte developed. Instead of painting pictures in which pictures of trees stand in front of real trees, you take a photo of a real tree in this weird, suspended, as-if state. Adding a background is basically commenting on how for an object to exist, there must already be some other object in the vicinity. For a mark to exist, there must be ink and paper. Meaning doesn't come from nothing. It comes from interactions between marks and inscribable surfaces. Facing us like gigantic, 1–1 scale picture postcards of themselves, the trees seem to threaten us with a clown-like artifice. The fact that you know that it's a stage set, that you can see the wrinkles in the cloth, makes them all the more intense. Like watching someone in drag, you know she or he is performing: queer trees.

Amongst Things

Molly Ann Rothenberg's book *The Excessive Subject* formulates a theory of retroactive causation based on the Lacanian concept "extimacy," a sort of "intimacy on the outside." We could quite easily extend some of its insights to non-humans and non-sentient beings. This is because objects are already within the phenomenon of extimacy. The extimate is an object-like presence that is "in you more than you yourself." It's your *agalma* (Greek), your "treasure." Rothenberg's own example is "Carl smiled as he gently stroked the skin of his lover with the keen edge of a knife."[64] The end of the sentence changes what we think of "him," retroactively rearranging the scene. Note that it's a *knife* that does this—an object that is "extimate." These clues are more than enough to imagine how to apply retroactive causation to non-human and non-sentient entities. Harman argues this precisely. When an iron bar clangs to the floor of a warehouse, it retroactively posits the warehouse floor in a certain way. That's what *translation* is. For Harman, the object is like a *retrovirus*, "injecting [its] DNA back into every object [it] encounter[s]."[65]

Consider the phenomenon of sampling in music. The sampler translates the sound into a regularly perforated version of the sound: the preferred sampling rate is 44 000 times a second, so there are 44 001 little holes in between and on either side of each tiny piece of sample. Every sample is a translation, in that it chops a sensual slice out of an object and thereby creates another object. To that extent, *causality is a kind of sampling*. Thus when we observe a phenomenon, we are always looking strictly at the past, since we are observing *a sample of another object*. To sample is to posit retroactively. This would account for the uncanny quality of objects. All objects have some kind of extimacy stuck to them, by dint of their being samples, and by dint of their sampling of other objects. *The excessive subject is simply one of a plenum of excessive objects.*

Beginnings are retroactive: they involve reverse causation. One finds oneself "in the middle of something," or as Horace says of a good epic, "*in medias res*"—quite literally, *amongst things*. This is a much more honest approach than inventing some middle object in which things appear, such as world, environment, Nature and so on. One simply wakes up on the inside of another object, amongst things. Existence is coexistence. Coexistence hollows out the being of a thing from within, since even a hypothetical isolated thing coexists with its parts. Heidegger assumes that this strange being-with applies only to humans, but there is no significant sense in which humans are any different in this regard than telephones, waterfalls and velvet curtains.

Thus the absolute beginning of something is ontologically unavailable, to any object in the universe. It is always already "there." Since no one is standing outside the universe equipped with a stopwatch or a starting pistol—since there is no metalanguage—the beginning of something is not only shrouded in mystery, it is itself the quintessence of mystery. The origin is a dark place. Here is a contemporary example. How can we tell that global warming is happening? Because we keep wondering whether it has started or not.

Beginnings thus involve a peculiar brand of irony that I call *apoleptic*. We're all fairly familiar with proleptic irony: the irony of anticipation in which we know something that a character in a narrative doesn't know yet. Now meet its weird sister, apoleptic irony. Apoleptic irony is the retroactive irony we feel when a narrative's ending causes us to look back differently at the narrative. The gap between what we thought we were reading and what we are now reading is exploited. (While teaching I describe irony as *gapsploitation*: the aesthetic exploitation of a gap between $1+n$ levels of signification. Which is more of a mouthful than "gapsploitation.") What is ironic about Alanis Morisette's song "Ironic"?[66] What's ironic is the fact that none of the examples she gives are examples of irony. There is a gap between what the song says it is and what it actually is. Since in my view there is an ontological gap between an object and its sensual manifestation, irony would seem to be a basic property of reality, not just a fun thing that happens in Jane Austen novels.

We must distinguish irony from sarcasm. Sarcasm can be without irony, and irony can be very gentle and not sarcastic. Sarcasm is the use of double or more levels of signification to cause pain. Like when my daughter uses air quotes when she says, "Daddy, I really 'love' you." This is not a trivial distinction, because there is also a distinction we can make within irony itself between a reified kind of irony, a slogan on a T-shirt kind, and a more open, fluid, hesitating irony. Sarcasm is an even more heavy-handed version than the T-shirt variety, and so it tends to fall outside the delicate system that is irony. Sarcasm and heavy irony imply a "meta" stance to things that OOO rules strictly impossible.

Irony is a system: it's interobjective. It has to do with gaps. Interobjectivity is the realm of gaps between objects, introduced when one object puts its footprint into another one, like a sound being sampled by a digital recorder. Irony always means that something is already there. Otherwise no gap could occur. Now there are various types of irony. There's proleptic irony, the irony of anticipation, in which a character anticipates something and the reader or audience know things will turn out differently. There's dramatic irony in which the audience knows something a character doesn't know. Romantic irony, specifically, happens when the narrator finds out that she is the protagonist. Now this knowledge is implicit in any first person narrative, since the I who is narrating is structurally different from the I who is the subject of the story. That's a 1.0 version of Romantic irony. But full Romantic irony is when this structural gap is thematized. Think of *Blade Runner*. Deckard finds out that he is the kind of person he has been pursuing throughout the story: a replicant, an artificial human with a four-year lifespan.[67] This is Romantic irony proper, version 2.0. There is also a version 3.0, in which the entire story is devoted to this discovery. Think of *The Shawshank Redemption*.[68] All the way through we are led to believe that Red, the cynical institutionalized narrator, is telling the story of the magnificent, liberated and liberating Andy Dufresne. But when Red opens the box under the tree, he and we discover simultaneously that the entire story was actually happening to him, that Dufresne's entire performance was devoted to setting free the inner Red, hence the "redemption" in the title. Both movies model beautifully a feature of OOO that Harman has linked with the thinking of Slavoj Žižek. Causation is in some sense retroactive, and apoleptic irony is thus responsible for the thrill of retroactive causation.[69]

At the end of *The Shawshank Redemption*, at the beginning of his "life" outside prison, Red finds that his cynicism has been collapsed. He is no longer outside. Cynicism is the attempt to find some kind of metalinguistic position outside the narrative. *Irony causes entities to be joined as well as separated*: they must join for causation to happen, yet nothing could happen at all if everything just swam around in glue. Apoleptic irony is not a form of sarcasm or cynical distance. It is the experience of total sincerity: of waking up inside an object, of being amongst things, *in medias res*. This total sincerity is the moment of birth, not as a moment "in" time, but as an event from which time gushes and spreads out into continuity and persistence, like the spreading fan of alluvial water melting from a glacier. It is to continuity that we must now turn.

Notes

1. Aristophanes, *The Frogs*, available at http://classics.mit.edu/Aristophanes/frogs.html, accessed June 27, 2012.
2. See Jakob von Uexküll, *A Foray into the Worlds of Animals and Humans*; with *A Theory of Meaning*, tr. Joseph D. O'Neil, introduction by Dorion Sagan, afterword by Geoffrey Winthrop-Young (Minneapolis: University of Minnesota Press, 2010), 44–52, 157–161, 190–191.
3. Uexküll, *A Foray*, 158–159, 190–191.
4. Giorgio Agamben, *The Open: Man and Animal*, tr. Kevin Attell (Stanford: Stanford University Press, 2004), 41.
5. John Donne, *Holy Sonnets* 5, line 1; *Major Works: Including Songs and Sonnets and Sermons*, ed. John Carey (Oxford: Oxford University Press, 2000).
6. Graham Priest, *In Contradiction: A Study of the Transconsistent* (Oxford: Oxford University Press, 2006), 28–38.
7. An extraordinary presentation of this fact is James Whitehead (JLIAT), "Deconstructing a Sine Wave," http://jliat.com/deconsine.html.
8. The most vivid exploration of this is found in Douglas Hofstadter, *Gödel, Escher, Bach: An Eternal Golden Braid* (New York: Basic Books, 1999), 418–424.
9. Aaron D. O'Connell et al., "Quantum Ground State and Single Phonon Control of a Mechanical Ground Resonator," *Nature* 464 (March 17, 2010), 697–703.
10. Aaron O'Connell, "Making Sense of a Visible Quantum Object," http://www.ted.com/talks/aaron_o_connell_making_sense_of_a_visible_quantum_object.html.
11. This is indeed the reasoning of Petr Horava, in "Quantum Gravity at a Lifshitz Point," *Phys. Rev. D* 79 (8): 084008 (2009), available at arXiv:0901.3775v2 [hep-th].
12. Edward Casey, *The Fate of Place: A Philosophical History* (Berkeley and London: University of California Press, 1997), 106–115.
13. Al-Kindi, "On Divine Unity and the Finitude of the World's Body," in *Classical Arabic Philosophy: An Anthology of Sources*, tr. and intro. Jon McGinnis and David C. Reisman (Indianapolis: Hackett, 2007), 18–22.
14. Martin Heidegger, "The Origin of the Work of Art," in *Poetry, Language, Thought*, trans. Albert Hofstadter (New York: Harper & Row, 1971), 15–86 (26).

15. Anton Zeilinger, *Dance of the Photons: From Einstein to Quantum Teleportation* (New York: Farrar, Straus and Giroux, 2010), 206–207, 208–217, 247–248.
16. Ibn Rushd in *Classical Arabic Philosophy: An Anthology of Sources*, ed. Jon McGinnis and David C. Reisman (Indianapolis: Hackett, 2007), 342, 349.
17. Aristotle, *Poetics*, available at http://classics.mit.edu/Aristotle/poetics.html, accessed June 28, 2012.
18. I adapt this term from Jean-Luc Marion, *In Excess: Studies of Saturated Phenomena* (New York: Fordham University Press, 2010), 37–40.
19. William Shakespeare, *Hamlet* 1.1.1; *Hamlet, Prince of Denmark*, ed. Edwards, Philip (Cambridge: Cambridge University Press, 1993).
20. Oscar Wilde, *The Picture of Dorian Gray*, ed. Robert Mighall (London: Penguin, 2003), 5.
21. Wilde, *The Picture of Dorian Gray*, 5.
22. Horace, *On the Art of Poetry*, in Aristotle, Horace and Longinus, *Classical Literary Criticism*, tr. T.S. Dorsch (Harmondsworth: Penguin, 1984), 84.
23. Emmanuel Levinas, *Existence and Existents*, tr. Alphonso Lingis, foreword by Robert Bernasconi (Pittsburgh: Dusquesne University Press, 1988), 51–60. See Graham Harman, *Guerrilla Metaphysics: Phenomenology and the Carpentry of Things* (Chicago: Open Court, 2005), 59–70.
24. Samuel Taylor Coleridge, *Coleridge's Poetry and Prose*, ed. Nicholas Halmi, Paul Magnuson and Raimona Modiano (New York: Norton, 2004).
25. Emmanuel Levinas, *Otherwise than Being: Or Beyond Essence*, tr. Alphonso Lingis (Pittsburgh: Duquesne University Press, 1998), 123.
26. I'm using Walter Benjamin's apt phrase: "Theses on the Philosophy of History," *Illuminations*, ed. Hannah Arendt, tr. Harry Zohn (London: Harcourt, Brace and World, 1973), 253–264 (261).
27. Martin Heidegger, *Being and Time*, tr. Joan Stambaugh (Albany, N.Y: State University of New York Press, 1996), 290.
28. Timothy Morton, *The Ecological Thought* (Cambridge: Harvard University Press, 2010), 38–50.
29. Edmund Burke, *A Philosophical Enquiry into the Origin of our Ideas of the Sublime and the Beautiful*, ed. James T. Boulton (Oxford: Basil Blackwell, 1987), 57–70.
30. Immanuel Kant, *Critique of Judgment*, tr. Werner Pluhar (Indianapolis: Hackett, 1987), 103–6.
31. Kant, *Critique of Judgment*, 106.
32. Kant, *Critique of Judgment*, 113.
33. Iain Hamilton Grant, *Philosophies of Nature after Schelling* (London: Continuum, 2006). Ben Woodard, *Slime Dynamics* (Winchester, UK: Zero Books, 2012).
34. Kant, *Critique of Judgment*, 130.
35. Kant, *Critique of Judgment*, 108.
36. Jacques Derrida, "Economimesis," *Diacritics* 11.2 (Summer, 1981), 2–25.

37. Longinus, *On the Sublime* tr. T.S. Dorsch, eds., *Classical Literary Criticism* (London: Penguin, 1984), 109.

38. Graham Harman, "Zero-Person and the Psyche," in David Skrbina, ed., *Mind that Abides: Panpsychism in the New Millennium* (Philadelphia: John Benjamins, 2009), 253–282.

39. Graham Harman, *Tool-Being: Heidegger and the Metaphysics of Objects* (Peru, IL: Open Court, 2002), 190–204.

40. Longinus, *On the Sublime*, in *Classical Literary Criticism*, 127.

41. Longinus, *On the Sublime*, in *Classical Literary Criticism*, 121.

42. Gilles Deleuze, *Cinema 2: The Time-Image*, tr. Hugh Tomlinson and Robert Galeta (London: Continuum, 2005), 66–97.

43. Longinus, *On the Sublime*, in *Classical Literary Criticism*, 123–4.

44. Harman, *Tool-Being*, 62–63.

45. Longinus, *On the Sublime*, in *Classical Literary Criticism*, 100.

46. Longinus, *On the Sublime*, in *Classical Literary Criticism*, 116 117; Doctor Seuss, *The Lorax* (New York: Random House, 1971), 49.

47. Longinus, *On the Sublime*, in *Classical Literary Criticism*, chapter 15.

48. Quintilian, *Institutio Oratoria*, 6.2.29. http://penelope.uchicago.edu/Thayer/E/Roman/Texts/Quintilian/Institutio_Oratoria/6B*.html - 2, accessed June 28, 2012.

49. Timothy Morton, *The Poetics of Spice: Romantic Consumerism and the Exotic* (Cambridge: Cambridge University Press, 2006), 33–8, 129–31.

50. On the seductiveness of phantasms, see Lingis, *The Imperative* 107–116.

51. Graham Harman, "Object-Oriented Philosophy," in *Towards Speculative Realism* (Winchester: Zero Books, 2010), 93–104 (94–5).

52. Timothy Morton, *Ecology without Nature: Rethinking Environmental Aesthetics* (Cambridge, MA: Harvard University Press, 2007), 29–78.

53. Harman, *Guerrilla Metaphysics*, 33–44.

54. Steven Lehar, "Gestalt Isomorphism," available at http://cns-alumni.bu.edu/~slehar/webstuff/bubw1/bubw1.html, accessed July 6, 2012.

55. Graham Harman, "On Panpsychism and OOO," available at http://doctorzamalek2.wordpress.com/2011/03/08/on-panpsychism-and-ooo/, accessed July 6, 2012.

56. Jacques Derrida, *Dissemination*, tr. Barbara Johnson (Chicago: University of Chicago Press, 1981), 54, 104, 205, 208, 222, 253.

57. Janet Murray, *Inventing the Medium: Principles of Interaction Design as a Cultural Practice* (Cambridge: MIT Press, 2011).

58. Brian Sutton-Smith, *The Ambiguity of Play* (Cambridge, Mass.: Harvard University Press, 1997), 1, 22.

59. Andy Clark and David Chalmers, "The Extended Mind," *Analysis* 5 (1998), 10-23.

60. Jacques Derrida, "Plato's Pharmacy," *Dissemination*, 61–171.

61. George Spencer-Brown, *Laws of Form* (New York: E.P. Dutton, 1979).

62. Jacques Lacan, *Le séminaire, Livre III: Les psychoses* (Paris: Editions de Seuil, 1981), 48.

63. Alan Turing, "Computing Machinery and Intelligence," in Margaret A. Boden, ed., *The Philosophy of Artificial Intelligence* (Oxford and New York: Oxford University Press, 1990), 40–66.

64. Molly Ann Rothenburg, *The Excessive Subject: A New Theory of Social Change* (New York: Polity, 2010), ix, 1–2.

65. Harman, *Tool-Being*, 212.

66. Alanis Morisette, "Ironic," *Jagged Little Pill* (Maverick, 1995).

67. Ridley Scott, Dir., *Blade Runner* (Warner Bros., 1982).

68. Frank Darabont, Dir., *The Shawshank Redemption* (Columbia Pictures, 1994).

69. Harman, *Tool-Being*, 205–216.

Chapter 3

Magic Life

> You have to play a long time to sound like yourself.
>
> – Miles Davis

This is my favorite part of *Anti-Oedipus*, the joyous, outrageous masterpiece by Gilles Deleuze and Félix Guattari:

> A schizophrenic out for a walk is a better model than a neurotic lying on the analyst's couch. A breath of fresh air, a relationship with the outside world. Lenz's stroll, for example, as reconstructed by Büchner. This walk outdoors is different from the moments when Lenz finds himself closeted with his pastor, who forces him to situate himself socially, in relationship to the God of established religion, in relationship to his father, to his mother. While taking a stroll outdoors, on the other hand, he is in the mountains, amid falling snowflakes, with other gods or without any gods at all, without a family, without a father or a mother, with nature. "What does my father want? Can he offer me more than this? Impossible. Leave me in peace." Everything is a machine. Celestial machines, the stars or rainbows in the sky, alpine machines— all of them connected to those of his body. The

> continual whirr of machines. "He thought that it must be a feeling of endless bliss to be in contact with the profound life of every form, to have a soul for rocks, metals, water, and plants, to take into himself, as in a dream, every element of nature, like flowers that breathe with the waxing and waning of the moon." To be a chlorophyll- or a photosynthesis-machine, or at least slip his body into such machines as one part among the others. Lenz has projected himself back to a time before the man-nature dichotomy, before all the co-ordinates based on this fundamental dichotomy have been laid down. He does not live nature as nature, but as a process of production. There is no such thing as either man or nature now, only a process that produces the one within the other and couples the machines together. Producing-machines, desiring machines everywhere, schizophrenic machines, all of species life: the self and the non-self, outside and inside, no longer have any meaning whatsoever.[1]

Machines, rhythms, speeds all moving with and against one another, like sitting in a train carriage watching different trains pulling into and out of a station, feeling tugged now this way, now that way, by the relative motion. The Rift between essence and appearance suspends itself against other Rifts: *an object persists*.

Forget the valuation of the schizophrenic against the neurotic, and focus on the descriptive language. This is the pure poetry of process relationism. It's perfect for evoking the persistence of objects, the way they stay themselves, for a time at any rate, before they break, before they die. OOO shouldn't abandon processes. It should think them as part of a larger configuration space. Processes are wonderful metaphors for existence: existing, continuing, flourishing, living. The very failures of process relationism, as we shall see—its failure to account for time as an inherent feature of objects—turns out to be a virtue, insofar as the magical illusion of the present is a feeling of being "in" time, just as one is immersed in the water of a swimming pool or the pulsing rhythms of a nightclub.

We shall use the technique developed in the previous chapter: let us look at art and see what it can tell us about how things remain what they are. To do so we shall have to think about the second of Aristotle's tripartite division of beginning, middle and end. What is *the feeling of being in the middle*? It is, I shall argue, precisely the feeling of being caught or suspended in a multiplicity of rhythms. Like being in a factory, a gigantic factory, hearing what Deleuze and Guattari memorably call "the continual whirr of machines." These rhythms are fundamentally composed of the irreducible difference between an object and its sensual qualities, as those qualities interact with the sensual qualities of other objects. Thus the most basic rhythm is *the difference of an object from itself*: a dialetheic phenomenon that we shall explore as we continue. This difference-from-itself is what constitutes persisting. When objects coexist without creation or destruction, this difference-from-themselves multiplies, like the expanding waves of a techno tune.

The Disco of the Present Moment

You can tell that you are in the middle of a classic realist story when the story seems to begin to circle. Again, note the difference between literary realism and ontological realism. My contention is simply that literary realism appears realistic *because there is a reality*—that realism in art is not simply a solipsistic human concoction. Realism simply exploits how humans anthropomorphize the real: there must be a real for this anthropomorphism to take place. So we can work backwards from the experiences granted to us in art to talk about reality as such. That this move seems counterintuitive is, as I have argued, a symptom of the problems that have beset modernity.

Narrative cycling, otherwise known as periodic structure, can be as simple or as complex as a storyteller wants it to be. But in general, the feeling of looping and cycling is achieved by introducing periodic forms: things repeat. Moreover, there is a feeling of being suspended: of moving while standing still, of stasis in movement. Somehow the storyteller achieves a feeling of relative motion, like being on a train waiting in a station, seeing another train beside you moving out, getting that feeling of movement even though your train is supposedly motionless.

How does our narrator achieve this? She introduces inverse ratios between the frequency and duration of events in the *narrated sequence* of events and the *chronological sequence* of events. What does this mean? Let's call the narrated sequence the *plot*, and the chronological sequence the *story*. For our purposes, let's make things easy and say that an "event" is anything in a narrative that has a verb attached to it. So "Humpty Dumpty decided to foment a revolution" is one event, the event "Humpty Dumpty decided." We can assign numbers to these events. Now one easy way to turn a story into a plot is to rearrange the sequence. Say my story goes 1, 2, 3, 4, 5 (it has to, because stories are chronological). But I rearrange it to obtain 2, 1, 5, 3, 4. You will see that I've introduced some flashbacks and forward jumps, little eddies in the recounting of the events.

So as a storyteller I can play with event sequencing. But I can also play with two basic features of narrating events: *frequency* and *duration*.[2] Frequency refers to how many times an event occurs. Duration refers to how long it takes. Now evidently an event that occurs just once in the story can be narrated many times, and vice versa. "Throughout the month of August, Humpty Dumpty kept on returning to that fateful square in Prague." An event that occurs many times can be narrated just once. In this case, we don't know how many times it occurs in the story, so let's call it n. The frequency is always expressible as a ratio, in this case $1/n$. Or we can have an event that only occurs once in the story being narrated many times. "Humpty Dumpty polished his gun … He picked up his gun and polished it … He cleaned his gun …" (he is something of an obsessive). Here the ratio is $n/1$.

The same goes for duration. An event that takes a very short time in the story can be stretched over many pages in the plot, and vice versa. We have already explored how aperture, the feeling of beginning, is a feeling of uncertainty. We can apply this to the rhythm of how events unfold in a story. The beginning of a story is marked by the coexistence of a chaotic flux of frequencies and durations. Aperture is the feeling that we don't know which end is up yet. In that case, what is typical of the middle of a story—that is, the *feeling* of being in the middle, in a realist story at any rate? It is a settling into a regular rhythm, a periodicity. Now the very core of the middle, which we shall call development, is like the development section in a sonata, in which all the themes and key signatures of the first movement are played out to their logical conclusions. This core of the development section immerses us in periodicity. How does a narrative achieve this?

It is through the exploitation of ratios between frequency and duration. In the middle of the middle of a realist novel, the frequency and duration ratios are in some kind of inverse form. That is, they take the form $1/n$ and $n/1$. What does this do to us readers? Time seems to dilate and compress. Days go past in a single sentence. Minutes go past like years. Thousands of repetitions become available in a single phrase. A single event is seen a thousand times. The reader loses track of time, not because there is no time, but because a host of crisscrossing rhythms is playing out. Time is *suspended.*

In cartoons, the effect of "being in the middle" is often achieved through a mechanical repetition that resembles what has just been described. Characters seem to be suspended in their actions, and these repetitions exude a comedic mechanical quality.[3] A joyous, disturbing repetition occurs. Beginnings are blissful or horrific, anamorphic distortions of existing appearances. But continuation is *comical*, as Bergson noted: acting like a machine is intrinsically funny. A dominant human aesthetic exploitation of "being in the middle" is found in many varieties of comedy. With their constant rapid rotation of characters and openings and closings of doors, farces arouse humor by prolonging suspension. In a romantic comedy movie, a pop song signifies being in the middle, accompanying the action with its regular verse-chorus-verse periodicity. The song says, "These events are carrying on for an unspecified time, many times more than this movie is now narrating them." In music, *suspension* is a technical term for an effect that resembles the narrative effect I've just described. A single note or chord, the pedal point, is held underneath or above a shifting melody. The melody constantly recontextualizes the pedal point. An affect of moving while standing still manifests. Disco music is famous for using such suspensions all over the place, since its aim is to keep us on the dancefloor for as long as possible. Dancing, which is a form of "walking while standing still," is itself an embodiment of suspension.

There is something strange about the disco of the present moment. The music seems to be emanating from the dancers themselves. To this extent, time is a verb: a clock *times*, in the way I might dance about architecture. On this view, clock time is a sensual effect, a play of periodicities that requires the existence of $1+n$ objects: an interobjective system. Clock time is an emergent effect of the time emitted by objects themselves. *To time* is intransitive, having to do with the Rift within the object itself. Moreover, dancers far away enough in the disco might not be dancing to anything like the tune in our neighborhood at all. The emergence of time from objects is just a physical fact. This fact puts severe constraints on the idea of a universal clock. Since the speed of light is strictly limited, even for a single photon, every event in the universe has a "light cone" within which events can be said to happen in the past or in the future, over here or over there. Events outside the light cone cannot be said to happen in the future or in the past or in the present, over here or over there.

This means that for every entity there is a *future future*—a radically unknowable one; and an *elsewhere elsewhere*—also radically unknowable. The notion of time as a universal container is a reification of a human sensual object, as if the whole universe were dancing to the same ABBA record. Even in our own vicinity, some objects have a much vaster present moment than we do. The German cartoon *Das Rad* presents the formation of a human road from the point of view of two sentient boulders by its side. Over the course of ten of thousands of human years, the rocks observe a few moments together, seeing wheels, cities and post-apocalyptic landscapes come and go.[4]

The disco of the present moment is a gigantic set of *transductions*. A record needle (magnetic cartridge) converts mechanical vibrations from vinyl into an electrical signal. A loudspeaker converts this electrical signal into sound waves. The piezoelectric effect transduces mechanical pressure into high voltage electrical energy, a jet of electrons. This jet of information is amplified further by butane, resulting in a flame. Electrons flow through a wire. A fluorescent bulb converts their energy into light. An electromagnetic wave propagates through space. An antenna focuses the wave and converts it into electrical signals. A transducer converts one kind of energy into another kind of energy.

A transducer is an object that mediates between one object and another, such that a transducer is an essential logistical component of vicarious causation. Input into the transducer is treated as information, which gives the energy in the transducer a specific form. The transduction energy then acts as a carrier wave for this information. On this view, "clunk causality" (mechanical causation) is a small region of the configuration space of transductions. Mechanical energy in one system is converted into mechanical energy in another, thus giving rise to the illusion for mechanical-scale objects (such as humans) that causality is only mechanical and that information is only ideal, not physical. Also, on this view, perception is just a small region of transduction space. Hearing, for example, depends on pressure cells in the cochlea. (Incidentally, these are the only plant cells in the mammal body.) Thus in any causal event we have two series, depending on whether we are thinking from the point of view of the transducer or that of the transduced. From the point of view of the transduced, the transducer is irrelevant (nonsensual, enclosed). This is in line with the reality of real objects. Reality doesn't "look like" anything.

Thus we have an asymmetry, an OOO asymmetry. It matters not one whit to the transduced whether it is picked up or amplified or whatever by an aerial or a microphone or a piezoelectric crystal. The electromagnetic waves go on propagating around the aerial, despite it. The aerial might as well not be there. Sign theories such as structuralism only deal with the point of view of transducers. To a transducer, everything looks like information. Rather than ignoring it or regressing from it (by substituting some form of new material for instance, such as a flow), OOO encapsulates linguistic turn theory in a wider configuration space that includes the physical. The era of the linguistic turn thought of information models such as signifiers and signified (structuralism). These were subject to various different kinds of analysis, such as deconstruction, which argues that there is no genuine signified, just an infinitely deferred chain of signifiers. When it makes this observation, what deconstruction implies, though this is not stated as such within deconstruction, is the presence of a withdrawn object ($1+n$ objects, precisely), outside the signifying system. The letters on this page don't care about the pixels they're made of, but without them the letters wouldn't exist. Thus to signifiers and signifieds, OOO introduces their mysterious twin brothers, the transduced and the transducers.

Suspension Machines

The present is not as real as some philosophers take it to be.[5] (In fact, when we get to Chapter 4, we will see a good case for its being less real than the past or the future.) Presence is the way an object *times*, in the intransitive sense I discussed. An object suspends itself, maintaining the Rift between essence and appearance. Thus presence is not like a box, or a street, or even a collection of streets that run in parallel. Presence is a wild chorus of times, a cacophony of *suspension machines*, populated with little islands of harmony. When we look for them, we find suspension machines all over the place, ticking out their syncopated rhythms. They are indeed best described as machines, since they involve overlapping periodic cycles. Such mechanisms include the *Clock of the Long Now*, a mechanical (rather than digital) clock being assembled in the Nevada desert. Once built, the clock will run for ten thousand years.[6] The clock forces us to see how the notion of the "present" is at bottom a reaction to a set of relations: a property of a sensual object. It could last for a microsecond, or for ten thousand years. Humans regard as simultaneous any two events that succeed one another by a tenth of a second or less ("the specious present").[7]

The impact of a thing can be measured according to how much periodicity it establishes. In music therapy, the therapist places the patient's mind in a hypnotic state through the use of repetition. In such a state, a person can be influenced. To place you in a state of suspension is for me to have power over you. To place in suspension is how what Ian Bogost calls "wonder" is engineered.[8] When I read a poem, I wonder about it. It begins to exert a power over me. When an acid drops onto a metallic surface, the metal wonders about it. Wonder is a state of suspension in which one being exerts a pull on another, an "allure" as Harman puts it.[9]

Suspension machines characterize the operation of what we call subjects. Consider melancholy, or depression, or grief. Melancholy is an object-like entity that inhabits our psyche without seeming to change. Grief seems to come and go in cycles. Melancholy is the footprint of another entity of whatever kind whose proximity was experienced as a trauma. The Freudian logic of the death drive is that periodic processes within the organism strive to digest external stimuli and maintain equilibrium. As stated earlier, Freud argues that the ego itself is nothing but the record of "abandoned object cathexes."[10] The ego is a sensual object. Melancholy by definition implies coexistence, which is why it's important for ecological thinking, since ecology is about coexistence thought as widely and as deeply as possible. This coexistence need not be with sentient beings, nor even with lifeforms per se: it can include all entities such as rocks, plutonium and carbon dioxide.

But just as importantly, melancholy doesn't imply anything about subjectivity. All you need for melancholy are various kinds of object. This is what makes it different, in traditional psychoanalytic theories, from other affects. Indeed, melancholy speaks a truth of all objects—recall that I here use the term "object" in a value-neutral way, implying any real entity whatsoever, not objectification or subject–object dualism. Melancholy doesn't require fully formed subjectivity. Indeed, subjectivity is a result of an abnegation of the melancholic thing, which Julia Kristeva calls the *abject*, in order to distinguish it from habitual concepts of subject and object.[11] The melancholy coexistence of objects predates the existence of the ego. Egos presuppose ancient layers of beings, fossilized remains.

The compulsion to repeat seems to outstrip the concrete needs of an organism.[12] Freud breaks the periodic cycling of the death drive down to a pre-sentient lifeform, a single-celled organism. It might be supposed that repetition goes a way farther "down" than this. DNA appears to be in a state of disequilibrium, like a paradoxical sentence such as "I am lying" or "This sentence is false." Why do replicators replicate? Isn't it because of some fundamental disequilibrium that the molecule is somehow "trying" to shake off? Isn't DNA also trying to "return to the quiescence of the inorganic world"? Isn't the death drive, then, far, far lower down than single-celled organisms, relative newcomers on the four and a half billion-year-old scene? Wouldn't it be unsurprising then that if the death drive were installed at this fundamental level, all levels above it would manifest it in different ways, until we reach self-reflexive levels of consciousness and the meaning-saturated worlds humans and other life forms spin for themselves—civilization, in a word?

In the process of trying to solve its inner disequilibrium, DNA and other replicators do the only thing they do—replicate. The trouble is, the more you pursue it, the more *life* you live. The death drive is precisely this momentum to cancel oneself out, to erase the stain of existence: death is the essence of life:

> The attributes of life were at some time evoked in inanimate matter by the action of a force of whose nature we can form no

> conception. It may perhaps have been a process similar in type to that which later caused the development of consciousness in a particular stratum of living matter. The tension which then arose in what had hitherto been an inanimate substance endeavoured to cancel itself out. In this way the first instinct came into being: the instinct to return to the inanimate state.[13]

DNA is involved in a noir plot in which the detective finds out that he is the killer. In attempting to solve the riddle of its existence, DNA redoubles existence. But why? Why do such things as DNA exist? How can a molecular string behave like a computer virus, reproducing itself in the attempt to (dis)solve itself? What if the reason for the existence of suspension machines such as DNA, the death drive, grief and melancholy were an inconsistency that lay deeper still towards the heart of an object? An inconsistency that applied not only to living systems, but to all entities whatsoever?

Consider again the achievement of continuity in narrative. When we think carefully about the model that compares the chronological sequence to the narrated sequence of events, we discover a telling fact. A chronological series is also strictly an arrangement. Who or what precisely is "telling the time" in such a series? What needs to be explained, time as a flow of events, seems to recede behind a certain storyline, even if that storyline is in strict chronological order. This devolves into further problems. Of course, who can say how long the Vietnam War really took? Counting in years seems reasonable but microsecond timing seems out of the question. Who could say how long it takes on average to brush your teeth or kill someone? The talk of duration and frequency, then, is vague. The "real events" seem to recede before us as we try to grasp them. Not to worry: might this recession of the real tell us something true about the nature of things? In other words, since in the words of one narratologist a chronological "reference zero" of total isochrony, total simultaneity between plot and story, is only an illusion, isn't it the case that what we are studying is the effect of the *chōrismos* between real and sensual objects?[14] Presence is an aesthetic effect.

Now we should make clear, as we close in on the notion of suspension, that the way an object is suspended is ontological. In other words, an object is not an objectively present block of something that then gets placed into relationships that are suspenseful. It's the other way around.

Suspenseful relationships are possible only on the basis that objects are irreducibly, intrinsically suspended. In other words, suspension is always already at work in the object, just one single object. An object is uniquely itself, observers or interactions notwithstanding. This means that what I here call *appearance* is not separable from the object; yet the object is not reducible to its appearance. At this point we face a choice. We could argue that a sensual object is a different object from a real object. Or we could suppose, as I do here, that the unicity of a thing requires that it defy the Law of Noncontradiction. Since there is a Rift (*chōrismos*) between the essence and appearance of an object, an object is suspended between "being itself" and "not-being itself" ($p \wedge \neg p$, a dialetheia). Without accepting this, we risk being stuck with a reality in which objects require other entities to function, which would result in some kind of undermining or overmining. All the needed fuel exists "inside" one object to have time, space, and causality.

This seems to be in line with what Heidegger says about persistence towards the end of *Being and Time*. Persistence, argues Heidegger, can't simply be continuing to exist "in" time, since that begs the question.[15] If we then apply Harman's generalization of Heidegger to encompass all objects, including nonhuman and nonsentient ones, we can assert that for an object to persist is for that object to be grasped by some other object, to become *vorhanden* (present-at-hand). But why is this the case? Again, it's the case because of the Rift between essence and appearance. In locking on to the appearance of an object—which includes anything at all we can say about it: its momentum, its density, its texture, as well as its color, shape, and so on ad infinitum—another object fails to grasp the essence of the object. The object is suspended between being-grasped and not-being-grasped. This is because the nature of objects is always already to be suspended, *to be the suspension* between essence and appearance. We shall revisit this paradoxical, complex issue in a while.

For now, let's note that we have already made quite a significant discovery. We are in a position to suppose that persistence is *persistence-for*: persistence, that is, is a sensual object. The "presence" of an object is never that object qua real object. Persistence is a significant problem otherwise: because objects are apparently themselves, how can their persistence be said to be a kind of causation? Yet how can it not, since there are clear examples of physical energy such as inertia that require a theory of causation in some sense?[16] Inertia is essentially the fact that objects remain what they are if nothing interferes with them. Newton's first law of motion states that an object will keep on moving unless something impedes it. This law grounds the Copernican turn in science. Yet understanding exactly what is happening, in a philosophical sense, is quite tricky.

To cope with persistence, Russell speaks of quasi-permanence, and Spinoza speaks of immanent causation. But these theories seem like supplements that are awkwardly tacked on to a substance-plus-accidents view of things. Furthermore such theories are not very congruent with contemporary physical science. If an object remains the same, nothing can happen to it—yet we see objects seemingly squirming about all over the place, remaining what they are. This is the deeper sense of "motion" that Aristotle grasps at when he talks about *phusis*, or "emergence" in Heidegger's fine translation.[17] *Phusis* manifests as *metabolē* or change. Even simply remaining-the-same is a subset of motion.[18] Thus Leibniz argues that things have an internal tendency to change, that a thing "is active by its own nature." This activity, or drive, can manifest as a soul-like or mind-like presence in a thing—in this respect, there is no intrinsic difference between a stone and a person.[19]

Unless we admit that there is a Rift between appearance and essence, it is very difficult to explain inertia. If things are just themselves, it seems as if they need other things in order to change. Nothing speaks to the illusory quality of objects like the fact of persistence. To alter Miles Davis, persistence is simply sounding like yourself after you've played for a long time. Consider an object such as a cascade of water: the water keeps changing though the waterfall is clearly identifiable as a waterfall. Consider me: many of my cells change over periods of several years yet I remain Tim in some sense. Or consider a species surviving over a stretch of millions of years: countless individuals come and go while the species remains vaguely the same as itself. To be *identical* is to be *the same as* (Latin, *idem*), and thus to be identical is to be slightly different. As strange as it sounds, there is some kind of difference within identity.

In a later section we will make some modifications to the disco of the present moment, since we are only borrowing from familiar, everyday things rather than looking deeply at ontology. For now, though, it's a pretty good image to be getting along with.

The Trouble with Lava

We should now be able to take stock of some theories of persistence that are on the market today. Problems arise when we start to take the joyous, frenzied periodic activity of the disco of the present moment for real aspects of real objects. The problem consists of turning this vision into an ontotheology. In this case, a process is just an atom, a lava-lampy kind of one, as I shall explain. The world is reducible to blobs and flows, hunks and chunks.[20] Inconsistency is gone, along with a lot of other things. Gone are the cats, the copper wire, the Oort Cloud at the edge of the Solar System. In their place we have flows of lava-like substance that only manifest as cats and copper wire in some vague sense—often, given the ravages of overmining, only for humans or for minds.

Most of what passes for acceptable ontology these days—when people dare to do it at all—is just a form of atomism. An atom is something that can't be cut any further. We think of them as little shiny ping-pong balls like the ones we saw in high school chemistry. This kind of atomism is deemed uncool. So various substitutes are invented, which I find only to be "new and improved" versions of the same thing:

> A process is an atom, just a lava-lampy one.
> A string is an atom, just a sub-quantal one.
> A quantum is an atom, just an indeterminate
> or "intra-active" one (to use Karen Barad's formula).[21]

Atoms reign supreme, two and a half thousand years after Democritus. These processes, despite the abundant PR in their name, are reifications of things.[22] Let us explore how.

If you really want to be a far-out materialist, you should go for monism, like Parmenides, Spinoza or David Bohm. Or drop matter and say that it's all controlled by mind, like Anaxagoras. If you change the names and substitute the latest findings for "water" and "fire" you pretty much get the pre-Socratics. The return to pre-Aristotelian scientism (where you make a decision about what constitutes the world—some kind of flux or some kind of apeiron, fire, water and so on), can't account for change in a thorough way. Change is fetishized at the level of appearance—but not explained. The materialist decision inhibits it. All you have to do is substitute names: for Heraclitus use Deleuze or Whitehead, for Barad say Anaximander and so on. Aristotle's response is as forceful now as it was to the pre-Sophists: if everything is a reflection, if everything is attributable to everything else, then nothing can ever change.[23]

That's where scientism gets you: right back where we started in the sixth century BC. It's about time humanists started telling scientists how to think again, as science seems to be defaulting to some quite old stereotypes. Which brings us again to OOO, the only non-reductionist, non-atomic ontology on the market, and one that is a lot more Aristotle-proof than the regular ones.

A majority of post-postmodern thinking is a regression, not a progression. It represents a desperate attempt to construct a "new and improved" version of the good old Nature that Derrida and others erased. This time it's autopoietic, processual, lava-lampy. I call it *lava lamp materialism*. It appears to evoke a certain form of contemporary joy: "Hey, look at me! I'm totally entangled with not-me!" "I *am* the walrus! And I've got the quantum theory to prove it." Do you though? A counter-argument might demonstrate that quantum theory is profoundly object-oriented.[24] Quantum theory decisively shows how objects really do exist separately from one another. It *positively guarantees* this: it would make a nonsense of entanglement, a basic property of (at least) tiny things, if they were the same thing. Furthermore, immersion in the not-me is frequently seen from an infinite distance, as if on TV. So if we follow the attitude this thinking implies, it turns out that there is *one* entity in the Universe that isn't entangled: consciousness. And I, the lava-lamp materialist, can judge it, from outside of itself ... Lava-lamp materialism keeps returning to the square one of Cartesian dualism. And in the end, it's just a form of atomism. Minds, pizzas and black holes become emergent effects of processes. It would be better to stop reinventing the wheel of Nature.

Process philosophy is in danger of not accounting for causality, only skimming along the phenomenal surface of events.[25] If instead we think processes as procedures (algorithm-like operations with definite steps) we

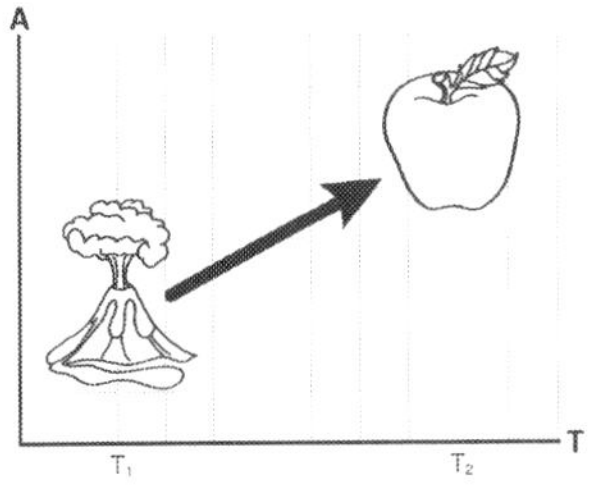

Figure 2: Genesis of an "Achievement." Image by Ian Bogost.

might get closer to causality. Lava lamps exhibit an aesthetics that appeals to process philosophy. But they also have to do with atomism and causality. Consider lava flowing through the lamp. At time T_1 the lava will be at lamp point *a*. At time T_2 the water will be at lamp point *b*. It seems elementary that on this view time is an external framework relative to the water flow. The lamp, on this analogy, is time, as the liquid travels through it in a decisive direction. Time is external to the process.

Process philosophy fails to account for the one thing that makes it attractive to people—escaping from the static. Every process requires a static frame (the lamp) in which the process can take place. The flow of water in a hose is an atomic unit of process. Of course it's not a little ball, but it has a temporal front and a back and it moves relative to a static container. Same thing with my lava lamp: it's a blob, not a ball, but it's consistently itself relative to a static container and a linear time sequence.

On the view of process-relational materialism, entities unfold in time. In keeping with the denigration of the static, we shall call them "achievements"—a gerundive, a noun based on a verb, and verbs are better than nouns, because they tell us more explicitly about the underlying process-stuff of which things are made. A mat is matting, and a cat is catting, and entities are achievements. Let's plot the evolution of an achievement:

The T axis is time. The A axis is achievement. It makes no difference how this achievement happens: other entities, one entity melting into different shapes. Perhaps this entity is evolution, God, novelty, or vitalism. Let's just assume it happens. A blob begins to somewhat resemble an apple. At the bottom of the lava lamp (time T_1) the blob is just a blob. By the time it's reached the top, the blob has morphed into an apple-like achievement (time T_2). At some future date it will melt into something else, perhaps. There may be other blobs that interfere with its apple-esque beauty, and so on.

Leave aside any concerns about the A axis. Ignore the fact that the apple-blob is more blob than apple (some more fundamental goo underwrites its appleness). Ignore the possibility that the apple-blob only resembles an apple-blob in the eyes of apple-blob users (you, me, some worms, and so forth). On this score its intrinsic appleness is simply a function of how it is "perceived," a classic case of overmining. Leave all that aside, and focus only on the terms internal to the diagram itself. Simply focus on the fact that at T_1 the proto-apple is a mere blob, while at T_2 it's an apple-oid blob. This explains everything we need to know about how apples come to be—*except for the temporal frame in which the becoming occurs.* We need T and A to account for the entities that manifest in the lava lamp. A major fact of our reality—time—can't be explained ontologically, it can only be assumed.

Relativity will not help here, if you feel like defending lava lamp materialism. Relativity simply means that the frame is also blobby (Gaussian) rather than rigid (Galilean). It's still a frame, still ontologically outside the entity. Imagine wrapping the graph around an orange. Congratulations. You now have the exact same problem, wrapped around an orange. Quantum theory won't help either. Make time's arrow reversible so that the apple-oid can speak to the blob faster than light and cause itself to achieve itself. Or invent a totally new dimension and let the blob jump out of the frame (into a different or larger frame) like in string theory. Same problem: no scientistic fact-candy whatsoever will make lava lamp materialism hold up against this refutation. This way of refuting materialism is roughly how Aristotle did it. Aristotle has problems, but let's not fix them by regressing to a pre-Aristotelian view.

The very thing that seems to be the case—we build Einstein-like temporality into our ontology—is the one thing that's missing. If you really want to do an Einstein, time has to emanate from the object itself. The fact that time is an external container for lava lamp activity is simply another way of saying that the lava is contained within the lamp. The lava finds itself on the inside of a lamp, suspended in the lamp's capacious medium. The lava lamp form of materialism, in short, can't account for time. All we now know is that the lava is in a lamp … which is the information with which we started. This leads to a wider question concerning the reductionism inherent in process philosophies. How come jumping away from the manifest is more realistic than staying with it? How come a flow of some lava-like substance is more real than a tabby cat?

No wonder lava lampism has taken off in eliminationist models of reality. Consider the following passage, and ask yourself: is this Deleuze, philosopher of flows; or is this Ken Wilber, New Age integrationist? Here it is:

> Our phenomenal world is not an elementaristic world made out of building blocks, it is not a Lego universe, because it possesses an organic structure; it is more aptly characterized as a quasi-liquid network.[26]

Yet I am unsurprised to find that neuro-eliminationist Thomas Metzinger is the author. Metzinger borrows notions of no-self from Buddhism, falling in line with the very many scholars who consider Buddhism a lava lamp religion.

Am I simply expressing an animus against liquids, fluidity, process, organicity, change? Isn't reality a (dare I say complex) mixture of stability and instability? In the real world of time and change, isn't it more useful to see stability as an achievement (as Latour would argue) rather than as the default position? To frame the debate in this way is precisely to have conceded to a reductive materialism that has no time for objects. On this view, "solidity" and "liquidity" are phases of the same underlying "thing," the die always weighted in the direction of liquid—so that solidity is only a metastable equilibrium of a flowing process, or whatever. Forget the inhibiting scientistic sheen of the issue. This is merely *an aesthetic image*: you are free to like it or dislike it, but there's no arguing with it. That's why I call it *lava lampy materialism*: some people just find lava lamps groovy. There's no accounting for taste. Of course there's nothing wrong with that: in fact, if the lava lampists were truer to their taste, rather than to scientism, we would have something to talk about. The literary critic Harold Bloom once wrote that all poetry interpretations are either paraphrase or metaphor. This is what the lava lamp discussion boils down to. If you want to paraphrase science then by all means go with lava lamp materialism. If on the other hand you aspire to more than that, then you must risk metaphor. And if the causal dimension is an aesthetic one, then paraphrase just is a version of metaphor. The real trouble with paraphrase is that it's information poor: the whole point of a good paraphrase is to lose information, to slim down. So paraphrases contain at least one inherent blind spot.

Beyond this, however, there is the matter of ontology. The lava lamp argument is just a version either of undermining—reducing objects to some object that is held to be more real (some overarching process of which cats and copper are instantiations). So I am simply unable to agree that things are made of processes and, worse, that some things are more true to the process than others. (More fluid, more groovy.) Do Lego bricks (to name the objects Metzinger mentions) require some kind of Stalinist show trial in which they admit their denial of their inherent meltiness? And beg to be melted down in the name of lava progress? "Some things are more processual than others." This is ontotheology.

Let's just start with the notion that objects withdraw. This means that everything is unique. It's my idea of the *strange stranger* applied to all entities. Although the idea was developed to cover lifeforms, it is elementary to apply it to non-living entities. This is because the difference between life and non-life is at many levels quite blurry: Sorites paradoxes abound when one tries to produce a thin, rigid boundary between life and non-life.

All entities are uncanny, even to themselves. *Unique* doesn't mean *individual*. Think of a front lawn. It's an expression of individualism, but not uniqueness. As a matter of fact there are some very strict rules as to what counts as a proper front lawn, just as there are rules about proper individualism. In Colorado you can be arrested in certain towns for not trimming your lawn just right. Since objects withdraw, there is no top object and no bottom object: no "matter," no lava, no holistic web, just a plenum of unique objects. Objects as irreducible units aren't like trillions of garden lawns or iPhones all "personalized" in different ways: that would be overmining. Nor are irreducible objects like various things all made of the same Lego bricks: that would be undermining. OOO is proclaiming this, *not* that we should favor solids over liquids.

OOO objects are *units*, in Bogost's elegant terminology.[27] A football team is a unit. A cloud is a unit. A quantum is a unit. Indeed, quantum theory works so beautifully precisely because it is unit based. Planck decided there were quanta in the first place to get around paradoxes of a relationist view. If everything is, at bottom, interlaced waves of energy (à la nineteenth-century physics), you get absurd results for black body radiation. (Above a certain temperature it looks as if the sum of those waves in your microwave is infinity!) A quantum is a unit par excellence: it's in the word itself. A system of quanta in coherence is *zuhanden*, not just "for me" or for some outside "observer," but within the system itself. "Measurement" (interfering with it) makes it *vorhanden*. A little particle qua tiny pingpong ball is a *vorhanden* parody of a *zuhanden* object. So a single quantum is a withdrawn object par excellence.

Quantum theory is about how there are independent things. As argued elsewhere in this book, to "measure" at the quantum level means "to hit with a photon or an electron" (and so on). When this happens the system is destroyed: it's an assemblage of quanta, if you like, that can be disassembled. The quanta are independent of one another. If they were fundamentally relational rather than units, quanta could not be wrested out of "coherence" when they are "measured," coherence being the term for the way quanta are smeared into one another in a closed system. If they were truly interlocked they could not be separated. But separating them is very easy. All that is required is some kind of interference. It is when quanta relate that their coherence is destroyed. There is something "underneath," "different from" (or what have you) relations.

Of course this hasn't yet stopped quantum physicists and philosophers from promoting quantum theory as the ultimate guarantee that things are relational all the way down. The constant pronouncement that quantum entities prove relationism correct is only a symptom of the age in which we live, not of quanta themselves. The Standard Model promoted by Niels Bohr is a good example of correlationism: quanta are only meaningful when they are measured, and it makes no sense to think any further about them. There is a longstanding taboo on ontological probing beneath the closed hood of quanta, which is why the "ontological interpretation" of David Bohm and Basil Hiley has been vilified. This is not the place to debate the merits of different interpretations of quantum theory. But it is evident that it is quanta themselves, as units, which make phenomena such as entanglement and coherence so astonishing.

These astonishing facts can easily be explained if we accept that units are ontologically prior to (aesthetic–causal) relations. Even process-relational ontological interpretations of quantum theory (de Broglie's pilot waves, Bohm's Implicate Order) rely on there being real entities that may enclose infinitesimal layers of smaller entities all the way down, below the size of an electron (10^{-17}cm). Of course, the big picture is that most adherents of quantum theory are underminers or overminers, so that Bohr's version is overmining, while Bohm's version is undermining.

I digress. Let's return to the discussion of process-relationism. Imagine that one could accede to some nice compromise between processes and non-processes: "Things are kind of melty but also kind of solid." Such a belief is still reductionism, eliminationism and so on. Lava lamps are precisely somewhere "between" melty and solid. I'm rooting for at least a fresh look at stasis for variety's sake, but because I do this, it doesn't mean that I think things "really are" static or that we prefer solids or whatever. That would be a childish misinterpretation, along the lines of "You prefer blue but I know purple is better." Or more precisely, "I prefer electrons to be orbiting quite a lot faster than you do, and that's a good thing." (The premise being that *we are all talking about different kinds of the same thing*, which isn't the case.) Quite the contrary: it's the lava lamp argument that suffers from superficial aestheticism. An aestheticism that it denies at a more fundamental level, since what really runs the show are machine-like processes, not colors and grooviness. The lava lamp theory is precisely attuned to human perception, rather than reality as such: if I were a four-dimensional being, I would see a flowing blob of lava as a static block.

If you want an ontology where aesthetics really does run the show, you need OOO. And that brings me to my final point. It's the lava lamp school that suffers from a static notion of time as a container—the lamp in which the lava gloops. OOO sees time as a feature of the sensuality of objects themselves. Ironically then, if you want stasis, stick with the lava lamps. If you've ever heard minimalist music, you'll recognize how all those flowing processes produce the precise effect of stasis, of running in place. The first Westerners to hear the gamelan noted this with wonder.[28] Or just plain old house music: it's a fluid dynamic of layered processes taking place in a four-to-the-floor container of mechanism, which makes you dance: that is, *move in place*. Colorful, beautiful, static machinery.

Fluid dynamics is perfectly mechanical. Fluids look lava-lampy to human eyes (a suspiciously correlationist fact). But the fluids push each other around much like cogs in a machine.[29] The concept of "organicity" began to exert its charm in Romantic poetry, the original lava lampy, process-not-product stuff. *Organon* (Greek) means *tool*, "component in a machine." A machine is precisely organic. Organicism is a form of mechanism, with soft components. The parts of an organic whole are replaceable: holism cares not a jot for unique objects. It's a form of mechanism.

With their quaintly aestheticized scientistic contraband (mechanism, protests notwithstanding), it's the lava-lampers who fail to explain causality, not OOO. Like lava lamps, process ontologies are a form of regressive kitsch, looking futuristic yet reassuringly passé, like a 1960s sci-fi concept of the twenty-first century. They leave humanism just where the linguistic turn left it: as the candy sprinkles on top of the cake of science. If, however, we take lava lamp processes to be a sensual phenomenon in the aesthetic dimension, that is the causal one, we can use them to think precisely about how objects persist. Lava lamp flows are not behind or underneath objects, but *out in front of them*. The deep problem with lava-lamp materialism is the problem with positivist theories of causality, the ones we explored in the Introduction. This is the anxiety to reduce or smooth out discrepancies between an object and its properties, so as to avoid logical and set-theoretical problems. The lava-lamp universe is pleasingly consistent. The price it pays is editing out whole chunks of reality and policing distinctions between real and pseudo, becoming brittle as it does so.

Lava lamps may ooze, but lava-lamp theory is brittle. It can't account for how things arise, without breaking the universe into an infinite of totally discrete entities—this is the trouble with Alfred North Whitehead, whose refreshing alternative to mainstream analytic and continental traditions has recently become evident to scholarship. For Whitehead, every interaction an entity has fundamentally changes that entity, creating a totally new one.[30] This is a form of cinematic change, in which change only appears to happen, based on a certain flow of static images—such a theory is also expounded by the Buddhist philosopher Dharmakirti. Coherence is bought at the price of fragmenting objects into tiny movie frames. When the movie is run (but for whom?) entities appear smooth and lava-lampy. But there is a mechanism, and an implicit production process, underneath. To parody The Wizard of Oz, lava lamp theories want us to pay no attention to the movie projector in front of the object on the screen, treating the object as a real object when everything in the theory says that it's made of relations or as Whitehead puts it, prehensions.[31] Again, the disturbing aspect of the aesthetic dimension—the fact that it lies, the fact that it pretends—is edited out, so that lava-lamp theories appear rather like those Hollywood sci fi movies that use the best special effects, then erase the trace that you are watching an illusion.

Behind the problem of process is a bigger problem of constancy. In this respect, lava-lamp theories take over from Cartesian theories of objects, which themselves rely heavily on notions imported wholesale from Medieval scholasticism. As we saw earlier in this book, this wholesale importation of substances encrusted with accidents is an intriguing moment in the history of philosophy and science, a moment with world-historical consequences. Descartes relied upon a medieval ontology of substance and accidents. Yet he took philosophy into the modern era by deciding somewhat unconsciously not to question this idea. Instead Descartes depends upon math and physics to "see" the kind of entity he thinks being is: "constant objective presence."[32]

To solve the problem that Descartes manufactured, some philosophy, in particular recent forms of process philosophy, have taken refuge in a kind of kluge of subject and object: as if gluing together the two fragments would result in something satisfactory. *Process* joins *environment* as what I've elsewhere called a "new and improved" version of Nature (which I capitalize to return to it the sense of artificiality it struggles to slough off). These terms float somewhere "in between" subject and object, as if one were trying to have it both ways, rather than fundamentally rethinking what an object is. The notion of a "between" in between subject and objects implies you have already passed over deep ontological questions concerning what "subject" and "object" are. For OOO, moreover, the notion of something in between *objects and objects* implies objectively present ontic contraband.[33] You already assume that there are certain kinds of self-consistent object, then you have to imagine a medium for them to float in, something Locke calls an "ambient fluid."[34] What surrounds the particles of ambient fluid themselves? If Nature is sandwiched between things, what medium keeps *that* sandwiched together? The ambient mayonnaise is at risk of leaking out of the ontological sandwich altogether.

To argue for a "between" such as an "ambience" or Nature that somehow accommodates subjects and objects, is already to have decided some things about said subjects and objects in advance, namely that they are reified "objective presence."[35] If you cleave to the withdrawal of things, you just can't do that. In fact, the OOO solution is that what is called the "between" such as "environment" is really *another object*. Thinking should be suspicious of approaches that claim to solve the subject–object dualism by positing a special adhesive that exists "between" them, or a special restaurant (nice ambience, nice music) in which they might finally hit it off and have "proper" sex.

Ideas about continuing to exist are frequently based on an unexamined assumption that the Law of Noncontradiction (LNC) holds for all things. Continuing to exist, according to this view, means continuing not to contradict yourself. On the view I am expounding here, the case is quite the opposite: *things continue to exist precisely by being in a state of constant contradiction*. When something fails to contradict itself, it ceases to exist: this is what ceasing to exist actually is. If objects must fail to contradict themselves to exist at all, we run into a very significant problem: how do things move? We shall explore this next.

Displacer Beasts: The Mystery of Motion

Now let's begin to modify the disco of the present moment by considering some ontological issues a little more deeply. By striving for coherence, lava lamp theories eliminate the intrinsic inconsistency of objects. Yet it is this very inconsistency that allows for things such as *persisting* and *moving*. Physical theories of matter take these phenomena to be related. Persisting, for physics, manifests in phenomena such as inertia, in which an object keeps going in the same direction at the same speed if it's moving through a vacuum at zero gravity. At the quantum level, persisting is simply the way in which quantum events inside an object cancel out. We have arrived at a strange insight. The persistence of a crystal lattice depends upon millions of quantum phenomena that subtend the relatively stable atoms and molecules in the lattice.[36] What are these quantum events? Nothing but the coherence of the quanta, that is, the way they occupy more than one place at once, "breathe" (in Aaron O'Connell's vivid term). At this scale, physics observes objects that occupy place x and place y at the same time. These objects are dialetheic. The disco of the present moment, in other words, only appears to spin its wheels smoothly. What is actually happening is that it is *constantly contradicting itself* in a periodic way.

When we consider motion, it first appears to be a very simple affair. Bertrand Russell argued that motion was simply the way an object occupies different places at different times. Yet when we examine motion more carefully, whole cans of worms seem to explode open. Zeno's paradoxes ruthlessly trip up theories of motion that think movement as occupying successive places at successive times.[37] These theories of motion must deal with the fact that, on their terms, a flying arrow is still at every single point on its journey. Then they are forced to argue that the whole sequence of now-points at which the arrow is still here and now here, is greater than the sum of its parts. The arrow is only changing its location of rest, not moving.[38] This doesn't feel very satisfactory. Or we could decide, like Parmenides, that motion doesn't exist. This doesn't feel right either.

What if the dialetheic status of objects underwrote motion? Hegel puts it this way: an object can move because it is both here and not-here at the same time. Graham Priest analyzes this idea of Hegel's. Suppose that an object really is displaced from itself by some length. Incidentally Priest wonders whether the length might be empirically measurable, and related to the Planck length; but this is not relevant to the discussion here. Although this is not strictly necessary for my argument, it's significant that Priest is ready to assert that the ambiguity of objects is installed at the most basic level of physical reality that we know. It would help to explain entanglement without recourse to a sub-quantum physical level or to strange faster-than-light communication between quanta.[39] Priest supposes that movement consists simply of the fact that "contradictions arise at the nodal points of certain transitions." Thus "motion is a continuous state of contradiction." When I am leaving a room I am both in and out of the room. When a cup shatters, it is "a cup and not a cup" at that instant.[40]

In this way, Priest is able to get around what he calls the "cinematic" theory of motion, which Priest associates with Russell, and which is what I take to be a problematic aspect of process relationism.[41] In detail, Priest argues that instead of being thought as occupying one point at one time, an object "cannot be localised to a point it is occupying at an instant of time, but only to those points it occupies in a small neighbourhood of that time."[42] If objects only occupy one location "in" space at any "one" time, then Zeno's paradoxes will apply to trying to think how an object moves. Yet motion seems like a basic, simple fact of our world. Either everything is just an illusion and nothing really moves at all (Parmenides). Or objects are here and not-here "at the same time."[43] This latter possibility provides the basic setup for all the motion we could wish for. Objects are not "in" time and space. Rather, they "time" (a verb) and "space" (a verb). They produce time and space. It would be better to think these verbs as intransitive rather than transitive, in the manner of *dance* or *revolt*. They emanate from objects, yet they are not the object. "How can we know the dancer from the dance?" (Yeats).[44] The point being, that for there to be a question, there must be a distinction—or there must not be ($p \wedge \neg p$).[45] It becomes impossible to tell, and perhaps it's time to wheel out Lacan again: "What constitutes pretense is that, in the end, you don't know whether it's pretense or not."[46]

An argument that objects "spread" rather than occupy a single time point is even easier in OOO, in which time emerges from objects themselves. Objects then are always a little bit out of phase with themselves and with one another. Isn't this why what Miles Davis says about music is so haunting? "You have to play a long time to sound like yourself." On this view, any creative activity is a tuning process. Since we have decided that causation just is "creative activity," we can apply Miles Davis's slogan to all objects. We need not confine the fun of being out of phase with yourself to human beings, as Heidegger does when he argues that Da-sein is always running ahead of itself.[47] Indeed, for an object to come into phase with another object in every respect is what we call destruction. The development phase of a narrative, for instance, is destroyed when the frequency of the narrated events comes into phase with the frequency of the events in the chronological sequence. An action movie is just that: a constant barrage of destruction at the formal level—never mind the exploding buildings and toppling bodies. The persistence of things is a strange unfolding of out-of-phase sequences of relations. When the sequences become synchronized, this is called an occurrence, which is always the death or destruction of something or other. A coyote is chasing a roadrunner around and around a mountain. One day, the coyote catches up with the roadrunner. With a quick gulp and a mess of flesh, the roadrunner is devoured. The roadrunner becomes the coyote. It comes into phase with the coyote's being. To coexist in harmony, the roadrunner and the coyote must be at least ever so slightly out of phase with one another.

Why? *Because objects are already ontologically out of phase with themselves.* The present moment of persistence is badly defined as a rigid box, for then it can be infinitely subdivided (Zeno's paradox). Objects don't sit in some kind of rigid temporal box. Instead, they are "internally" out of phase with themselves, and this is what produces time and the possibility that they can interact. It's as if they were just a little to the left or just a little in front of themselves. In the role playing game *Dungeons and Dragons*, there is a monster called a Displacer Beast, a sort of tentacled panther. A Displacer Beast can project an image of itself slightly to one side of its real position, thus cloaking itself. All objects are Displacer Beasts, riven from within between essence and appearance.

Thus when an object exists, when it persists, we can say that it is like a quantum object. It breathes, moving and not-moving at the same time, emanating a certain tempo with which other objects may or may not synchronize. The present moment, then, is only a fiction imposed on a strange "nowness" that is a phenomenological sensation of time that takes place within and between objects themselves. This nowness can be relatively extended or narrow, depending on how the object in question is breathing. It just isn't true to say that there is a rigid reference frame for measuring time, whether we think of this frame as encompassing all entities, or whether every entity has its own unique frame. For an entity to "be in" a frame, some interaction with some other object(s) must have occurred. We can't specify the dimensions of nowness in advance.

Bardo 1

The interobjective space is the aesthetic dimension in which the appearances of objects interact in what we call causality. There is no way to determine the boundary of this space in advance. The space can't be thought as being "in" something in the way that a jack-in-the-box features a jack inside a box. The space has no center or edge that we can determine in advance, because to do so would have been to exert some kind of causal influence, *within that very space*. When we delimit a region of interobjective space, even if we just think of doing so, without police tape or calipers or GPS, we do so within that very interobjective space itself. The interobjective space exceeds any particular grasp of it, precisely because it is the possibility space of causality as such. It is strictly not possible to visualize the interobjective space, so instead we must use metaphors: "interobjective space" itself is a metaphorical term.

One metaphor we might use is *abyss*. Schelling's philosophy of nature (for Schelling nature just is everything, whatsoever) posits a whirling abyss of dynamism below the products we encounter such as stars, Earth and speculative realist philosophy books.[48] By contrast, object-oriented ontology locates this abyss not behind or before but *out in front of* objects. When I reach for the toast, I plunge my hand into an abyss of causality. When a stranger smiles at me in the street, her smile opens a whirling vortex in the abyss of things: the abyss floats in front of her smile. The human tendency to reduce objects to "things over there," the ersatz definition of objective presence, may simply be a defense mechanism against the surging abyss that confronts us at every turn. Just talk to someone who has a major mental illness such as schizophrenia. The slightest causal event is experienced as a disaster. Threads seem to tie the schizophrenic to the objects in his world, abolishing the illusion of distance.[49] What if this semblance were actually the case, so that what is called causality—the dull clunking of billiard balls on a smooth green baize surface—is the hallucination? It's not called *the schizophrenic defense* for nothing.

What I've been calling the interobjective abyss in which causality occurs—the aesthetic dimension—is what Buddhism calls the bardo. Bardo means in-between. Traditionally there are six: the bardo of this life, the bardo of dying, the bardo of the moment of death, the bardo of luminosity, the bardo of dharmata, and the bardo of becoming. Each of these interstitial spaces is configured according to the mind of the person in them. These spaces are causal. In other words, what you do in them affects what happens next. And what you have done affects what happens in them, now. But like in a nightmare, the causality is aesthetic. What happens to you is an aesthetic event that you take to be real because of your conditioning.

In the bardo, you are blown around by "the winds of karma," the patterns that you have accumulated. Where do those patterns reside? In the interobjective abyss itself. On this view, what is called *mind* is simply an emergent property of interobjective relations. Mind is thrown into the abyss, it discovers itself there. Mind is not some special demon or transcendental vapor lurking inside the "cabinet" of self.[50] It is simply produced in interactions between objects. This view of mind is highly congruent with enactivist theories of intelligence, for which mind is a retroactive positing of a certain quality of "mind-ness" on a sequence of actions. A baby doesn't simply have language imposed on her, but engages in a physical back-and-forth with others that is already charged with meaning.[51] I look clever when I walk over the surface of a moraine glacier: but perhaps I'm just trying not to fall.[52] Such a hypothesis accounts for the evolution of the brain as a kluge of devices held together by projects of lizards, mice and apes in an interobjective space. What are called *subject* and *object*, "inner" and "outer" existence, are simply retroactive positings of relations between events in the abyss of causality.

The bardo of this life is like coexisting with seven billion people, all having slightly different nightmares. We affect one another across these nightmares. The view is not solipsism or idealism. These nightmares are happening in a shared space and they happen because we exist. And what happens in them is real. It affects you. Now OOO argues that what nonhumans do is not all that different from what humans do. And "nonhuman" can mean frog, pencil or electron cloud. So the bardo now includes the dreams of trillions of entities.

As I walk across my dream of the lawn, the lawn is dreaming about me. When I drink this Diet Coke, I'm drinking my fantasy Coke, while the Coke is sliding down its Coke-fantasy of my throat. It's like that moment in *Alice Through the Looking Glass* in which Alice wonders whether she is a character in the Red King's dream.[53] It's as if every entity in reality—salt crystals, the Sombrero Galaxy and Take That—are hooked up to *Inception*-like dream machines. It's scary and complex. There is no one single stable background "world"—not just because there is a plenum of entities dreaming, but also because such backgrounds are only ever artificial constructs that delimit the interstitial space, the bardo.

The bardo, the in-between in which objects inevitably find themselves, is a space in which the formal properties of objects—strictly, what happened to them in order for them to end up that way—determine their fate. Objects dream. Think of a footprint. It's sand's dream of a foot.

First, let's revisit some aspects of the OOO view:

A. There is very little ontological difference between what we call a mind does when it's thinking and what a pencil case does when it's holding pencils.

B. Objects are what Harman calls "vacuum-sealed" from one another. They never touch each other ontologically, only aesthetically.

C. What goes on inside an object are all kinds of sensual impressions of other objects. Bryant has revised Jakob von Uexküll's *worlds* in this regard.

Now let's consider what we know about the unconscious. Freud argues that it's some kind of inscribable surface. He uses the analogy of the mystic writing pad. Derrida has a marvelous, McLuhan-like essay on it ("Freud and the Scene of Writing"): Freud is in effect admitting that the unconscious is what Derrida calls *arche-writing*, namely, a technological device that subtends meaning.[54] When you use a mystic writing pad, you erase the wax paper, but the impression of the writing stays on the wax tablet beneath. Script is inscribed in an object. Think of your hard drive, which works in a similar way.

There are some interesting physiological theories of memory to throw in here. Perhaps memories are distributed holographically, that is nonlocally, in interference patterns.[55] Or perhaps memories are inscribed directly into discrete locations in the body. Dylan Trigg explores how these memory traces go beyond the lifespan of the body in question.[56] It's beginning to be quite well accepted in contemporary medicine that we store traumas in our bodies. So what do we have so far?

1. Objects only comprehend sensual translations of other objects.

2. Memories are inscribed on an object-like surface, of the body or of some more general unconscious, either locally or nonlocally.

Doesn't there seem to be something like a chiasmic link between (1) and (2)?

Now dreaming is a neurophysiological process in which memories are mixed with somewhat random neuron firings and a virtual experience of the world is lived through by the dreamer, who is often trying to make sense of the traumas (un-cathected objects) that have occurred to her. She feels her way around her interactions with other entities in a virtual space. You can call the unconscious a mystic writing pad, because mystic writing pads themselves hold memories and impressions in a meaningful sense. As tough to swallow as it might sound, then, I see no immediate obstacle to allowing for the possibility that objects—nonhumans, that is, including nonsentient nonhumans—dream in some meaningful sense.

Consider these lines of Percy Shelley:

> Thou who didst waken from his summer dreams
> The blue Mediterranean, where he lay,
> Lull'd by the coil of his crystàlline streams,
>
> Beside a pumice isle in Baiæ's bay,
> And saw in sleep old palaces and towers
> Quivering within the wave's intenser day,
>
> All overgrown with azure moss, and flowers
> So sweet, the sense faints picturing them!
> (*Ode to the West Wind*, 29–36)[57]

The ocean is dreaming, writes Shelley. What is it dreaming of? A submerged city. The water laps around the sunken palaces and towers of Baiae. It tries to comprehend (OOO aspect [A]) these alien, encrypted objects (aspect [B]), in its ocean-centric, oceanomorphic way (aspect [C]). These human structures that now rest within its domain are strangers in the ocean's world—Shelley conveys this strangeness by alluding to Shakespeare's *The Tempest*: "Full fathom five thy father lies; / Of his bones are coral made."[58] It's a marvelous image of how consciousness is never simply a neutral container, a void. It's colored; it quivers. Consider the typical Shelleyan inversion of "the wave's intenser day." More blue than the blue of the sky. More sky-like than sky. An image of phenomenological sincerity. ("Wherever you go, there you are.") But this is also an image of an object wrapped in another object: the OOO universe is one of "objects wrapped in objects wrapped in objects" (Harman).[59] An object that accesses another one by dreaming about it. In this way, an object suspends its Rift between essence and appearance relative to other objects. Persistence, life, periodicity, just is the suspension of a Rift between essence and appearance.

Perhaps I don't seem to have given an account of the active work of dreaming and remembering. What disturbed Freud was his discovery that the unconscious actively edits incoming stimuli. Now this agency can perhaps be thought of in two distinct ways. The first is that some supervenient property such as imagination or will or creativity adds something to the mix. The second is that there is a physiological process that does roughly the same thing.

Two propositions are handy at this point:

1. The binary opposition activity–passivity is, according to OOO, somewhat overrated. OOO is predisposed to disregard the opposition, to some extent, since it seems to map onto human–non-human, or perhaps sentient–nonsentient. Or, looking to Aristotle, animal–vegetable (and mineral).

2. There are deeper reasons why OOO would be chary of the active–passive binary. If as Harman puts it, "free will is overrated," I believe we're signaling that what is called activity and passivity are both as-structured: they are both of them sensual phenomena that occur between objects. And there are reasons to suppose the binary is just spurious, as I shall try to demonstrate.

To return to the activity of memory and dreaming: we need to think these activities in such a way that ontologically subtends both the hypothesis of a supervenient entity and that of a physiological process. It is actually fairly simple, now that we have everything in place. If every encounter between every entity is a parody or a translation, we have all the fuel we need for the things that look like action, passion, imagination, memory and so on. So we are always dealing with an object's dream of another object. The unconscious is precisely that: not what we call "subject." It's automatic. It seems as if we have all we need then for a theory of how objects dream.

An object is already dreaming about itself, even when it is "sleeping" (to use Harman's term), unaffected by another object. This is because of the profound Rift between essence and appearance. This Rift provides the impetus for movement and continuity. Just persisting, just remaining the same, is a strange phenomenon in this regard. The real problem with non-OOO theories of objects—default lumps sprinkled with accidents or cooler flows—is that, as we've seen, they are unable to think movement or time without recourse to some non-examined concept that is brought in as a kind of patch. One way this works is that the interobjective space is taken as the actual reality of objects, when it functions more like the Lacanian concept of the Big Other: just as I am a person called Tim by others (in the Big Other in Lacanian terms), so objects are defined by their relations in interobejctivity. This gives rise to the illusion we call relationism. One reason OOO is hard to accept for some people is also the reason why psychoanalysis or ecological awareness is hard to accept: what is found is a profound lack in the Other, the realization that "the Other does not exist": there is no Nature, no deep background of meaning—what we took as real is really a projection. What we assumed to be real is just a manifestation of the as-structure.

Belief in interobjectivity as the sole space of objective meaning gives rise to a further illusion that objects are consistent lumps of whatever, or just bundles of qualities.[60] But as we have seen, there are deep reasons why objects appear, and why they move. These reasons have to do with the fact that objects are never just lumps that relations paint into meaningful existence, or qualities floating around. If persistence is only "continuity of form," it becomes difficult to explain how things change without getting involved in Sorites paradoxes. Exactly when does the continuity kick in? What counts as an iteration of a quality or a quality-bundle?[61]

There is no difference between stillness and movement, "stasis" and "process." This is not a superficial lack of difference. Some contemporary philosophy is concerned about how you could tell the difference between a static disc and a "homogenous rotating" one, supposing for a moment that such a thing could exist.[62] These discs are totally uniform in color and to perceivers they appear to be still. On this view, something in the way science intuits objects must be flawed. But such arguments about scientific intuition are pitched towards appearances only, from the OOO standpoint. They think they are talking about the essence of things, but rotation and non-rotation are appearances.

There is a Rift between the substance and its appearance: this Rift is what makes the disc plausible or not, not whether it's rotating or still (and the dilemma about whether you can tell the difference). What does this mean? Very simply, if you can destroy it, it's real, because destruction intervenes in the Rift between essence and appearance. It is to this subject that we must now turn: how do objects end?

Notes

1. Gilles Deleuze and Félix Guattari, *Anti-Oedipus: Capitalism and Schizophrenia*, tr. R. Hurley, M. Seem and H. Lane (Minneapolis: University of Minnesota Press, 1983), 2.
2. I am adapting the structuralist narratology of Gerard Genette. See *Narrative Discourse: An Essay in Method*, tr. Jane E. Lewin, foreword by Jonathan Culler (Ithaca: Cornell University Press, 1983).
3. See Henri Bergson, *Laughter* in George Meredith and Henri Bergson, *An Essay on Comedy/Laughter* (New York: Doubleday, 1956), 62, 158–161.
4. Chris Stenner, Arvid Uibel and Heidi Wittinger, *Das Rad* (Film Academy Baden-Württemberg, 2002).
5. Arda Denkel, *Object and Property* (Cambridge: Cambridge University Press, 2007), 96–97.
6. See longnow.org/clock/.
7. David Bohm, *The Special Theory of Relativity* (London: Routledge, 2006), 247–248.
8. Ian Bogost, *Alien Phenomenology: Or What It's like to Be a Thing* (Minneapolis: University of Minnesota Press, 2012), 113–134.
9. Graham Harman, *Guerrilla Metaphysics: Phenomenology and the Carpentry of Things* (Chicago: Open Court, 2005), 141–144.
10. Sigmund Freud, *The Ego and the Id*, tr. Joan Riviere, revised and ed. James Strachey, intro. Peter Gay (New York: Norton, 1989), 24.
11. Julia Kristeva, *Powers of Horror: An Essay on Abjection*, tr. Leon S. Roudiez (New York: Columbia University Press, 1982).
12. Slavoj Žižek, "How to Read Lacan 5. Troubles with the Real: Lacan as a Viewer of *Alien*," http://www.lacan.com/zizalien.htm.
13. Sigmund Freud, *Beyond the Pleasure Principle*, tr. and ed. James Strachey (New York: Liveright, 1950), 32.
14. Gérard Genette, *Narrative Discourse*, 88.

15. Martin Heidegger, *Being and Time*, tr. Joan Stambaugh (Albany, N.Y: State University of New York Press, 1996), 385, 386.

16. Phil Dowe, *Physical Causation* (New York: Cambridge University Press, 2000), 50.

17. Martin Heidegger, *What Is a Thing?* tr. W.B. Barton and Vera Deutsch, analysis by Eugene T. Gendlin (Chicago: Henry Regnery, 1967), 83.

18. Heidegger, *What Is a Thing?* 82.

19. Martin Heidegger, "From the Last Marburg Lecture Course," *Pathmarks*, ed. William McNeill (Cambridge: Cambridge University Press, 1998), 63–81 (77, 75, 73–74).

20. See for instance Mark Heller, *The Ontology of Physical Objects: Four-Dimensional Hunks of Matter* (Cambridge: Cambridge University Press, 2008), 47–51.

21. Karen Barad, *Meeting the Universe Halfway: Quantum Physics and the Entanglement of Matter and Meaning* (Durham: Duke University Press, 2007), 139–140, 178, 214, 235.

22. Martin Heidegger, *Contributions to Philosophy (From Enowning)*, tr. Parvis Emad and Kenneth Maly (Bloomington: Indiana University Press, 1999), 332.

23. Thanks to Joseph Goodson for talking this through with me.

24. Timothy Morton, "Here Comes Everything: The Promise of Object-Oriented Ontology," *Qui Parle* 19.2 (Spring–Summer, 2011), 163–190.

25. Ian Bogost, "Process vs. Procedure," paper given at the Fourth International Conference of the Whitehead Research Project, Claremont College, December 2–4, 2010. Bogost uses the term "firehose materialism," analogous to my lava lamps.

26. Thomas Metzinger, *Being No-One: The Self-Model Theory of Subjectivity* (Cambridge: MIT Press, 2004), 145. See Graham Harman, "The Problem with Metzinger," *Cosmos and History* 7.1 (2011), 7–36.

27. Ian Bogost, *Unit Operations: An Approach to Videogame Criticism* (Cambridge: MIT Press, 2008), 3–19; *Alien Phenomenology*, 22–29.

28. David Toop, *Ocean of Sound: Aether Talk, Ambient Sound and Imaginary Worlds* (London and New York: Serpent's Tail, 1995), 13–20.

29. David Bohm, *Wholeness and the Implicate Order* (Abingdon: Routledge, 2008), 11–14, 87, 137, 143–146, 153–155.

30. Alfred North Whitehead, *Process and Reality* (New York: Free Press, 1978), 75–78, 210, 214–215.

31. Whitehead, *Process and Reality*, 18–20.

32. Heidegger, *Being and Time* 88–89 (89).

33. Heidegger, *Being and Time*, 124.

34. John Locke, *An Essay Concerning Human Understanding*, tr. Peter H. Nidditch (Oxford: the Clarendon Press, 1975, 1979), II.23.23–24 (308–309).

35. See Heidegger, *Being and Time*, 124: "In which direction must we look for the phenomenal characteristics of being-in as such? We get the answer to this question what we were charged with keeping in view phenomenologically when we pointed

out this phenomenon: being-in in contradistinction to the objectively present insideness of something objectively present 'in' an other; being-in not as an attribute of an objectively present subject effected or even initiated by the objective presence of the 'world'; rather, being-in essentially as the kind of being of this being itself. But then what else presents itself with this phenomenon other than the objectively present *commercium between* an objectively present subject and an objectively present object? This interpretation would come closer to the phenomenal content if it stated that Da-sein *is the being* of this 'between.' Nonetheless, the orientation toward the 'between' would still be misleading. It colludes unawares with the ontologically indefinite approach that there are beings between which this being as such 'is.' The between is already understood as the result of the *convenientia* of two objectively present things. But this kind of approach always already *splits* the phenomenon beforehand, and there is no prospect of ever again putting it back together from the fragments. Not only do we lack the 'cement', even the 'schema', according to which this joining together is to be accomplished has been split apart, or never as yet unveiled. What is ontologically decisive is to avoid splitting the phenomenon beforehand, that is, to secure its positive phenomenal content." This was an argument I made in *Ecology without Nature* (Cambridge: Harvard University Press, 2007), 47–54.

36. David Bohm, *Quantum Theory* (New York: Dover, 1989), 20, 352–353.

37. Graham Priest, *In Contradiction: A Study of the Transconsistent* (Oxford: Oxford University Press, 2006), 172–181.

38. Priest, *In Contradiction*, 180.

39. Priest, *In Contradiction*, 160.

40. Priest, *In Contradiction*, 170–171.

41. Priest, *In Contradiction*, 173.

42. Priest, *In Contradiction*, 177.

43. Priest, *In Contradiction*, 172–181.

44. William Butler Yeats, "Among School Children," *Collected Poems*, ed. Richard J. Finneran (New York: Scribner, 1996).

45. Paul de Man, "Semiology and Rhetoric," *Diacritics* 3.3 (Autumn, 1973), 27–33 (30).

46. Jacques Lacan, *Le séminaire, Livre III: Les psychoses* (Paris: Editions de Seuil, 1981), 48. See Slavoj Žižek, *The Parallax View* (Cambridge, Mass.: MIT Press, 2006), 206. While we are on the subject of Hegel, let it be noted that for a philosophy of dialetheias to bestow much of its affection on Hegel is a little bit flawed. If you really want to go with dialetheias you have to go with discrete objects. You really don't want to go with a hide and seek game of the Absolute in which the result is known at the very beginning.

47. Heidegger, *Being and Time*, 304–306, 310–311, 312, 321–322.

48. Iain Hamilton Grant, *Philosophies of Nature after Schelling* (New York: Continuum, 2008), 37–38, 79, 92, 99, 130–131, 146–147, 162.

49. Paul Fearne, *All in the Mind*, ABC, September 9, 2010; see Paul Fearne, *Diary of a Schizophrenic* (Brentwood: Chipmunka Publishing, 2010).

50. Martin Heidegger, *Being and Time*, 56–58.

51. Stephen J. Cowley, "The Cradle of Language," in Danièle Moyal-Sharrock, ed., *Perspicuous Presentations: Essays on Wittgenstein's Philosophy of Psychology* (New York: Palgrave, 2007), 278–298.

52. See Herbert A. Simon, *The Sciences of the Artificial* (Cambridge, MA: MIT Press, 1996), 51–53.

53. Lewis Carroll, *Alice Through the Looking Glass*, in *The Annotated Alice:* Alice's Adventures in Wonderland *and* Through the Looking-Glass, ed. and intro. Martin Gardner (New York: Norton, 1999), 189.

54. Jacques Derrida, "Freud and the Scene of Writing," *Writing and Difference*, tr. Alan Bass (London and Henley: Routledge and Kegan Paul, 1978), 196–231.

55. Karl Pribram and E.H. Carlton, "Holonomic Brain Theory in Imaging and Object Perception," *Acta Psychologica* 63 (1986), 175–210.

56. Dylan Trigg, *The Memory of Place: A Phenomenology of the Uncanny* (Athens, OH: Ohio University Press, 2012).

57. Percy Shelley, *Shelley's Poetry and Prose*, ed. Donald H. Reiman and Neil Fraistat (New York and London: W.W. Norton, 2002).

58. William Shakespeare, *The Tempest*, ed. Frank Kermode (London: Methuen, 1987), 1.2.399–400.

59. Graham Harman, *Guerrilla Metaphysics*, 23, 158.

60. Arda Denkel, *Object and Property* (Cambridge: Cambridge University Press, 2007), 12–13, 37, 152.

61. Denkel, *Object and Property*, 132–140.

62. See for example, Craig Callender, "Humean Supervenience and Homogeneous Rotating Matter," *Mind* 110.447 (January 2001), 25–43.

Chapter 4

Magic Death

> Dust in the air suspended
> Marks the place where a story ended.
>
> – T.S. Eliot[1]

In order to exist, objects must be fragile. This sounds obvious but when we think the deep ontological reasons why, it becomes quite mysterious. It turns out that objects are dying around us all the time, even as they give birth to other objects. An object's sensuality is an elegy to its disappearance.

What Harman calls allure, the way one being exerts power over another, is a sign of possible death.[2] The aesthetic dimension, in other words, is where death happens. If birth is the sublime, beauty is death, as this chapter shall make clear. To be born is to be thrown into an always-already, to find oneself in a set of relations subtended by some object(s). To be born is for a fresh Rift between appearance and essence to *open up*. To persist is for a Rift to *suspend itself* in relation to other riven entities.

In turn, to end is *to coincide with one's sensual appearance*. Disappearing into a black hole, I leave behind a rapidly fading image of myself on the event horizon.[3] When a glass shatters, it has been matched by the sensuality of another object. Ending brings to light the withdrawnness of a thing. We can't point to the absent glass—we only see fragments, splinters. When I die, you can't point to my death: rather I become memories in someone's head, a collection of jpegs, the way some people think about things, objects that they handle, wounds.[4] When a realist novel ends, the frequency and duration of the action on the page synchronizes ever more tightly with the action in the chronological sequence of events: ashes to ashes. Again, notice that "realist novel" and "philosophical realism" are different. Nevertheless, since realist fiction is intended to induce a feeling of reality as an aesthetic effect, and since the aesthetic dimension is the causal dimension, it seems appropriate to use it to exemplify how things end.

The reader's heart beats faster as the police mount the staircase, only to find the stretched-out body of Dorian Gray, and a picture of him into which a knife has been thrust.[5] A dead crow becomes the dust and trees that surround it. When a Dzogchen yogini dies, in one of the spaces between existences (the Bardo of Luminosity), it is said that she allows her being to dissolve into the Clear Light "like a child leaping into its mother's lap."[6] Or she allows her body to disintegrate into rainbow light (Tibetan, *jalu*). From her point of view, it is as if the body wants to dissolve in this way. Only fragile ego is preventing the inevitable from happening.

Imagine a good old-fashioned vinyl record player. Now imagine a record called *I Cannot Be Played on This Record Player*. When you put the record on, the sounds that are recorded on the disk cause the record player to vibrate in such a way that it falls to pieces. Douglas Hofstadter, author of the wonderfully capacious and multilayered *Gödel, Escher, Bach*, talks about the exploding record player as an analogy for Gödel's Incompleteness Theorem. You just can't design a record player for which there is no nemesis record, just as Gödel showed that you can't design a coherent logical system that isn't capable of producing a weird, dialetheic sentence that says, "This sentence cannot be proved in this system."[7] In order to be coherent, a system must be incomplete. Let us extend this axiom to physical things: in order to exist, objects must be *fragile*.

This doesn't mean that theories are never true. It means something far stranger. The theorem states that any well-formulated system will be unable to account for at least one statement that is *true* on the terms of the system itself. This put paid to Russell and Whitehead's attempt to systematize mathematics, which relied on a strict and ultimately brittle adherence to the Law of Noncontradiction. Gödel showed how logical systems must self-contradict at some point in order to be true, while Alan Turing showed how physical systems can exemplify Gödel's Incompleteness Theorem, by imagining Turing Machines that compute data, visualizing them as spools of tape read by a machine head. Turing Machines provide a graphic, physical version of the Incompleteness Theorem, and in the process exemplify how fragility applies to objects in just the way Gödel applied it to logical systems. You can't design a Turing Machine that will be able to predict whether all algorithms will halt or go into an infinite loop: "Not-All algorithms are predictable." In order to be a system that is coherent, there must be at least one sentence that cannot be proved by the system, within the system. The sentence, "This sentence is not provable within this system," is in a loop.[8] If it is correct, then it is possible to prove it; but what is says is that it is not provable, so it is impossible to prove it. In the view expounded here, dialetheic sentences are symptoms of the double-truthed quality of objects.

The record player is more than just an analogy. If you make a record that produces the right tones, you could blow up a record player. In fact, this was a specialism of creators of rave music in the early 1990s. I remember going to several raves where the speakers would explode because of a tune called "LFO"—Low Frequency Oscillator, a boondoggle on old synthesizers, but also a joke metaphor for "I Cannot Be Played Through These Loudspeakers."[9]

Hofstadter gives the example of a virus. A virus is a piece of RNA or DNA code in a protein packet that says to your genome, "Hey, there's a version of me somewhere in your system. Go fetch it will you?" This is a version of a Henkin Sentence.[10] The trouble is, this Henkin Sentence comes bundled with a Liar, along the lines of "It is true that I am lying in this sentence." So you go into overdrive producing copies of the virus in a desperate attempt to solve the paradox, then you die—just like your computer. Thus begins the race between viruses and other lifeforms to detect and destroy viruses and, conversely, to slip through the defenses of lifeforms. The record player story is thus also a story about lifeforms. There is at least one entity out there (it could be lurking in your genome) called something like "If Tim Downloads This, He Will Auto-Destruct." That's what mortality *means*. Life forms exist precisely to the extent that they are fragile.

Consider objects in general—not just living ones, but all objects. There is an *even less* metaphorical sense in which the record player story is true for objects. There is at least one other object out there that could bring it about so that a certain object was annihilated. Not only this: it is also the case that the sensuality of an object is what might finally destroy it, which is why even black holes, fatal to other objects, eventually evaporate under their very own steam. As I've been arguing, sensuality is not simply decorative candy on the surface of something "more real," so we should expect this to be the case.

Objects are fragile, not superficially, but all the way down, ontologically. And this means that they are *weak*. I mean this without a trace of sneer: we are one of those weak objects. Consider human language. That languages do not beam the thing down in full presence is not some local quirk of language, but a fact about reality. Words such as "this" and "is" are symptoms of a long and jagged history of relationships with nonhumans. Some of the inconsistencies of language are symptoms of our coexistence with other objects. This makes our language inherently weak. Unlike those theorists who want to posit human language as powerful or rich, I claim it is weak and flexible. That the reason why one can say things such as "This statement is false" in English is not because English is rich, but because English is weak. Like the branch of a willow tree, it bends. Software languages are not less expressive than English, but in a way, they are *more* expressive. Every term really means something. Or really does something. When you try to dissipate the Liar paradox ("This statement is false" and variants) you end up having to jump to another language. This language can also generate the Liar paradox, in a modified form that might even be stronger. Paradoxically, the more rigidly one tries to exclude contradiction, the more virulent become the dialetheias that are possible.

I can get around "This sentence is false" by imagining that there are metalanguages that explain what counts as a sentence. Then I can decide that "This sentence is false" isn't a real sentence. This is the strategy of the logician Alfred Tarski, who invented the notion of metalanguage specifically to cope with dialetheias.[11] A Tarski adherent might say that " 'This sentence is false' is not a sentence." But I can subvert her ploy with the following: "This is not a sentence." My sentence-virus is worse for the Tarskian than the one she was trying to eliminate. Then she might claim that sentences such as "This sentence is false" are neither true nor false. But in turn you can imagine a strengthened version of the Liar such as: "This sentence is not true"; or "This sentence is neither true nor false." And we can go on adding to the strengthened Liar if the counter-attack tries to build immunity by specifying some fourth thing that a sentence can be besides true, false, and neither true nor false: "This sentence is false, or neither true nor false, or the fourth thing." And so on.[12]

The metalanguage tries to tamp down the problem, but in doing so it becomes more brittle than English. Fundamentally, this is because *there is no metalanguage*, which is the argument for what Harman has called "sincerity" (see the discussion earlier in this book). And *that* is because *there are objects*. A metalanguage would function as a "middle object" that gave coherency and evenness to the others—and there are no middle objects, as we have seen.[13] Since there is no metalanguage, there is no rising above the disturbing illusory play of causality. This issue is more than adjacent to Gödel's Incompleteness Theorem. Inconsistencies such as the Liar are archaeological evidence of a fundamental inconsistency in objects: the irreducible gap between real and sensual objects.

The irreducible gap Lacan discovers between the *subject of the enunciated* and the *subject of enunciation* is made clear in the Liar.[14] There is the I who is saying the sentence and the I about whom the sentence is said. Novelists exploit this gap, knowing full well that all first-person narratives are intrinsically untrustworthy. If you want to play with irony and paradox, write in an autobiographical mode. Why else is *Frankenstein* written that way? This literary gap is only one among trillions.

Gödel argues that because of the inherent inconsistency of all theories, you need another theory to explain the semantics of one theory. Each theory requires $1+n$ others. Doesn't this sound awfully like the OOO theory of translation, that objects are apprehended in an interobjective space that consists of 1+n objects? You never hear the wind in itself, you hear the wind in the chimney. I part company with most computational linguists, who hold that computational languages are less expressive than English. I think this is not the problem. I think that computational languages are more explicit and therefore more rigid. English has the advantage of being weak, because it evolved to be spoken by flesh and blood objects who were trying to keep on keeping on.[15]

Closure: This Is the End, Beautiful Friend

The experience of beauty and of the sublime, argues Kant, is one of tuning yourself to the object. But what is this tuning (*Stimmung*)? Let's think about the extreme of tuning. When an opera singer matches the resonant frequency of a glass, the glass explodes. The Tibetan Buddhist analogy for dying is a vase. When a vase explodes, the space inside the vase merges instantly with the space outside. We can briefly surmise that beauty is death.

Watch a slow-motion video of the opera singer's effect on the glass. Watch how the glass in the video shudders just before it ceases to exist. "It was so beautiful I almost died." Theodor Adorno argues that this is what the aesthetic is supposed to do: start a subject-quake, *Einschütterung*, a little death.[16] An earthquake is when the rhythms between tectonic plates become extremely regular. A stroke is when brainwaves become isometric. Closure is when the frequency and duration of the plot synchronizes with those of a story in a 1/1 ratio. These quakes cancel the difference between a thing and its resonance, its appearance.

Kant argues that beauty is an experience of coexisting with an object. In this experience, it's as if the object and the subject suddenly fuse, like the space inside and outside a vase. It's only a short hop, skip, and jump from here to an object-oriented theory of beauty. Beauty is the end of an object, because in beauty, two objects fuse. Sound waves match the resonant frequency of the glass. When they reach a critical amplitude, the glass ceases to exist. It becomes its environment.

What is the feeling of being at the end of a story? The feeling of beginning (aperture) is uncertainty. The feeling of middle (development) is cycling and suspension. The feeling of ending is *closure*. How do stories achieve closure? They begin to correlate the plot to the story in an isochronous way. The frequency and duration ratios begin to match one another. The more they match, the more tension is generated. An action movie is a narrative that reaches closure as soon as possible, and stays there. The Bourne trilogy, for instance, involves almost isochronous narrative sequences throughout. That's what "fast-paced" and "mounting suspense" mean. You know you have exited the development section in a classic realist fiction when one single event happens and it is narrated one single time, with a roughly isochronous duration. You pop out of the maelstrom of development. You can feel the end approaching. The beginning of chapter 12 of *The Picture of Dorian Gray* is a masterpiece of economy. By narrating one single event, the narrator exits from the exotic perfumed worlds evoked in the seductive reading and rereading of the decadent book by Huysmans that Dorian is obsessed with in the development section:

> It was on the ninth of November, the eve of his own thirty-eighth birthday, as he often remembered afterwards.
>
> He was walking home about eleven o'clock from Lord Henry's, where he had been dining, and was wrapped in heavy furs, as the night was cold and foggy. At the corner of Grosvenor Square and South Audley Street, a man passed him in the mist, walking very fast and with the collar of his grey ulster turned up.[17]

In three crisp sentences, closure begins. Somehow we anticipate that Dorian will die at the end of the story; or at least, there will be an end, and it is coming. A quake is on its way. Now it's "only a matter of time." The story's ending is included right here, like a splash of cold water.

Closure is the feeling of death. The feeling of death is a feeling of isochrony: of the two channels of plot and story synchronizing with one another. The plot attunes itself to the story. In so doing, it vanishes, leaving only a few corpses for the police to come and clear things up. The end of *The Picture of Dorian Gray* is exemplary in this regard. Dorian slashes the picture, and dies—the police run up the stairs to find his corpse—the last few pages seem to be unfolding before our very eyes, as the plot synchronizes with the story. One event is narrated one single time. It's enough to break the spell of suspension ever more tightly.

Consider how a drama handles closure. In a play or an opera, closure is when the *fourth wall* dissolves: the aesthetic screen that separates the audience from the players. This is the moment in the drama at which the audience is made to sense that they are part of the play. It's formalized in a Shakespeare tragedy when a character speaks directly to the audience in the final scene. In *The Tempest*, Prospero makes a speech that marks the end of a masque within the play, but which also speaks knowingly to the audience behind the fourth wall:

> Our revels now are ended. These our actors,
> As I foretold you, were all spirits, and
> Are melted into air, into thin air:
> And, like the baseless fabric of this vision,
> The cloud-capp'd towers, the gorgeous palaces,
> The solemn temples, the great globe itself,
> Yea, all which it inherit, shall dissolve,
> And, like this insubstantial pageant faded,
> Leave not a rack behind. We are such stuff
> As dreams are made on; and our little life
> Is rounded with a sleep.[18]

After this, the play is "dying." The artifice of the play is destroyed, by being heightened: "This is only a play, and you are watching it." The sensual space in which the play occurs overwhelms the play itself. At the end of *The Tempest,* Ariel repeats the closure, just to make sure we feel the quake of ending: he asks for our applause to release him from the confines of the stage. *The Tempest* stretches out the feeling of closure, a long goodbye.

Dying is a sensual event that occurs in an interobjective space. Closure demonstrates how when one object comes into phase with another, annihilation is near. Death is when a virus, for instance, starts to replicate itself in your genome, using your cells like a photocopying machine. If the cells do this very efficiently, it is called death. Then your body disintegrates. Bacteria eat your rotting flesh. You become bacteria. The bacteria bacteriomorph your body, translating you into bacterian. Worms and fungi eat through the residue. At the time of writing I'm watching a tree stump in my backyard. A rather too big pine tree was cut down at the back of my garden last year. Fungi have been eating into the stump. As the fungi digest the sugars in each ring of the tree, they grow a little bit. What results is a mushroomogram of the tree rings, a series of spreading fungi with rings, quite like the rings of the old tree. It's quite uncanny: the ringed fungi look like the tree, yet they don't. The fungi are fungimorphizing the tree. It's as if the tree rings are being translated into fungese before my eyes. The more complete the translation, the more complete the death of the object.

Bardo 2

Yet every translation is necessarily imperfect. There is an element of parody in every death, an uncanny resemblance, as in the figure of the zombie, a corpse that resembles me in every feature, except that it's a walking dead version of me. The zombie both is and is not me. We argue about whether a human in a "vegetative state" is alive or dead. Fingernails continue to grow after what medicine calls death. And some religions hold that some kind of soul or consciousness exists after physical death. There are all kinds of everyday squabbles about what constitutes death, and this is because of the ontological Rift. When an object is dying—namely, throughout an object's existence—is it existing or is it simply ceasing to exist? When I stand in a doorway, am I inside or outside the room? By existing, objects have one foot in the grave.

Nothing dies completely. The physicist Roger Penrose suggests that when entropy reduces everything to massless particles, they will be photons, and the universe can begin again.[19] Evolution turns a swim bladder into a lung.[20] There are more drastic cases of ghostly half-life. Some objects seem to be "waiting for" a new use: objects that clutter attics, kept perhaps as heirlooms but never seen, even by those who inherit them. Underlying all these is an inherent property of all objects whatsoever: *objects are already ghosts* of themselves, because of the Rift between appearance and essence. On this view, death, birth and continuity are happening "simultaneously," or more accurately, "equiprimordially."[21] An object just is a "black hole" with a fading photograph of itself on its surface.[22] As stated in the Introduction, Lucretius, the arch-atomist, is compelled to supplement his atomism with aesthetics: objects are seen in their past as if they all disappear into a black hole: "To see something else is to be affected by an emanation, not the thing itself, such that whatever we do see is an effect of what took place in the past as films or simulacra take time to travel in the void."[23] An object is self-referential: "What I do is me" (Gerard Manley Hopkins). Yet this self-reference is of the order of the Liar: "This sentence is false." *I* and *me* are subtly different.

David Wiesner rewrote *The Three Little Pigs*. In this version, the pigs escape from the book by somehow exiting the page.[24] They find themselves in a curious interstitial space populated with other characters. They bring a dragon back to their world and defeat the wolf. What can we learn from this about our ideological and ecological situation? One is that when we exit from our ideological "world" with its familiar contours, we are still somewhere. Isn't this the lesson of those interstitial moments in David Lynch movies, in which we see a transition between seemingly coherent worlds? These transitional spaces are not just a void. Maybe philosophy and ideology only thinks these spaces as voids from within a certain kind of philosophical or ideological framework. OOO and Buddhism share something very interesting. They both hold that the interstitial space between things is not a blank void. In fact, it's charged with meaning, even with causality.

Objects have an ego, and this ego is fragile. Since the ego is nothing but a palimpsest of "abandoned object cathexes," as Freud puts it, why couldn't we apply this theory to every object?[25] Let's think it in an Aristotelian way. Formal causes are in for a return both in quantum theory and in OOO, for somewhat similar reasons. In what sense is the form of an object its "ego"? The formal cause of an object, rather simply, is just the record of everything that has "happened to" it. A blob of molten glass is blown and cooled, resulting in a wine glass. The form of the glass, its ego if you like, is the record of the objects that struck it, blew on it, snipped it while it was molten, left it to cool. What in rhetorical theory is called *memoria* is formal cause just as delivery is the sublime.

Just as the chapter on beginnings rethought the idea of rhetorical *delivery*, this chapter rethinks the rhetorical art of *memory*. Memory was a part of rhetoric that came under fire in early modernity. First Erasmus underplayed, then seventeenth-century English Puritans downright banned the art of memory, the various mnemonic techniques practiced down the ages, as it was thought to resemble magic.[26] In the Middle Ages, by contrast, memory, not imagination, was held in awe.[27] The human practice of memory, as a handling and offsite storage of an object in an interobjective (mental) space, often imagined as a building with many floors, eroded.[28] This aided the restriction of rhetoric to mere style (*elocutio*), as Chapter 1 explored. The absence of memory from rhetoric further depleted the ability of thinking to cope with objects.

The formal cause of something is its past, its memory, as in the memory inscribed in a silicon wafer. Memory precisely is a state in which "everything is there, but nothing is ever present."[29] We have already encountered the question of memory in thinking the continued existence of objects in the previous chapter. It seems appropriate then that the notion of bardo would come around once more, since bardos are the repetition of memories. This time, however, we are dealing with the bardo of dying, the way in which repetition is caught in something deadly. The (superficial, given) appearance of an object *just is its warping by another object*, which is another way of saying that the "past life" of an object is its form.

What Hegel says about the abstractness of the *I* cannot be said about how an asteroid piles into Earth, causing a gigantic molten chunk to blurt out the other side and become the Moon. The asteroid never encounters Earth as just a blank screen, onto which it projects its own fantasy, its form—its warping by other objects. The asteroid does not perform a negation of every positive content, a Hegelian "abstraction from all determinateness."[30] The ego of an object is simply the record of the traumas that happened to it—this goes for the objects called human, for whom the ego is a virtual, sensual object. Thus there are no blank screens in reality whatsoever.

Hamartia

While the aesthetic mode of beginning is horror–bliss, and the mode of continuing is comedy, the mode of ending is tragedy. This is because, like the protagonist of a Greek tragedy, objects all possess an intrinsic flaw or wound, which, after the Greeks, I here call *harmartia*.

Somewhere out there, there exists at least one bullet with your name on it, could be a virus, could be your own DNA. Why? The truth is closer to home than a bullet burrowing into one's flesh. Consider an explosion. An explosion is frightening not only because it threatens me. An explosion is frightening because it's ontologically uncanny. This uncanniness underlies the physical threat. What uncanniness? Quite simply, an object that just functions in "my world"—a plane, a skyscraper—suddenly comes to life in a very different way. My world wavers for a moment—even collapses.

An object affects another object by translating it, as best as it can, into its own terms. A plane gouges a plane-shaped hole in a skyscraper. A perfect translation of one object by another object would entail the destruction of that object. Consider again the glass. When an opera singer sings a certain note very loudly, the sound stirs up the resonant frequencies of a wine glass. In slow motion, you can see the wine glass rippling. Then the glass explodes. Why? Of course we know physically, or we think we know. But how about ontologically?

The sound was able to reduce the glass to a pure appearance. There is an ontological Rift between essence and appearance. This has nothing to do with the spurious gap between substance and accidents. What is called *substance* and what is called *accidents* are both on the side of what this book calls appearance. The Rift is irreducibly part of a thing: a thing is both itself and not-itself. I call this double truth of a thing its *fragility*. The inner fragility of a thing is why a thing can exist at all. Fragility is also why anything at all can happen. Existence is incompleteness. This fragility is activated in what is called destruction. Somehow something interferes with the Rift between essence and appearance and translates the object so radically that the Rift collapses. Nothing can physically insert itself into the Rift. Since objects are enclosed, secret and withdrawn, interference with the Rift must be caused when the object in question aesthetically attunes to its translator, in a process resembling the manner in which my genome creates more viruses under certain conditions. The difference between immanent and external causation does not exist for this theory. This is more efficient than claiming that things are totally destroyed ontically, which would imply that objects are just lumps of blah decorated with accidents, or nothing but bundles of qualities, and so on. On the "ontic destruction" view, an object requires some other object to do the dirty work. Tracing the whodunit story of destruction via another object, we soon return to prime movers and first causes.

An explosion reveals the fragility of things. But it also reveals the strange inconsistency of things. Beginnings are anamorphic, while endings are beautifully symmetrical. Life is distortion; death is peaceful, as Freud argues concerning the death drive. To begin is to distort; to end is to become consistent. To kill or destroy is *to reduce something to consistency*: the theory advanced here is the inverse of Badiou, for whom to destroy is to make inconsistent. When I die, I become memories, some crumpled paper in a wastebasket, some clothes. I become my appearances. Yet there can be no perfect translation of an object, because the translator is also an (inconsistent) object. There would be no trace of a perfect translation. Thus there appear cinders, fragments, debris. New objects are uncanny reminders of broken objects. A culture of mourning might arise around them.

The Rift between essence and appearance is why an object has an outside. The Rift is why an object exists. The Rift is also how an object can die: its inner, irreducible fragility. Every object has some feature labeled "I am not part of this object." A *hamartia* (Greek, "wound"). An inner silver bullet, like a physical version of a Gödel sentence.[31] The inner fragility of an object allows it to be destroyed by another object. Much more importantly, however, inner fragility means that *an object can "die" all by itself.*

Every object is wounded. A hamartia constitutes the object as such in its determinacy. Impermanence is an intrinsic feature of why an object is an object. When an object comes into phase with its own fragility, it is destroyed. Consider the Hawking radiation emanating from a black hole. Not everything remains caught within a black hole: even a black hole, the densest object in the physical Universe, is internally inconsistent. At some point, the black hole will expend itself. Its hamartia, its inner fragility, causes it to cease to exist. Hamartia is what Aristotle calls a tragic flaw.

It's mistaken, then, to see:

1. Objects as solid lumps in a stream of time that gradually wears them down.
2. Objects as reifications of a temporal flux.
3. Objects as decomposable into parts (undermining).
4. Fragility/death as an occurrence that "happens to" an object from without.

Fragility is an ontological condition of objects. It doesn't depend on non-objects. By contrast, (1) through (4) explain fragility by adding to or subtracting from the object. The fact of fragility is due to the simple yet counter-intuitive fact that objects are what they are, and not what they are, at the same time. They are *dialetheic*, double-truthed.

Objects have one foot in the grave. The fact that an object can cease all by itself is very satisfying from the standpoint of fundamental ontology. No other objects, let alone relations, are required for an object to "die." This means that theoretically at least an object can die alone, unknown and unloved. All an object needs to cease existing is to coincide with itself. Once it does that, it evaporates. Reduced to sheer simplicity, the object dies, leaving behind only memories, cinders, sensual impressions. The Rift between essence and appearance collapses. The object evaporates into its appearance-for another object(s).

Let us delve into the question of fragility a little further. The intrinsic fragility of objects has to do with why we can derive time and space from them. For Kant, the experience of beauty is an object-like entity that seems to inhere both in oneself and the beautiful object: this is what makes it impersonal, or beyond ego. Beauty is universalizable, that is, the kind of interaction that beauty is could be extended to include any other object in the vicinity. If I find the *Mona Lisa* beautiful, the feeling consists in the idea that everyone should find it so. If I find a particular piece of dance music incredibly beautiful, I want to put speakers on top of the tallest buildings and embarrass my family by broadcasting it to the surrounding world, because everyone should be able to find it beautiful. Yet when I do this, when I threaten people with my beauty, I am no longer within the beautiful experience.

Why? Kant argues that it's because beauty is also nonconceptual: it has a certain *je ne sais quoi*. As soon as I put my finger on it, it's gone, like Eurydice disappearing back into Hades when Orpheus looks back at her. I grasp at the object as if the object in itself were beauty, and I lose beauty. Or I specify some aspect of the object. Nothing in the object can be specified this way: not the parts, and not the whole. Beauty then is irreducible. I can't dissolve it into smaller components and I can't dissolve it upwards ("overmining") into some holistic vision. Beauty is unique and contingent. Beauty is unspeakable, which is why Kant's beauty provides the conditions for Humean taste, and not the other way around. It seems as if nice colors and smells and sounds are the condition for beauty, but really the profound freedom glimpsed in beauty is ontologically prior to those things. Why would we even care about those things if it were not for this freedom? That beauty is irreducible is a clue that beauty might tell us something about OOO objects.

We are driven to the realist conclusion that beauty is evidence of the existence of 1+*n* objects: myself, the *Mona Lisa*, the dry air between us. Yet beauty is in none of these objects. What is uncanny and slightly frightening at times about beauty is that it can't be located, yet it appears to emerge in interactions between things. Beauty then is a kind of lie that is told of an object when it interacts with another object: a beautiful lie. It is as if beauty is everywhere, everyone, for all time. Yet it emerges from a pure contingency. It is timeless only insofar as it is based on objects that seem to be fleeting.

The mysterious quality of artworks is a signal about the mysterious quality of objects in general. Beauty is a secret that we know exists but whose content we don't know. When we share it with others, it's as if we are in on the same secret. We look at each other in amazement or with a knowing look. But it's impossible to specify what this secret is. Only *the fact that there is a secret* is of any importance. Beauty is based on the raw fact of the secret as such. The contours of the secret are felt like the coolness of a marble surface to a blindfolded person. Throughout this book I have been using the term *secret* to account for withdrawal. The secret then is simply the objectness of the object: the fact that objects appear, yet they withdraw from appearance, a double-edged quality that means that there is a permanent Rift in the universe, for any object whatsoever, not just sentient beings and certainly not just humans. This Rift happens both within and between objects. Or rather: it becomes impossible to specify whether the Rift is *inside* or *outside* an object. The Rift cannot be located ontically, that is, we can't point to it anywhere on or inside the object. Yet there it is. This Rift accounts for what I call *fragility*.

Now fragility shouldn't be confused with the fact that things do break. While this is true, its truth is just a symptom of a deeper ontological fact. In other words, objects don't exist in time like porcelain dolls on a conveyor belt: when they reach the end, they drop off onto a concrete floor and smash to pieces. No: the object is riven in order to be an object. Time as a succession of instants emanates from objects themselves. That is, linear time as we (and whoever or whatever else) experience it is a product of a certain set of interactions between objects, based on their fragility. We can think of physical analogues quite easily. Time emanates from the decay of a radioactive particle; or from the vibrations of a piezoelectric crystal; or from the massiveness of a planet. In a sense, the radioactive particle, such as the carbon used in carbon dating, provides the best example. *All objects are isotopes of themselves*, uncanny and unstable doubles. Theories of objects and causation that rely on faceless substances or bundles of qualities have trouble with isotopes—real isotopes, not just figurative ones—precisely for this reason.[32]

Fragility is what explains beauty. Kantian beauty is slightly sad, because it isn't you. (I indulge here in a little anthropomorphism, since as Jane Bennett argues, this may be a net benefit to our understanding of things.)[33] It's also a little bit scary because you can't tell whether it's pretense or not. It's the same way with nonhuman and with nonsentient objects. In some sense objects are sad, because they contain kernels of not-themselves, in order to be what they are. Objects just can't be consistent and coherent at the same time. It seems as if Gödel wrote the rules for existence. Objects could shatter into a million pieces—a million new objects that is—at any moment. Their *possibility* is predicated on their *impossibility*. In this sense, objects are not very different from what Heidegger calls Da-sein.[34] We should explore this.

Heidegger strongly influenced Lacan with his idea that anxiety is the emotion—or *attunement* as he puts it—that never lies.[35] Angst is a bottom line attunement of being that doesn't "hinder and confuse" a person who is tuned to their authentic being (Da-sein). It's what the Buddhist teacher Chögyam Trungpa, echoing Heidegger, calls *basic anxiety*.[36]

Now this talk of Angst all seems a long distance from objects. But is it far away from OOO? Is it not because Da-sein is both potential and "impossible" that Angst appears? This is a slightly subtle argument, so we shall have to bear with each other for a few paragraphs to get it right. But we shall see as we proceed that what characterizes Da-sein, far from being a special human property—or worse, the special property of specific humans (Germans)—is a quality shared by all objects. This quality is *dialetheic*:

double-truthed. Objects are themselves and not-themselves, $p \wedge \neg p$, as the Introduction argued.

Within objects are differences from themselves, which is why objects can appear: namely, why they can appear-to some other object. A star-nosed mole smells a thousand delicate perfumes emanating from the soil, because those perfumes are not the soil. The soil perfumes are "isotopes" of the soil, unstable bearers of soil-information to other entities, such as the receptors in the noses of star-nosed moles. This is precisely how Heidegger characterizes Da-sein, "being-there." Da-sein isn't objectively present, yet it manifests in all kinds of tunings such as fear and anxiety. In particular, anxiety is a clean attunement to Da-sein since it resonates only with the simple fact of Da-sein as such. In anxiety, the world becomes flat and meaningless. Objects seem to lose their significance for us: they have "nothing more to 'say' to us," in Heidegger's telling phrase.[37] That is, it is as if we are able to catch an impossible glimpse of their secretiveness.

Tuned to Da-sein itself, Angst has one foot in the sensual ether and one foot outside of it, in some impossible no-space. This is a point at which language breaks down unless we are willing to admit that (some) things can be dialetheic, both p and not-p at the very same time. For instance, Hegel explains motion, as we saw in the previous chapter, by supposing that objects are here and not-here simultaneously. We could explain being in a doorway like this: we are both inside and outside the room. It becomes impossible to specify, using objectively present, reified measuring devices such as tape measures and stopwatches, just what "being inside the room" is as opposed to "being in the doorway." If we do, all kinds of Zeno's paradoxes arise that tempt us to say that nothing is happening, or that there is no movement. The trouble is, we are so habituated to imagining beings existing "in" time that it becomes hard to see how time and therefore events as such flow from objects. This flow occurs when objects emit isotopes of themselves, riven from within by fragility. In this sense, death is all around us. Since the universe just is a huge object, we exist inside death, just like in the Buddhist paintings of the Wheel of Life, in which the whole of samsara takes place within the jaws of Yama, god of death.

"It was so beautiful I almost died." Is there more than metaphorical truth in this statement? Is beauty an experience of death, or near-death?

Adorno writes that the shudder of beauty shatters the encapsulated subject.[38] When an opera singer sings just the right note, at just the right pitch and volume, the sound waves resonate with the wine glass in such a way as to destroy it. On slow-motion film, we can see how just before it is destroyed, the glass undergoes a shudder. The resonant frequency matches the glass perfectly.

From the perspective of the alien phenomenology of the glass itself, might this indeed be an "experience" of suddenly losing a sense of boundary? And isn't this what beauty is? In the event of beauty, a non-self part of my inner space seems to resonate in the colors on the wall, in the sounds pouring into my ears. Hugely amplified, might this resonance actually kill me? "A beautiful way to die"—to be destroyed by vibrations that removed myself from myself.

For beauty to work, then, there must already be a surface capable of receiving the wound. It seems that the knife of beauty is able to insert itself into the slit between an object's essence and its appearance. Beauty "works itself in" to the already existing Rift between an object and that same object, the fact that objects are dialetheic, fork-tongued. This Rift is an inconsistency in the object that enables the object to end. When an object is entirely sundered from its appearance, its *hamartia* gets the better of it: that is called *destruction* or *death*.

Beauty, then, is a nonviolent experience of near death, a warning that one is fragile, like everything else in the universe. Beauty is the shadow of the threat to objects, *the threat that is objects*. Objects as such carry an inner threat, because of the Rift between essence and appearance. Beauty is the call of the vulnerable flesh and the fragile glass. This explains perhaps why beauty is associated with experiences of love, empathy and compassion, themes that preoccupy pre-Kantian theories of aesthetic affect such as Adam Smith, and that also preoccupy ethical theories based on the Buddhist view of anatman (no-self). It is the reason why we can articulate an ethics of nonviolent coexistence based on beauty. This ethics cannot truly be grounded in the cool Kantian version of aesthetic experience, with its rigid anthropocentrism and sadistic shadow side. It must instead be founded in the project of coming as close as possible to our already shared, disturbing intimacy. Let us begin to explore this.

When I experience beauty, I resonate with an object. The object and I attune to one another. Kant describes beauty as a tuning process. "Beautiful" is what I say to myself when an impersonal, "object-like" cognitive state arises that seems to emanate from the object itself. It is as if the object and I are locked together in inseparable union. In common prejudice, one supposes that when having no ego means not being able to brush your teeth. But according to this argument, you brush your teeth all the time without an ego. That's happening already. It's perfectly possible to have a non-ego experience. You are having one now.

The beautiful object fits me like a glove. Kantian beauty, however, is unlike Aristotelian and Horatian decorum, the traditional way in which the aesthetic is said to be like clothing.[39] Decorum provides objective rules for what a beautiful thing should wear, an external, systematic set of criteria for what counts as beautiful, a checklist. Kantian beauty, by contrast, is a symptom of something more disruptive. Kant thinks this discovery as the transcendental subject, but OOO thinks the discovery as the withdrawal of objects. Yet there is an affinity between these thoughts, because they both imagine some kind of transcendental crack or Rift to be intrinsic to reality. Beauty is not a glove fitting a hand, but more like Death taking you by the hand.

Beauty is nonconceptual. Nothing in the object directly explains it: not the parts, because this would be sheer positivistic reductionism; not the whole, because that would be another kind of reduction (the parts are now expendable). Yet beauty seems to emanate from this thing. Just this particular, unique thing, is the locus of beauty. Everyone in their right mind should find it beautiful, I think, yet if I were to impose this on others, it would ruin the experience. I know my particular experience of beauty is not shared, but I know that you know what beauty is. A certain unconditional freedom opens up, along with a certain coexistence without content. No wonder Kant considered the experience of beauty to be an essential part of democracy. Beauty is an event in being, a sort of gap, a gentle slit. Beauty allows for a cognitive state that is noncoercive and profoundly nonviolent.[40]

But what are the conditions of possibility for the experience of beauty to occur? What, as it were, are the phenomenological physics of beauty? As we explore these conditions we uncover a remarkable body of work. The name of this body of work is Alphonso Lingis. Kantian beauty tacitly presupposes a being that can be wounded by colors, sounds, smells, textures and tastes: affected by them, so as to resonate such that the tuning process of beauty can commence. This being is what Lingis explores, in a series of remarkable studies. This is not simply a realm of mere appetite, as Kant suggests, because that would reproduce a difference between humans and nonhumans (animals, for instance) that is untenable and problematic.[41] Moreover, in appetite I roam like a hungry wolf over the carcass of things—it seems as if powerful objects at the very least suspend this aggressive craving, always already suspend it before the event of beauty takes hold. And stranger still, as Lacan noted well, there is a symmetry between Kantian beauty and sadism, a cold lust concerning an infinitely opaque object.[42] Before the gentle slit of beauty is made, then, the knife must be ready and the arm must be in range. It is this dimension, a dangerous and uncanny dimension of "levels" and "directives," that the thinking of Lingis addresses.[43] Since ego just is the formal cause of an object, what we are talking about when it comes to beauty is an aesthetic resonance with the Rift between essence and appearance. What Lingis shows is that experiences that are beyond our ego do exist, and are profoundly physical. The insights of Lingis inform many of the proposals made in this book.

Since beauty doesn't depend on ego, it must be incredibly default to human cognition. OOO argues that this default-ness is present in any interaction between any objects, not just humans and other things. Let's walk through this rather startling idea. A sample of an object is not the object. An attunement is not the object. Yet it can dial itself very close to the object. If an object were to tune itself perfectly to another object, at least one of them would be destroyed. Think again about the glass. An opera singer sings a note of a certain pitch. The pitch vibrates with the resonant frequency of the glass. The sound is like the glass, but not the glass. The pitch is tuned to the glass. The glass begins to dance, it has a little glass orgasm—don't they call it the little death?—then it explodes into non-glass. Again: sound waves attuned to the resonant frequency of the glass fit the glass so perfectly that it is destroyed. A tune shatters an object.

Art can create and destroy things, quite literally. Causality is an illusion-like play of a demonic energy that has real effects in the world. Perfect tuning of an entity to that which is not the entity means destruction: this is what happens when you die—you become your environment. Enveloped perfectly by the soundwaves, does the glass itself experience a kind of beauty? A sudden dissolution of boundaries between the glass and the not-glass, an experience Adorno calls the core shattering that makes the ego disappear? For Kant, beauty is a nonconceptual experience of coexisting with an object. It's a virtual experience, as if my inner state were emanating from the object. In this experience, it's as if the object and the subject suddenly fuse, like the space inside and outside a vase. What if the agency comes from the object, from the not-me or the not-glass? What if the as-if quality that Kant sees as a projection of my inner space into the object is indeed an emanation of the object, or based on such an emanation? What if beauty is when an object tunes to our vulnerability? When you hear that deathly musical box sound in that P.M. Dawn song we explored in the Introduction, you really are hearing the possibility of your own death. That beautiful, uncanny musical box, wound up and playing over and over, executing itself. The tip of an iceberg. Beauty is how objects end. Beauty is death.

Objects Without Presence: Objects Without the Present

Heidegger argues that the end of something is the beginning of something else.[44] Now this is trivially true: when a wine glass smashes, a thousand fragments are born. But Heidegger means something stranger than this. He means that the end of authentic Da-sein is the "*beginning* of … something objectively present."[45] Ends, in other words, are not simply to be found on the outer edges of things when we measure them with tape measures or Geiger counters. Ends of things are within things. Appearance, as appearance-for, is a kind of death. We are living in a universe of death, in which interactions between the isotopes of objects, their uncanny, ghostly apparitions, determines size, shape, duration, momentum, gravitational pull, color, taste and emotional state. Things appear because some kind of death happens. A photon "measures" an electron by changing it. I make the poem real for me by misreading it. Every step on the sidewalk wears it away. Time crumbles from the collapsing of carbon-14 as the atoms become something else.

The measurement of a quantum destroys its "coherence," namely its existence in a dialetheic state in which different positions and momenta are "superposed" one on the other. Something definitely exists before measurement, which is why measurement can happen at all. We are not dealing with *esse est percipi* here. Yet measurement destroys the fragile, wavering quality of an object as it oscillates and not-oscillates: as it breathes, as Aaron O'Connell says (see Chapter 2).

In Chapter 1 we briefly explored Percy Shelley's *A Defence of Poetry*, a stirring text on the revolutionary value of poetry. Shelley argues that poetry is an event whose meaning is irreducibly to-come. What makes a poem a poem is that we don't know what it means yet. Thus poets are "the hierophants of an unapprehended imagination, the mirrors of the gigantic shadows which futurity casts upon the present."[46] Poems are "timeless" insofar as they ontologically subtend time itself, opening up hitherto unknown possibilities of meaning and action.

Shelley bases his argument not on idealism, but on a beautifully worked out physicalism that can account for thinking on its own terms. Humans and probably "all other sentient beings," he writes, are like Aeolian harps, wind lyres that resonate to the motion of the wind. It's strange to imagine that these harps were common pieces of eighteenth-century household equipment. Imagine Jane Austen's characters listening to one. The sound is not unlike contemporary drone music by Sonic Youth or La Monte Young. As in Plato's *Ion*, the wind is channeled by the strings of the harp, which in turn are channeled by our ears. When the wind stirs the strings, a process of translation is going on. Then these translations are themselves translated: this is Shelley's image of thinking, the translation of a translation. Since any translation is a *transduction*, a mistranslation via another object, Shelley's Aeolian lyre image provides all the tools we need for including thinking in a physicalist realism.

The essence of the wind withdraws. Thus the "apprehension" of the wind is an elegy for a lost thing. There is no wind in the sound of the wind. Yet what is the essence of the elegy? The elegy's essence also withdraws. Each vibrant, phasing note of the Aeolian lyre talks about the wind in lyre-morphic ways. There is no end of the series of (mis)translations. The (mis)translations of the wind are as open-ended, then, as the wind itself is withdrawn. Yet the wind is finite, determinate: it's the wind, it's not a shrimp cocktail. What we encounter here is a *non-teleological finitude* of objects. Objects are specific, yet open; they are not a vague blur, yet they refuse to be pinned down. They are already dead, their fate sealed by their inner fragility: dead objects walking. They are undead, spectral and haunting: not quite alive, but not quite brute and inanimate. At a deep ontological level, the future of an object is uncertain. Not because "the future" is hard to predict, but because of the inner chasm, the *chōrismos* between an object and its sensuality. Contra Heidegger, then, for whom objects are simply props for the human drama and have a history insofar as they are encountered within human worlds, objects of all kinds spread open the future, like mysteriously parting red theater curtains.[47]

We think of essence as buried away "behind" or "before" an object. But it should by now be fairly clear that the essence of things is *in front of objects*. However paradoxical this may sound, the *essence of a thing is the future*, while *the appearance of a thing is the past*.[48] This rather startling conclusion deserves some further thought.

What is called *matter* is on the OOO view simply matter-for. In other words, "matter" is a sensual object, an aesthetic phenomenon that appears as part of causality. What Aristotle calls the material cause of a thing is the being(s) that compose the thing: "what it's made of." *Matter* is a retroactive positing of the thing that was carved, wrought, melted, entangled, to produce the object in question. On this view, materialism is strangely non-materialist, even somewhat "correlationist" or even idealist: correlationism is the dominant post-Kantian view that reality itself only meaningfully inheres in a correlation between a mind and a thing or a world.[49] That is, matter requires some "observer" (sentient or not, human or not is irrelevant) "for whom" matter is posited. "Observing" here does not mean predicating or making some conscious decision. Suppose the "observer" is only the object in question, and that the object is not sentient or intelligent. Its matter is still matter-for, retroactively posited by the existence of the object as such.

Matter implies the existence of at least one other entity from which the matter in question differs. Think about Derrida's infamous line: *il n'y a pas d'hors-texte*.[50] Happily, Gayatri Spivak gives us two translations. The second, parenthetical one is my preferred one: "there is no outside-text." What this means is not that everything is reducible to pure language. That would be structuralism, which indeed reduces things to their relations. What Derrida is saying, by contrast, is that a text is a closed system (in the terminology of Roy Bhaskar) that is predicated on some kind of externality that it includes–excludes, which it just can't talk about but which it can't help talking about in the negative.[51] A word for example depends upon an inscribable surface, ink and a history and culture of writing, various protocols of spelling and so on. The existence of a text is its coexistence with at least one $(1+n)$ withdrawn entities. This is not the whole OOO truth—for OOO, there is a real hammer. But from an OOO standpoint, perhaps Derrida's insight is the tip of an object-oriented iceberg. OOO is the first and only truly post-Derridean view, rather than a relieved regression from Derrida into an affirmative or positivistic process relationism or some other form of materialism.

What is called the past is really some other object(s) that coexist with the object in question. The OOO universe just can't be monistic, nor can it be solipsistic. Though objects are unspeakable, I know they exist. My very existence is predicated on them, not simply because "I am made out of" them, but because an object just is coexistence, even if only with itself, because of the Rift between essence and appearance.

So much for one aspect of the past, which we have shown is coterminous with matter-for and is retroactively posited by the existing object. Now consider again the ugly duckling of Aristotle's four causes, formal cause. For many reasons formal causation has been down on its luck in the post-scholastic consensus (otherwise known as "science"). One main reason is that formal causation is often interpreted in a teleological way, and much science acts as a powerful repellant against teleology. If anything, consider the harm that teleologies have done: non-white races are "for" being dominated; cows are "for" eating; and so on. Marx wrote Darwin a fan letter simply because he recognized how *The Origin of Species* seriously undercut a teleological view of lifeforms.[52] The deeper OOO reason to be suspicious of teleology is that it turns objects into blobs that are given meaning by some "for-which," some purpose. On this view, until objects are purposed in this way, they just float around in some interstitial realm: to be is to have a purpose-for some other entity.

Nevertheless, as I have shown, contemporary discoveries in quantum physics may be bringing formal causes back. Might it be possible to revise formal causation while unplugging it from teleology? For OOO, the physical shape of an object, its form, is a form-as and a formed-by: in other words, it is interobjective and thus aesthetic. A glass is shaped the way the breath and hands of a glass blower, a tube and a blob of molten glass interacted. Its shape is the record, the trace of what happened to it. Freud argues that the ego is just the "precipitate of abandoned object cathexes."[53] Freud's use of *precipitate* is marvelously physical, and by evoking a chemical stew rather than a living organism, it opens the way to thinking his discovery beyond the human and beyond life.

What then if we were to invert this phrase, and argue that the form of objects was as it were their ego? If ego is object-like, then the inverse surely applies. The identity of this glass is the way I use it as a glass by pouring water into it, and the way it was shaped as a glass. And again, there is a profound Rift between the identity of the glass and the essence of the glass, which is not the same as the difference between an undifferentiated blob and a defined shape with stem, neck, weight, sparkle and so on. For lack of a better way of putting it, it's *the difference between the glass and the glass*. ("What is the difference between a duck? One of its legs is both the same.") The glass is a glass and an uncanny not-glass: $p \wedge \neg p$.

When we hold a glass, we are holding the past, in a "formal" and "material" sense. What then of the present? What is existing, or continuing, or persisting? It just means being in difference from oneself. Existing thus is futural. It is not-yet. The "present" is not a bubble in between past and future, or a blinking cursor, or a point. The present is difference-from-itself. Presence is a sensual construct imposed on an uncanny intermeshing of appearance and essence. What is called *present* is hollowed out from the inside by "past" and "future." We are approaching an OOO interpretation of the end of Shelley's *Defence of Poetry*, in which Shelley regards poets as "the hierophants of the gigantic shadows which futurity casts upon the present."[54]

Because causality is aesthetic, it's legitimate to use the thinking of poetry to think causality. Only consider what Harold Bloom says about a poem: "the meaning of a poem can only be a poem, but *another poem—a poem not itself*."[55] Likewise, *the meaning of an object is another object*. We can slightly modify this to argue that the "other object" could uncannily be the very same object, since objects are dialetheic. In other words, the very appearance of an object could be the "meaning" of an object. But this is not the meaning of limpid givenness: not in any sense WYSIWYG meaning (in an age before Microsoft Windows, this meant "what you see is what you get"). This is a shifting, deceptive, illusory meaning. Startlingly, we are beginning to see that *the past just is appearance*. Contrary to the commonly held belief that appearance is "now," the formal and material cause of a thing just is its pastness. That must mean that *the future is the essence of a thing*.

Let's pause to repeat that again: appearance is "the past," essence is "the future." This is a very strange discovery. Traditionally, the essence of a thing is associated with the past. What was this thing before I looked at it, before it interacted with that other quantum? The quantum theoretical definition of "measure" is "deflect with another quantum." At this level, the link between perceiving and causing is undeniable, though many consider this to be an invitation to idealism or New Age fantasy. Many of the problems of Aristotelian–scholastic substance theories and post-Kantian correlationism (the Standard Model descended from Niels Bohr is just such a view) stem from thinking essence as past. Thus is born the light-in-the-refrigerator anxiety of the correlationist and the idealist. When a tree falls in the forest… First the tree falls, goes the story, then someone hears it. Or conversely: Maybe if I stop thinking about the light in the refrigerator, there is no light in the refrigerator. But already this is to think time as a "middle object" that gives meaning to the other objects by containing them in its ether.

We know that OOO holds this to be illegitimate. OOO returns to the substantialities of Aristotle, without the teleology implicit in the idea that things come from some kind of prime matter and are exclusively defined by their telic function: forks are for spearing, ducks are for swimming, Greeks are for conquering barbarians and so on. Form is delinked from telos. Matter becomes just a retroactive positing of the object that was formed, resulting in the "present" object. Form and matter then are different ways of talking about the past, and the past is just the appearance-for of an object. To repeat, on the surface of the black hole into which I have fallen, you see a rapidly fading photograph of my horrified face.[56] The appearance of an object is the past: a simple consideration of special relativity will show this to be trivially the case.[57] A black hole is the densest possible object in the universe, an object from which no information escapes. In their appearance aspect, all objects are like the photograph on a black hole's event horizon.

Fancifully, appearance just is the event horizon of an object, the point ontologically "in front of which" causality becomes meaningful. Yet even black holes radiate (Hawking radiation). Why? Because they do not coincide with their appearance. Eventually, a black hole evaporates. Its essence collapses into its appearance. When I die, I become your memories of me, the crumpled pieces of paper in my waste paper basket.[58] The shifting, swirling abyss is not surging behind objects, as it does in some Schellingian accounts of primordial stuff.[59] For OOO, the abyss is right before our very eyes. When I reach for an apple in a red plastic bowl in my kitchen, I am reaching into an abyss; even to look at the apple, to speak about it or write a poem about it, is to plunge into the abyss.

Gerard Manley Hopkins writes:

> Each mortal thing does one thing and the same:
> Deals out that being indoors each one dwells;
> Selves—goes itself; *myself* it speaks and spells,
> Crying, *What I do is me: for that I came.*[60]

We have seen how even here, in the midst of a reaffirmation of the Aristotelian haecceity of Duns Scotus (the last time the term *ontology* could be spoken without a slight blush), there is a difference between "I" and "me": "*What I do is me: for that I came.*"[61] What is a thing saying, what is the *me*? For OOO, what the thing is saying is something like the Liar, "This sentence is false." Appearances are liars, but in lying they tell the truth. The bottomless play of appearances is paradoxically grounded: the endless dream of causality is subtended by objects that lie too deep for dreams.

The meaning of a poem is (in the) future. A poem's "*What I do is me*" is to have been read, recited, placed in an anthology, ignored, remembered, translated. This future is not a now-point that is *n* now-points away from the current one. This future is what Derrida calls *l'avenir*, the to-come, or what I call the *future future*. In a very strict sense, then, poetry does come from the future. A weird Platonism is in effect, beaming the shadows of objects down from their unspeakable existence in the future future into sensual–aesthetic–

causal coexistence. The future future is not some transcendental beyond: there is no beyond in OOO, since this would be a top object par excellence. Nor is the future future a "time" in which the object "resides." Rather, the future future is the pure possibility of the object as such.

Withdrawal is this futurality, not as a predictable time, because then it would be ontically given. Nor is futurality an *excess*, since this concept, beloved by poststructuralism, implies a for-whom the thing is excessive ("whom" could be a telescope or a teabag as much as it could be a human or a fish). Excess is sensual, and belongs to the realm of appearance. If anything, excess belongs in an object's pastness. Nor is futurality a void, a gap. Perhaps the term *openness* expresses it best. Withdrawal is openness. Now we can discern more clearly the *chōrismos* between essence and appearance. It is a Rift between openness and pretense.

Time is not a series of now-points "in which" objects exist, but instead time flows out of objects in two different ways. The unknown, unknowable essence of the thing is the future; how something appears is the past. This is in accord with physics, since the speed of light guarantees that any sensual impression of a thing is an impression of its past. What I am arguing here is that there is an ontological reason for this, namely that time pours out of objects. The fixity of things, their history, definition and so on, is the past. The openness of things is the future. The present is an "objective" fiction of something immediately "present at hand" (Heidegger, *vorhanden*). Presence is difference-from-itself, the thing hollowed out from the inside by past and future.

Measurement gives meaning to the unspeakable secretiveness of things by setting up relationships with the isotopes of those things. The meaning of a thing, then, is caught in its relations, that is, they are past. We just can't know what an object is until we've handled it, tasted it, shot it around a particle accelerator, written a poem about it. Neither can a photon know what an object is until it's adjusted it in some sense. Yet even then, we do not have the object: we have our knowledge of its feel, its voltage, its flavor. Relations are what establish the significance of an object, and these relations are irreducibly the past. Just as the meaning of a dream or a poem is in the future, the essence of a relation in the sensual ether that is the causal dimension is also in the future: it hasn't happened yet. The tape measure rests against the child, but in order to know her height, I must read the tape measure with my eyes. The photon is deflected from a crystal lattice, but in order to tell us about it, the photon must record a trace on a photographic plate. Thus time unfolds from relations between and within objects. And thus we can't specify (except in some ontic or ontotheological way) what happens with relations.

Process relationism tries to reduce the intrinsic ambiguity of relations. The significance of an event is to come. There is something that appears process-like about this; hence the illusion that things are processes. Relations are uncanny and hollow; there is a not-yet quality to them. Process relationism reduces this uncanniness, which is ironically a feature of the realness of relations. For relations are inherently doppelgangers of objects, and thus they have the quality of demons, intermediaries between things. And so for object-oriented ontology, art is strikingly like what Socrates says about art in the *Ion*: art is an attunement to a demonic force, akin to the way a magnet resonates with an electromagnetic field.[62] Why? Because when a relation gives something meaning, it skates over the ontological surface of an object, unable to plumb its secret depth. (I use the surface–depth image fancifully: this skating also applies to two-dimensional objects, and so on.) To give meaning is to mistranslate. And furthermore, the meaning of a meaning is another mistranslation: the meaning of a relation is another relation. Time is born from this fundamental error.

The fact that the "meaning" of a relation is *yet another relation* is an object-oriented way of extending Heidegger's argument about the futural quality of Da-sein to all beings.[63] The significance of things to one another is unspecifiable, irreducible to smaller components or to larger wholes. Yet this significance does exist, haunting objects like a ghost. "Futural" doesn't mean that at some point *x* the significance of relations will be settled. It means that relations have a strange hollowness and openness throughout their being. Like paintings or pieces of music—just like them, since relations just are aesthetic—relations between objects are weirdly unclosed and cryptic. Yet they are determinate: they just are this painting, that tragedy, these musical notes. When we specify what they are, all we do is add another set of relations.

Something like death happens in the act of specifying. Specification forecloses sets of possibilities. When a subsequent relation perfectly tunes to the physical form of an object, that object is destroyed. Every object is a Kantian. Hume derives beauty from having a nervous system. But for Kant, beauty is a signal from something ontologically upstream of nerves and brains. And so Kant will, despite his correlationism, provide material for an OOO theory of beauty and causality. On this theory, beauty is an interobjective state in which one object attunes to another one.

Tuning exploits the Rift between essence and appearance. Kant refuses to locate beauty "in" any specific entity such as colors or sounds. To do so would be to allow for the possibility of making a pill that would give me all the sensations of beauty, and Kant has already decided that beauty is not reducible to nerve firings. Yet beauty is there, even though we can't specify it. Kant's theory of beauty, then, is irreductionist. An OOO theory of causation should be very interested in it indeed. Like a knife with a diamond blade, beauty works its way into the Rift between essence and appearance. Somehow beauty is able to turn an object inside out, as if we could for a second glimpse its essence in its appearance. It is no accident that Lacan associates Kantian beauty with sadism, then. For Keats to posit the Grecian Urn as a "still unravish'd bride of quietness" is to fantasize a world in which an object can be destroyed over and over again without deterioration.[64]

Tuning ruthlessly exposes the *harmartia* of an object, its inner wound, its non-identity with itself. Just before it shatters, the glass quakes, resembling for a moment that breathing tuning fork that Aaron O'Connell made. It ripples, then it ends "for real." Beauty cruelly ignores the coherence of the object, its "ego." In beauty, an object is vaporized. It loses its memory. As I argued above, it is hard to avoid the conclusion that beauty is death.

When the glass ends "for real," we can never specify when exactly this moment takes place. We are faced with a Sorites paradox: is it when the glass loses a certain number of coherent features? How many? We can only conclude that just like the experience of Kantian beauty, death happens outside time construed as a linear sequence of moments. Strictly, nothing has happened. There is no glass. The form, the memory of the glass, has vanished. Yet this impossible, timeless moment of beautiful death is also the birth of a host of other objects. The glass shatters. Twenty shards of glass lie strewn on the dining room floor. One has penetrated my hand. In this death, a kind of reincarnation takes place. The formal properties of the glass are transmitted into different objects that bear an uncanny resemblance to the original. "Matter" is just the term for previous life of an object: these are shards *of* glass; this is a picture frame *of* wood; that is a mountainside *of* granite; this is the sound *of* the wind in the treetops. An object becomes matter-for. Form deliquesces into matter. I see anamorphic pieces of glass in my hand—something has been born, and from that I infer the death of the glass, which I can't point to anywhere in my given space. The "impossible" symmetry of ending is strictly nowhere in ontically given spacetime. Small wonder then that many philosophers are tempted to conclude that beauty is nonphysical, ideal and so on. What I see around me in ontic space are distortions, cracks everywhere, suspended over one another like lines of music.

In the moment of an object's ending, two distinct modes of time emanating from two kinds of object relations intersect. The futural not-yet-ness of relationality looms, but is cut off by the objectifying power of a destructive relating. The opera singer tunes her pitch just right—suddenly the glass is at an end. Yet a cone of time emanates into the "past," retroactively positing a whole new set of objects: hey, that's a shard of glass in my finger. Recall that the sublime is the discovery of the proximity of an object (Chapter 2). The object is always already there, before I reach out towards it with another set of relations. It isn't the case that the glass disappears, and "then" the shards are born. The two events occur in different ontological dimensions. The glass forgets that it's a glass, gives up its glassness when the destructive tuning exposes its not-glass qualities. Watch a slow-motion video of a glass shattering to a perfectly tuned soundwave. The glass wobbles, breathes; then the glass stops breathing and just shatters. We can't specify when the glass becomes the not-glass. This becoming happens outside of linear time, in what Heidegger calls the *Moment*.[65] Yet something else is happening. New relations are being born that constrain and limit things, giving a whole new "for" to matter-for. The glass is forgotten—not by us, but by the shards, which now carry anamorphic traces of glass memory. Time flows out of the shattering and the new objects blissfully ignore their fragility, caught in the temporal wake of surrounding things. Something died, yet this death is nowhere to be found in objectively present things. Almost everything goes blithely on its way: there's no use crying over spilt milk.

Notes

1. T.S. Eliot, *Little Gidding*, 2.3–4, *Collected Poems 1909–1962* (London: Faber and Faber, 1983).
2. Keiji Nishitani, *On Buddhism*, tr. Seisaku Yamamoto and Robert E. Carter (Albany: State University of New York Press, 2006), 156.
3. Roger Penrose, *The Emperor's New Mind: Concerning Computers, Minds, and the Laws of Physics* (Oxford and New York: Oxford University Press, 1990), 334.
4. Jean-Paul Sartre gives an elegant account of this in *Being and Nothingness: An Essay on Phenomenological Ontology*, tr. and ed. Hazel Barnes (New York: Philosophical Library, 1984), 41–42, 61–62.
5. Oscar Wilde, *The Picture of Dorian Gray*, ed. Robert Mighall (London: Penguin, 2003), 212–213.
6. Padmasambhava, *The Tibetan Book of the Dead: The Great Liberation by Hearing in the Intermediate States*, tr. Gyurme Dorje, ed. Graham Coleman with Thupten Jinpa, introductory commentary by the Dalai Lama (New York: Viking, 2006), 176.
7. Douglas Hofstadter, *Gödel, Escher, Bach: An Eternal Golden Braid* (New York: Basic Books, 1999), 75–81.
8. Graham Priest, *In Contradiction: A Study of the Transconsistent* (Oxford: Oxford University Press, 2006), 39–50.
9. LFO, *LFO* (Warp Records, 1990).
10. Robert M. Solovay, "Explicit Henkin Sentences," *The Journal of Symbolic Logic*, 50.1 (March, 1985), 91–93.
11. Priest, *In Contradiction*, 9–27.
12. See Graham Priest and Francesco Berto, "Dialetheism," *The Stanford Encyclopedia of Philosophy (Summer 2010 Edition)*, ed. Edward N. Zalta.
13. Jacques Lacan, *Écrits: A Selection*, tr. Alan Sheridan (London: Tavistock, 1977), 311.
14. Jacques Lacan, Jacques Lacan, "The Agency of the Letter in the Unconscious or Reason Since Freud," *Écrits: A Selection*, tr. Alan Sheridan (London: Tavistock Publications, 1977 (French 1966)), 146–178.
15. Mark Changizi, "Why Even Data from Star Trek Would Have Fuzzy Language," http://changizi.wordpress.com/2011/01/04/why-even-data-from-star-trek-would-have-fuzzy-language/, accessed October 8, 2011.
16. Theodor Adorno, *Aesthetic Theory*, tr. and ed. Robert Hullot-Kentor (Minneapolis: University of Minnesota Press, 1997), 245–246, 331; see also 113, 281, 323–324, 346.

17. Wilde, *The Picture of Dorian Gray*, 141.
18. William Shakespeare, *The Tempest*, ed. Frank Kermode (London: Methuen, 1987), 4.1.148–158.
19. Roger Penrose, *Cycles of Time: An Extraordinary New View of the Universe* (New York: Knopf, 2011), 146, 150, 212; Roger Penrose, *The Road to Reality: A Complete Guide to the Laws of the Universe* (New York: Vintage, 2007), 436–437, 541, 978.
20. Charles Darwin, *The Origin of Species*, ed. Gillian Beer (Oxford and New York: Oxford University Press, 1996), 160.
21. Heidegger's term for the features of Da-sein.
22. Graham Harman, *Guerrilla Metaphysics: Phenomenology and the Carpentry of Things* (Chicago: Open Court, 2005), 95, 184.
23. Levi Bryant, "Lucretius and the Wilderness," http://larvalsubjects.wordpress.com/2011/08/26/lucretius-and-the-wilderness/.
24. David Wiesner, *The Three Pigs* (Clarion Books, 2001).
25. Sigmund Freud, *The Ego and the Id*, tr. Joan Riviere, revised and ed. James Strachey, intro. Peter Gay (New York: Norton, 1989), 24.
26. Francis Yates, *The Art of Memory* (London: Pimlico, 2007), 57, 121, 133, 137, 201, 233, 267, 274.
27. Mary Carruthers, *The Book of Memory: A Study of Memory in Medieval Culture* (Cambridge: Cambridge University Press, 2008), 1.
28. Carruthers, *The Book of Memory*, 18, 38, 50, 107, 139.
29. Michel Henry, "Material Phenomenology and Language," *Continental Philosophy Review* 32 (1999), 343–365 (351).
30. Martin Heidegger, *Being and Time*, tr. Joan Stambaugh (Albany: State University of New York Press, 1996), 395.
31. This is based on Harman's argument that *Angst* is not that different from the tool/broken tool structure. Graham Harman, *Tool-Being: Heidegger and the Metaphysics of Objects* (Peru, IL: Open Court, 2002), 95–97.
32. Arda Denkel, *Object and Property* (Cambridge: Cambridge University Press, 2007), 204.
33. Jane Bennett, *Vibrant Matter: A Political Ecology of Things* (Durham: Duke University Press, 2010), 199–120.
34. Heidegger, *Being and Time*, 134–135.
35. Heidegger, *Being and Time*, 316.
36. Chögyam Trungpa, *The Truth of Suffering and the Path of Liberation*, ed. Judith Lief (Boston: Shambhala, 2010), 9–10.
37. Heidegger, *Being and Time*, 315.
38. Adorno, *Aesthetic Theory*, 245–246, 331.
39. Horace, *On the Art of Poetry*, in Aristotle, Horace and Longinus, *Classical Literary Criticism*, tr. T.S. Dorsch (Harmondsworth: Penguin, 1984), 82–83.
40. See Theodor Adorno, *Aesthetic Theory*, 241.

41. Immanuel Kant, *Critique of Judgment: Including the First Introduction*, tr. Werner Pluhar (Indianapolis: Hackett, 1987), 45–46, 51–52.

42. Jacques Lacan, "Kant with Sade," tr. James B. Swenson Jr., available at http://www.lacan.com/kantsade.htm, accessed July 11, 2012.

43. Alphonso Lingis, *The Imperative* (Bloomington: Indiana University Press, 1998), 25–38.

44. Heidegger, *Being and Time*, 221.

45. Heidegger, *Being and Time*, 221.

46. Percy Shelley, *A Defence of Poetry*, in *Shelley's Poetry and Prose*, ed. Donald H. Reiman and Neil Fraistat (New York and London: W.W. Norton, 2002), 509–535 (535).

47. Heidegger, *Being and Time*, 355.

48. Heidegger, *Being and Time*, 353, 355–356.

49. The locus classicus is Quentin Meillassoux, *After Finitude*, 5–7.

50. Jacques Derrida, *Of Grammatology*, tr. Gayatri Chakravorty Spivak (Baltimore and London: the Johns Hopkins University Press, 1987), 158.

51. Roy Bhaskar, *A Realist Theory of Science* (New York: Routledge, 2008), 56, 82, 85, 124, 212.

52. Gillian Beer, "Introduction," in Charles Darwin, *The Origin of Species*, ed. Gillian Beer (Oxford: Oxford University Press, 1996), xxvii–xviii..

53. Freud, *The Ego and the Id*, 24.

54. Shelley, *Defence*, 535.

55. Harold Bloom, *The Anxiety of Influence: A Theory of Poetry* (Oxford: Oxford University Press, 1997), 70.

56. Roger Penrose, *The Emperor's New Mind*, 334.

57. David Bohm, *The Special Theory of Relativity* (London: Routledge, 2006), 158–174.

58. See Jean-Paul Sartre, *Being and Nothingness*, 41–42, 61–62.

59. Iain Hamilton Grant, *Philosophies of Nature after Schelling* (New York: Continuum, 2008), 37–38, 79, 92, 99, 130–131, 146–147, 162.

60. Gerard Manley Hopkins, *The Major Works*, ed. Catherine Phillips (Oxford: Oxford University Press, 2009).

61. For haecceity, see John Duns Scotus, *Philosophical Writings*, tr. Allan Wolter (Indianapolis: Hackett, 1987), 166–167.

62. Plato, *Ion*, tr. Benjamin Jowett (Cambridge, Mass.: Harvard University Press,), available at http://classics.mit.edu/Plato/ion.html (accessed October 7, 2011).

63. Heidegger, *Being and Time*, 298–303.

64. Lacan, "Kant avec Sade."

65. Heidegger, *Being and Time*, 311.

Conclusion

A Weird Aristotle

Graham Harman discovered a gigantic coral reef of mysterious entities beneath the Heideggerian submarine of Da-sein, which itself is operating at an ontological depth way below the choppy surface of philosophy, beset by the winds of epistemology and infested with the sharks of materialism, idealism, empiricism and most of the other -isms that have defined what is and what isn't for the last several hundred years. At a moment when the term "ontology" was left alone like a piece of well chewed old chewing gum that no one wants to have anything to do with, object-oriented ontology (OOO) has put it back on the table. The coral reef isn't going anywhere and once you have discovered it, you can't un-discover it. And it seems to be teeming with strange facts. The first fact is that the entities in the reef—we call them "objects" somewhat provocatively—constitute all there is: from doughnuts to dogfish to the Dog Star to Dobermans to Snoop Dogg. People, plastic clothes pegs, piranhas and particles are all objects. And they share affinities, at this depth. There is not much of a distinction between life and non-life (as there isn't in contemporary life science). And there is not much of a distinction between intelligence and non-intelligence (as there is in contemporary artificial intelligence theory). Many of these distinctions are made by humans, for humans (anthropocentrism).

Causality is a zone where a certain action is taking place: heat radiates, bullets fly, armies are defeated. What action is taking place? Let us call on

Alphonso Lingis: "[N]ot something that just is what it is, here and now, without mystery, but something like a quest...a tone on its way calling forth echoes and responses...water seeking its liquidity in the sunlight rippling across the cypresses in the back of the garden."[1] If as suggested earlier there is no functional difference between substance and accidents; if there is no difference between perceiving and doing; if there is no real difference between sentience and non-sentience—then causality itself is a strange, ultimately nonlocal aesthetic phenomenon. A phenomenon, moreover, that emanates from objects themselves, wavering in front of them like the astonishingly beautiful real illusion conjured in this quotation of Lingis. Lingis's sentence does what it says, casting a compelling, mysterious spell, the spell of causality, like a demonic force field. A real illusion: if we knew it was an illusion, if it were just an illusion, it would cease to waver. It would not be an illusion at all. We would be in the real of noncontradiction. Since it is like an illusion, we can never be sure: "What constitutes pretense..." The ambiguity of the aesthetic dimension is a radio signal from the dialetheic being of objects.

His unwillingness to accept illusoriness might have been what pushed Heidegger into Nazism. Heidegger understands that truth is not simply making "objectively present" assertions about "objectively present" things. Truth is an event in the world, a kind of "truthing," in which truth and untruth are coemergent: "All new discovery takes place not on the basis of complete concealment, but takes its point of departure from discoveredness in the mode of illusion. Beings look like ..., that is, they are in a way already discovered, and yet they are still distorted."[2] Heidegger descended to this ontological depth without much protective gear. He thought he had hit some kind of authentic bedrock, and in a bitterly ironic way, he had. But voyaging at these depths requires some kind of cognitive protection—this is territory that Buddhist mystics swim in, as Heidegger himself intuited. The depth could drive you crazy. Why? Because there are no guarantees. The protection that a Buddhist has at this depth is the protection of emptiness: not a hard suit of armor or tough diving gear, but a light-touch sense of the openness and illusoriness of things, without cynicism.

Unable to tolerate illusion, Heidegger relegates it to a function of Da-sein being confused, caught in "the they" and so on. In other words, he reinvents the wheel a little: he himself reinstalls some of the "objective substance" software that got us into trouble. Despite thinking that (especially thinking that) he has gone beyond objective presence he reifies being into an authenticity that means ripping the illusion away. There is a fantasy of seeing a real underneath. In a perfect political storm, this authenticity-speak matched the authenticity-speak of Nazism.[3] This is a true tragedy, because the tunnel to the future lies through some kind of engagement with Heidegger. But his very name gives people an allergic reaction.

Heidegger's story is a cautionary tale about correlationism, in fact. Right after his discussion of illusion and the tearing away of illusion by authentic Da-sein, Heidegger lays out his most explicitly correlationist thought: "Newton's laws, the law of contradiction, and any truth whatsoever, are true only as long as Da-sein *is*."[4] Now to put Newton's laws—which passed muster with a certain kind of mathematical proof—next to the Law of Noncontradiction, which is too often taken as gospel, is itself telling. It seems of a piece with the fact that Heidegger insists that he is not saying that truth is merely "subjective." For a view of Da-sein that clung to LNC would be almost enough to get you into trouble, as we have seen. Heidegger insists that truth is not "subjective" even though it is "relative to the being of Da-sein."[5]

Correlationism itself only works if there is some kind of phobia of illusion. So one trajectory of correlationism culminates in Nazism. Correlationism itself is a breeding ground for Nazism, because in order to escape its paradoxes one might retreat still further into an extreme form of anthropocentrism: Da-sein is human, and German Da-sein is the best ... Heidegger goes on to a brilliant critique of skepticism—has there ever actually been a *real* skeptic, the assumptions of dialectical critiques of skepticism notwithstanding? But it is just here that Heidegger brings up the "despair of suicide." To be a skeptic is to have "obliterated Da-sein, and thus truth."[6] One wants to say, as one might say to a lover who yelled a cuss word unexpectedly, "Where the heck did *that* come from?" One wants to say, "Wait a sec Martin. You were just saying how no 'attunement', no conceptual or emotional stance really ever got rid of Da-sein." One moment we were exploring truth and the flimsiness of skepticism, the next moment the "obliteration" of truth and suicidal despair. The refutation of skepticism is *too* brilliant, overdone: something is overlooked—if there has never been a true skeptic on God's good Earth, why in heaven's name worry about suicide all of a sudden? It's a case of overkill, a symptom of some deep anxiety about truth and illusion. Why kill something that couldn't really exist?

OOO provides another kind of protective gear at precisely the point of "seeing truth." Since all causal relationships, including seeing, happen in an aesthetic dimension, there is no way at all to see the "real" thing "underneath" the illusion. Heidegger fails to see that illusoriness is where all the action is. *Realist Magic* has wanted to say just the same thing—in a positive sense.

Aristotle decided that "coming-to-be" is "a change into [the] perceptible material" of an object. In turn, ceasing to be, "passing-away," is "when there is a change into invisible material."[7] *Realist Magic* has argued something that seems like the inverse. The coming to be of an object is the opening of a fresh Rift between essence and appearance. This Rift is unique, just as the object is unique. The Rift is not a void or a chasm: it is "What constitutes pretense." It is the collapse of the Rift, not a change into invisibility, that spells the end of a thing. In death, things appear: ashes, photographs, fingernails that carry on growing, hollow grief inside another person. In a larger sense, however, *Realist Magic* simply places Aristotle in a wider conceptual space, yet not in a way that Aristotle would have anticipated. It is just that the positive appearance and disappearance of things happens in the sensual realm, not in some quality-free zone "beneath" it. And this is not because there are no real substances, but because indeed there are.

Likewise, *Realist Magic* has situated Hume's devastating assault on causality in a wider space. Post-Aristotelian science is indebted to Humean accounts of causation, but this raises a problem. Science that relies on probability theories lacks a theory of causality precisely since, like Hume, it is only able to say that data are statistically correlated.[8] And philosophy has since tended to view objects as bundles of qualities.[9] The reason why we only ever have associations and statistical correlations is because causality is indeed an illusion-like play of perceptions at the phenomenal level. But this is for a reason that Hume could not have grasped. The reason for the play of illusion is the existence of real objects.

Kant transcended Hume insofar as he discovered a region of synthetic judgments that is always already in place prior to analytic judgments. These synthetic judgments are based on experience. Kant argues that there must always already have been a positing of things as … in order for the experience to take place.[10] Kant does not quite understand what he has uncovered here.[11] *Realist Magic* has specified that what Kant calls synthetic judgment is part of a causal space that is intrinsically aesthetic. This space only exists as an open, secret manifestation of irreducibly withdrawn objects. The Kantian Thing, then, is already an aesthetic effect, a fact that Kant's *Critique of Judgment* seems to underwrite when it posits aesthetic experience as the ground of synthetic judgments. Kant ironically allows certain phenomena such as space and time to be object-like in the sense that this book describes, because they are reflexes of consciousness. They are *quanta*, units that are not yet divisible until some analytic machinery goes to work.[12] In *Realist Magic*, however, space and time are simply emergent properties of objects in general, not simply the way the "pure form of sensible intuition" (and so forth) manifests.[13] Caught in the correlationist circle, Kant was incapable of realizing that his discovery of pure consciousness could develop into a phenomenological account of intention, which would in turn be folded into Harman's account of objects as intensely, openly-secretly themselves.

What has happened in *Realist Magic?* There has been a return to a weird non-theistic Aristotle. This Aristotle was left behind at the start of the modern age, when Descartes, Newton and Leibniz (among others) broke with scholasticism. Science as we know it appeared with its rigor and doubt, based on mathematics. At the same time, epistemology became the dominant philosophical game, based again on the doubt that Descartes put at the center of his *Meditations*. This paved the way for the correlationism of Kant. Kant thought he had finished the job by placing traditional metaphysics on a small island of analytic judgments in the midst of a wide ocean of synthetic judgments. This event also marked the moment at which rhetoric and logic parted company, giving rise to the contemporary discourse of aesthetics. *Realist Magic* has returned to an Aristotle without Nature, without material and final causes, and without a Prime Mover.

This Aristotle also does not rely on the Law of Noncontradiction. This is not only the Aristotle of formal causation, but also of the *Poetics* with its still misunderstood argument concerning beginning, middles and ends. *Realist Magic* has, like other forms of OOO, radicalized Kant by de-anthropocentrizing him. The human–world correlate is only one of trillions of thing–world correlates. In so doing, *Realist Magic* has bypassed the Hegelian "solution" to Kant: I cannot know the thing in itself, but here I am, thinking that, so I can. And yet, I have retained Hegel's sense that things can be self-contradictory.

Realist Magic has returned to Aristotle, but not out of some atavistic desire to wipe away the achievements of modernity and return to an oppressive theocratic regime. It is simply that modernity has now reached a certain limit. This limit is characterized by, to cite only too brief examples, the decisive appearance of nonhumans in human social, psychic and philosophical space. The current ecological emergency consists in this appearance. Some deep paradoxes concerning the Law of Noncontradiction have also emerged, within the very thinking of mathematics that grounds modern science (Cantor, Hilbert, Russell, Gödel, Turing).[14] The contradictory beings that this lineage of mathematics and logic discovered has necessitated an attentiveness to ways in which logic itself might need to violate LNC, the Law of Noncontradiction, especially when it comes to thinking objects. That this appears to be the case despite the founding of modern thinking upon LNC, provides more evidence that humans are now exiting the modern. Meanwhile, physics has discovered formal causation in the shape of nonlocal quantum interactions. I take these events to be symptoms of the pressure exerted by real beings on the glass window of epistemologically-inclined modern knowing.

These beings press on the glass like the uncanny faces in a painting by the Expressionist James Ensor. They are what OOO calls objects, and it's time to let them in—or rather, to let ourselves out.

Notes

1. Alphonso Lingis, *The Imperative* (Bloomington: Indiana University Press, 1998), 29.
2. Martin Heidegger, *Being and Time*, tr. Joan Stambaugh (Albany, N.Y: State University of New York Press, 1996), 204.
3. Theodor Adorno, *The Jargon of Authenticity* (London: Routledge, 2003).
4. Heidegger, *Being and Time*, 208.
5. Heidegger, *Being and Time*, 208.
6. Heidegger, *Being and Time*, 210.
7. Aristotle, *On Generation and Corruption*, tr. H.H. Joachim (forgottenbooks.org, accessed August 18, 2012), 19.
8. Judea Pearl, *Causality: Models, Reasoning, and Inference* (Cambridge: Cambridge University Press, 2010), 41, 134–135.
9. Arda Denkel, *Object and Property* (Cambridge: Cambridge University Press, 2007), 37.
10. Immanuel Kant, *Critique of Pure Reason*, tr. Norman Kemp Smith (Boston and New York: Bedford/St. Martin's, 1965), 45–48, 48–51, 71–74, 129–140.
11. Martin Heidegger, *What Is a Thing?* (Chicago: Henry Regnery, 1967), 113–114, 128–129, 137–140, 146.
12. Kant, *Critique of Pure Reason*, 68, 69–70, 71–72, 74–75, 77–78, 201-202.
13. Heidegger, *What Is a Thing?*, 198–199.
14. See Heidegger, *What Is a Thing?*, 106–108.

Permissions

Figure 1 is available at http://cns-alumni.bu.edu/~slehar/webstuff/bubw3/bubw3.html, accessed November 21, 2012. Permission granted by the author.

Figure 2 Permission granted by the author.

66347513R00130

Made in the USA
Middletown, DE
10 March 2018